UNITING
BY DESIGN

The Architecture of Creative Collaboration

for Organizations...Teams...and Groups

By Mark D. Bennett

For Solor & Renata
with my best wishes
in all your collaborations
Mark Bennett
August 2021

Uniting by Design LLC
www.unitingbydesign.com

Mark D Bennett
505.660.8806
mark@unitingbydesign.com
www.unitingbydesign.com

...you better start swimmin' or you'll sink like a stone
For the times they are a-changin'
Bob Dylan

Dedication:
For the leaders who placed their trust in me
and provided opportunities to learn together.

Brief Table of Contents

Full Table of Contents

Definitions

UNITING

- joining together, combining so as to form a single whole, acting in concert or agreement

Design

- a plan to form or build something, the intention to act, invent

Architecture

- knowledge framework, structural imagining, the process of building

Creative

- imaginative approach, fearless exploration, resourceful engagement

Collaboration

- unified strength, empowered partnership, synchronized action

Force

- power, dynamism, influence

Author's Note on cover logo The double quatrefoil of 8 linked hearts symbolize the synergy of heartfelt commitment in organizations. The plus sign at the center represents the power of unity in creative collaboration. The four primary colors represent human diversity of personalities, perspectives, cultures, and work styles. Beautiful, unique colors have also been used by the Birkman Method® of leadership styles, the Situational Leadership® model, and others that promote diverse ways to work well together.

The logo was developed by Tania Jackson and her talented team at RedIdea, Digital Marketing Agency, https://redidea.co.uk/

Introduction

The Times Call for a New Level of Collaboration

The 21st century is a dramatically new and strange landscape. As I write this in late 2020, we are in a dynamic vortex of five powerful waves of change that challenge the capacity of organizations to respond.

- An unfolding disease pandemic has no end in sight.

- A weakened global economic system leaves many unemployed and vulnerable.

- Changes in the Earth's climate generate large social, political, and economic impacts.

- Billions more people arriving in the next thirty years will tax the capacity of Earth's ecosystems to sustain human, animal, and plant life.

- Global social and political movements for racial justice challenge governments to address historic and current inequalities.

We can see the fragility of the structure of global systems that many of us believed were more stable and predictable. Business as usual has ended and we have to relearn together in order to move forward. We do not yet know what the long-term impacts will be. And, as if all this is not enough to challenge every organization, veteran observers of the pipeline for global technology development forecast that the world will see 100 years of technology change in the next 10 years. It is hard to imagine the scope of so much change so fast. The world of 1920 bears almost no resemblance to 2020. Could our world look so different in 2030 that we don't recognize it?

In *The Future Is Faster Than You Think*, Peter Diamandis and Steven Kotler candidly acknowledge the scope of the challenges facing humanity. Then, they sum up the situation by diagnosing where the solutions will come from. The authors describe specific, remarkable innovations that are not distant dreams, but emerging practical options to reverse climate change, regrow the ocean's coral reefs, reforest the disappearing forests, and more "We must be all in right now….We already have the tech to meet these challenges…. Our innovations may have caught up with our problems. ***Collaboration is the missing piece of the puzzle….We the people are the obstacle and the opportunity.***" (my emphasis added) (1)

I refer to the "all in" level of collaboration needed to meet the challenges of so much change as Creative Collaboration. About 60 years ago, in another time with powerful waves of cultural shifts and disruptive change, the songwriter, Bob Dylan, wrote his anthem, "The Times They Are a Changing." The song's refrain has a prophetic ring for these times. "You better start swimmin or you'll sink like a stone." (2)

The core belief that guides this book is that successful navigation of these waves requires that we *swim* alongside others in the communities and organizations where we live and work. The times and circumstances demand all the creativity, resourcefulness, and synergy we can muster, lest we sink separately.

Despite the turbulent waters we are in and a stormy weather forecast, this is a book of hope. As Vaclav Havel wrote, "Hope is definitely not the same thing as optimism. It is not the conviction that something will turn out well, but the certainty that something makes sense, regardless of how it turns out." (3) Real hope is not a fuzzy, idealistic wish for better days. It is a muscular and pragmatic force in the heart that strengthens the will to act.

Hope is action that makes sense. In these times, intentional actions make sense when they build the capacity for Creative Collaboration. There are three practical strategies.

- Use intelligent design principles like open forums and cross-functional teaming that shape the environment to increase individual and collective capacity to communicate, engage, and innovate together.

- Embrace core values that provide ethical orientation and build trust.

- Apply common-sense practices that enable organizations and teams to join together, learn together, and stick together.

The process of UNITING and dividing is as old as human history. However, the stakes have never been this great. We must face what divides us and come together in the organizations in every community that are essential to the health of civil society. *Design principles, core values, and shared practices enable us to swim together with strong, confident strokes in the seas of anxiety and uncertainty.*

How Creative Collaboration Can Change the World

In 2018, I received an introduction to speak with the employees and leaders of an organization that changed the way I understand how the practical power of an organization's commitment to creative collaboration can change the world.

This inspiring story at the leading edge of a major healthcare challenge began in 2003 in Albuquerque, New Mexico in the southwestern United States. Dr. Sanjeev Arora was a liver specialist on the medical staff of a major academic medical center. He saw the overwhelming need of his patients with Hepatitis C from this perspective. Many of these patients had limited means and lived in rural areas. They had to overcome substantial barriers to receive their care including: the cost of travel, missed work, childcare arrangements, and the lack of reliable transportation. It was often difficult and sometimes impossible for patients and their families to make the necessary long trips from distant rural homes. He was only one doctor and there were many patients.

Dr. Arora envisioned a low-cost, high-impact model of practice as an alternative way to serve his patients and many others. He took the well-established practice of tele-medicine and transformed it into a breakthrough practice, *tele-mentoring.* In tele-medicine, one expert treats one patient at a time via video link in real-time. This is the traditional framework for healthcare. There are still a limited number of expert doctors and there are still many patients who remain underserved. In contrast, *tele-mentoring* solves the immediate needs of one patient who needs expert help. Then, it exponentially multiplies the resources available to serve many more.

Expert specialists in large urban areas link with groups of community physicians and other health practitioners to grow their capacity to treat patients in their home communities. Imagine a medical expert on a video conference call and a computer screen filled with thirty doctors in remote locations in parts of the United States and other countries. A local doctor (or other health practitioner) presents a detailed case about a patient with a difficult medical condition, protecting the patient's identity. The problems and challenges with successful treatment of the patient are carefully assessed and examined with the help of the expert. The local doctor leaves the call with increased expert knowledge and capacity to help the patient. All the other participants on the call have the same opportunity to grow their capacity. They can ask related questions about their patient challenges. For others, the patient's consult becomes a master class. The paradigm of "one-to-one" transforms to "one-to-many."

Dr. Arora's vision became an organization called Project ECHO which stands for **E**xtension for **C**ommunity **H**ealthcare **O**utcomes. Like many organizations with noble missions, Project ECHO started with a large problem to solve, an idea about the solution, and limited resources.

- The problem: many people with limited resources and serious medical needs lack access to quality medical care.

- The solution: reverse the process. Instead of bringing the people to where the necessary medical care is located, use an elegantly simple, powerful, and cost-effective approach to move the quality medical care to where the people are.

- The resources: develop a digital collaborative network model to accelerate the learning and multiply the force of one expert to reach many.

Project ECHO's vision is to change the world fast, reaching One Billion people with help by 2025. The only way to achieve this bold vision is by reframing the process of knowledge sharing. ECHO's two major principles are "demonopolize knowledge" and "move knowledge, not people." The experts openly share their specialized knowledge so the knowledge moves quickly to many more practitioners in far-flung communities.

In order to move so much knowledge to so many people so fast, Project ECHO is UNITING by design in a flexible, scalable, worldwide computer network of collaborative learning. It is a creative community of practice without borders that is continuously learning, circulating lessons, spreading best practices, growing, and adapting to accelerate impact.

The ECHO model is scaling rapidly to treat many more serious conditions where high levels of expertise are necessary to provide patients with quality care. What began as a focus on patients with liver disease is now being used to address high levels of need among underserved patients with over 100 complex medical conditions such as HIV, chronic pain, tuberculosis, diabetes, and COVID-19.

At this writing, ECHO has over 135 collaborative partnerships with major healthcare organizations and more than 80 global partners in 31 countries. ECHO's noble mission to serve those in great need is inspiring. In an era of so much partisanship about health care needs and solutions, Project ECHO has been recognized by a bipartisan resolution of the United States Congress as a model of hope! It is idealistic AND it is pragmatic! A recent PBS documentary released in 2019, tells the full story, "Project ECHO: A Democracy of Knowledge." (4)

ECHO is a fitting way to begin this book because it is an organization that is wisely UNITING to adapt to an operating environment of rapid change, high levels of needs, and limited resources. We will return to ECHO in Lesson Nine to see how organizations outside of healthcare are adapting its proven model to rapidly share knowledge and best practices via a collaborative network and help underserved populations.

Organizations Need Leadiators More Than They Need Leaders

I have encountered quite a few leaders who can't or won't build Creative Collaboration. They are committed to the status quo with fixed ideas of what is possible and desirable. They may be afraid of change. They often favor a top down approach to management that fails to engage others and elicit their creative contributions. Sometimes, they are neither open-minded nor fair-minded. They are unable to adapt to the waves of change and show others how to do so.

This book is a field guide for people who want to become more resourceful to meet the challenges of the times. You may be a veteran leader who recognizes the need to reinvent your leadership approach and help others navigate the big waves. You may be an emerging leader with an open mind about adaptation and collaboration who is willing to step forward and lead in your organization and community. Or, you may not see yourself as a leader, but want to be part of a collaborative organization.

In the turbulent waters of disruptive change, anxiety, and increasing polarization, we need leaders who believe in UNITING instead of dividing. These leaders believe in the value and power of diversity. They are willing to address racial injustice and power differences. They want to act to increase equity and inclusion.

We need a better term for the adaptive leader who can show people how to join together and *swim* together. A mediator is a peacemaker who acts without bias or favoritism to help individuals and groups address their differences constructively, explore common ground, and seek agreement. The times call for leaders with the values and skillset of a mediator who can acknowledge conflict, remain centered amidst polarization, bridge differences, and bring people together in common cause.

Throughout this book, I will use the word, leadiator to describe a leader who is willing and able to adapt and meet the unique challenges of our times. A leadiator has the courageous heart of a peacemaker and the capacity for UNITING people in Creative Collaboration.

- A leadiator commits to fairness and justice.

- A leadiator helps people face divides of fear and anger and build bridges of understanding with intelligent questions and intentional actions.

- A leadiator encourages everyone's voice and creative contributions.

In three decades of work with organizations, teams, and groups across sectors, I have introduced the practical mediator skillset to many leaders and change agents. I have witnessed this transformation of leaders into leadiators. They are usually unsung heroines and heroes, because they act as servant leaders who want to bring others together and bring out the best in everyone. Their quiet, eloquent examples inspired the design of this book as a field guide.

In an earlier period of national crisis and bitter division in the United States, Abraham Lincoln said, "The dogmas of the quiet past are inadequate to the stormy present." (5) This observation seems apt for our time. Leadiators need to show others how to *swim* in stormy conditions. Leadiators act intentionally to inspire, build, and sustain the collaborative capacity necessary to overcome the challenges of a rapidly changing, polarized environment.

A practical design for Creative Collaboration can be part of a necessary upgrade to an organization's social *operating system*. It must be open source, widely available, and easy to update based on user experience. Like Project ECHO's innovative network model, the design of Creative Collaboration must rapidly scale up to the size of the challenges and continuously encourage innovation. Any leadiator can help an organization develop collective understanding of the actions necessary to tap the potential of each individual and build the capacity of the whole organization.

In this digital, knowledge economy, we have open access to a cornucopia of developments in neuroscience, positive psychology, and successful organization models. Leadiators can act confidently with unprecedented, practical understanding about the effective design of human collaboration in organizations, teams, and groups. I have used my experiences with diverse organizations to field-test and curate the best of these developments and resources for leadiators to build a collaborative organization that learns together and adapts.

Leadiators Need a *Vehicle*

Metaphors help us better understand by using a different reference point to see more clearly. This book is a *blueprint* for an organization *vehicle*. In novel, challenging territory, you have to stick together and cross challenging terrain. To stick together, every organization needs individuals who can work resourcefully with others to design and maintain the organization as an *all-terrain vehicle*. Collaborative structure in organizations is something that can be designed to carry people together through this challenging landscape. As you will learn in Lessons Five, Six, and Seven, this vehicle needs to be equipped with an effective *global positioning system* to navigate and guide the organization.

A leadiator with a blueprint can show others how to build and maintain the organizational *vehicle* to make this journey. A *vehicle* that is suitable for a rapidly changing environment must be designed to deliver a level of collaboration that exceeds its past capacity. This increase in capacity comes from three capabilities that support improved processes and practices.

- *Collective learning to increase wisdom*
- *Creativity to innovate*
- *Unified resourceful effort to overcome challenges*

The capacity to learn together has always provided human communities with an evolutionary advantage. Learning, creativity, and resourcefulness make sense and can help people in an organization remain hopeful to meet the challenges now and those that lie around the next corner.

Read This Book as a Co-Creative Partner

I invite you to assume the role of a creative partner. This book is for current and emerging leadiators of the organizations that are a vital force in our civil society.

Imagine you are holding this book in your hand as you stand in your organization right now, facing the uncertainties of the future. There is no clear path forward. So, what do you do? *The most robust strategy that any organization can pursue amidst change and uncertainty is to increase adaptive capacity.* When an organization doesn't know what lies ahead, it increases the odds of success when it has the capacity to respond, adapt its approach, and shift its course when necessary. This book helps leadiators work together with others to build adaptive capacity.

> *Adaptive capacity is your North to orient and move ahead.*

The path of Creative Collaboration is shaped intentionally by a leadiator. If you are already a natural, intuitive leadiator, this guidebook will enhance your capacity with a blueprint and language to engage others. It will also help anyone at any level in an organization design and implement actions to establish the underlying conditions that support the *emergent* property of collaboration. This term comes from the study of natural, human, and social systems that are complex and adapt. *Collaboration is emergent because it is always increasing or decreasing based on the interaction of the underlying organizational conditions with the surrounding environment that includes social, technological, environmental, economic, and political forces.* (6)

Most books about organizational development and collaboration focus on the rarefied environments in the boardrooms and leadership teams of Fortune 500 corporations and large government agencies. This is a very small slice of reality! Too many of these leaders have out-sized egos and powerful ambitions that prevent them from becoming leadiators.

9

The lessons for huge organizations with more than 100,000 employees distributed in operations around the world may not be relevant and practically applicable in much smaller organizations. For every giant corporation and mammoth federal government agency, there are hundreds of thousands of small and medium-sized businesses, nonprofits, and local government agencies. They have many hundreds of thousands of presidents, executive directors, agency supervisors, mayors, city councilors, county managers, and school district superintendents. In every community, legions of committed citizens serve on the governing boards of faith-based organizations, nonprofits, schools, and neighborhood organizations.

It would be cumbersome to continually repeat a list of the broad variety of organizations and other groups where collaboration is important. Therefore, I will use the term "organization" throughout this book in a generic sense to refer to many different forms of operation.

- Formal organizations of all sizes in all sectors (business, nonprofit, government, education)

- Departments, divisions, and teams (leadership, management, and work) within larger, formal organizations

- Coalitions, alliances, and partnerships among independent organizations

- Ad hoc groups that come together around a specific issue or concern

Leadiators in small and medium-sized organizations face unique dilemmas, often without access to skilled advisors and consultants. I wrote this book for these leadiators and the small and medium-sized organizations they serve. These organizations are the frontlines of civil society. They face tough challenges and choices while seeking ways to bring people together. Their capacity to respond effectively affects the health, vitality, and livability of their communities.

I will use a few examples of very large organizations that have built Creative Collaboration. However, most of the examples in this book will be about people working in small and medium-sized organizations in a community like yours.

You can be a leadiator! I have come to recognize leadership as an asset of the highest value in every organization of any size, and in every sector of operations. This is a book for leadiators who want to help any organization learn to work together and adapt to change.

Leadiators come in many forms.

- With formal titles and without

- From every age, race, ethnicity, gender, and orientation

- Experienced and inexperienced

- Already recognized by others or just emerging to step up in a crisis

- Situated at the top, middle, and bottom of organizations

There are leaders with formal authority who are leaders in name only because they fail to provide the leadership needed. ***Leadiators show who they are by their principled actions, not by their words or their titles.***

Leadiator Action Principles

- Align words and deeds to do the right thing.
- Speak up courageously and show up to face difficulty together.

- Bring fresh energy and ideas to challenge a stagnant status quo.

- Lead the necessary action for positive change.

- Be accountable to earn trust and remain credible.

- Admit mistakes readily and continue to learn.

- Be vulnerable, acknowledge interdependence with others, and ask for help.

Your current role may be as a leader with formal authority. You may be a person without formal authority but with some influence who wants to promote actions that lead to beneficial change. You may be an employee, a volunteer, or a follower who sees a leadership gap and wants to be part of the solution.

> **There are leaders and there are those who lead.**

Use this book to identify emerging opportunities to lead Creative Collaboration. You can make a difference in the organization where you work, in the voluntary group to which you belong, and in the community where you live. If you do not yet believe this to be true, I respectfully challenge you to read this book before accepting the limiting belief that you cannot be a leadiator. Some of the stories you will encounter in this book involve people without formal authority or leadership experience who stepped into the gap. They became leadiators, UNITING others who needed to come together.

The Creative Collaboration Blueprint

This book presents a practical, flexible blueprint to improve the Creative Collaboration of any organization. With this blueprint, you will have a common reference with a shared language for UNITING. You can speak this common language with clarity, conviction, and courage. You can teach this language to others. With it, critical conversations become more focused and productive.

The basic blueprint has four components and begins to build from the bottom up.

Figure 1

Blueprint for Creative Collaboration

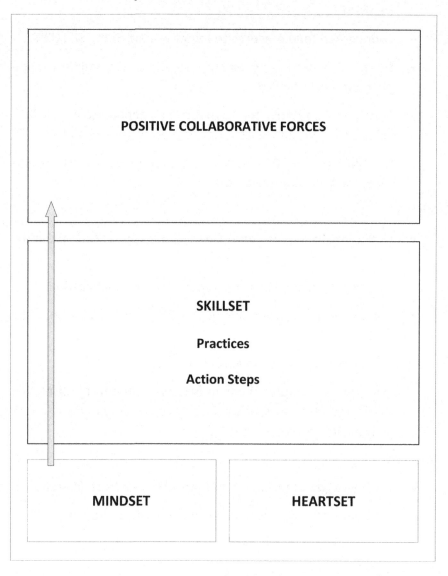

The complete blueprint layers in detail to build a strong, flexible structure that can sustain components that will build and sustain a collaborative organization. See Figure 2.

- Resources to develop (MINDSET, HEARTSET, SKILLSET)

- Cultural characteristics* to cultivate as part of MINDSET and HEARTSET

- Four cornerstone practices to follow as part of the SKILLSET

- **D**esigned **N**ecessary **A**ction steps as part of the SKILLSET to implement each practice

- Positive collaborative forces that can be generated with MINDSET, HEARTSET, and SKILLSET to produce positive results

- MINDSET and HEARTSET provide the foundation. SKILLSET provides the behavioral structure.

Mindset

- Use common sense to think clearly and pragmatically about the work together.

- Follow a disciplined process to build strong collaboration.

- Communicate so everyone understands the whole and the parts.

- Assess effectiveness to improve results.

- Develop the cultural characteristic of a Growth Mindset that uses mistakes, errors, and failure to generate learning and turn learning into improvement.

Heartset

- Have enough humility to admit mistakes and learn lessons.

- Have enough patience to listen and learn from others.

- Be willing to work out differences and conflicts.

- Face challenges with courage.

- Develop the cultural characteristic of Integrity by articulating and being guided by core values and guiding principles.

- Develop the cultural characteristic of Psychological Safety by maintaining a trustworthy environment where everyone's voice matters and people can count on each other.

Skillset (Practices and Action Steps)

- Use Dialogue to generate respectful learning conversations.

- Use Wise Planning to coordinate and focus collective effort.

- Use Values-Based Decision Making to put core values and principles into action.

- Use Principled Negotiation to build bridges and make peace.

MINDSET, HEARTSET, AND SKILLSET enable leadiators to resourcefully guide, encourage, and educate others to build Creative Collaboration. These elements work like a 3-D printer to build the resourceful organization in layers from the bottom up.

Creative Collaboration always requires learning by doing. Therefore, instead of chapters, I have structured this book as nine lessons. These resources are layered into each lesson and can be adapted to organizations in all sectors.

The Skillset resource is divided into two parts. The first part includes four cornerstone practices. Each will be the primary focus of a lesson.

- Dialogue (Lesson Four)

- Wise Planning (Lesson Six)

- Values Based Decision Making (Lesson Seven)

- Principled Negotiation (Lesson Eight)

The second part includes the ongoing skillful action steps that leadiators must take to guide organizations and implement these practices. In the aggregate, these **D**esigned **N**ecessary **A**ction Steps are the remainder of the skillset. Like the DNA of our bodies, these constructive behaviors are the life force of a healthy organization. Each lesson describes action steps and action-oriented questions to move an organization forward together.

The development of Creative Collaboration over time is a dynamic process because the power of collaboration comes from nine interconnected forces. When these forces develop, there is synergy that multiplies the power of collective effort to overcome obstacles, innovate, and adapt to change. An organization that harnesses the collective power of these forces has a *spirit* that is palpable. This *spirit* unleashes creativity and possibility.

Each lesson addresses one of these forces.

1. *Clarity* to reason, assess, and think well together
2. *Perspective* to see the big picture and recognize the path forward
3. *Connection* to stick together in a climate of safety and trust
4. *Understanding* to learn together, improve, and grow capacity
5. *Moral Imagination* to envision a positive future to work toward together
6. *Leverage* to align collective effort for excellent results
7. *Conviction* to act with integrity, earn credibility, and build trust
8. *Reconciliation* to bridge differences and make peace
9. *Agility* to adapt to change, innovate, and shift direction to navigate difficulty

Figure 2

Blueprint for Creative Collaboration

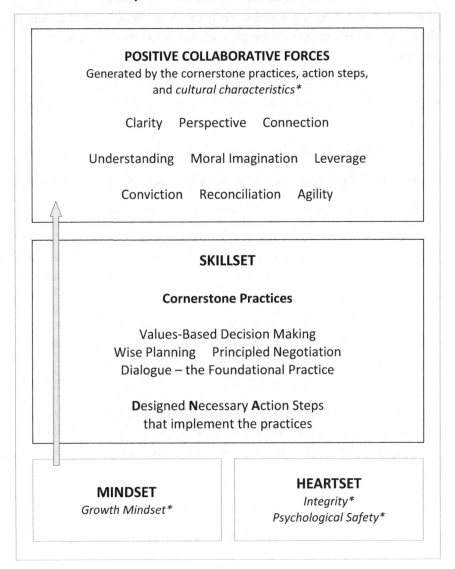

POSITIVE COLLABORATIVE FORCES
Generated by the cornerstone practices, action steps,
and *cultural characteristics**

Clarity   Perspective   Connection

Understanding   Moral Imagination   Leverage

Conviction   Reconciliation   Agility

SKILLSET

Cornerstone Practices

Values-Based Decision Making
Wise Planning   Principled Negotiation
Dialogue – the Foundational Practice

Designed **N**ecessary **A**ction Steps
that implement the practices

MINDSET
Growth Mindset*

HEARTSET
Integrity*
Psychological Safety*

Along with recommended action steps, each lesson ends with questions to engage others in a dialogue about your organization's situation and ways you and others can put these ideas into practice. With questions to engage others and steps to follow, you can adopt the Mindset and Heartset of a Leadiator. Through practice, the organization grows the Skillset to succeed. *The leadiator role is to point the organization toward TRUE NORTH, the continuing growth of its adaptive capacity. Then, the organization will be able to navigate change, uncertainty, and risk.*

The nine lessons for organizations are separated into three parts of the book. Each part represents a basic developmental phase of creative collaboration.

- FORMING (joining together with the intention to collaborate)

- BECOMING (learning and growing full capacity to work together)

- EVOLVING (maturing, reinventing, and adapting over time)

You can follow the book sequence from beginning to end, or read Lessons One and Two to understand the framework and then turn to any lesson that attracts your interest. There is a summary of the lesson's core ideas on the last page.

This is a book of HOPE because it provides something that makes common sense: a practical blueprint that you can adapt to your organization's challenges UNITING others in the essential work of these times.

Build sustainable, creative collaboration in your organization, team, group, or community to increase the capacity to learn together, innovate together, and adapt together.

H umans

O rienting through

P ositive

E ngagement

Core Ideas from the Introduction

Throughout this book, I will use the word, leadiator to describe a leader who is willing and able to adapt and meet the unique challenges of our times. A leadiator has the courageous heart of a peacemaker and the capacity for UNITING people in Creative Collaboration.

Collaboration is emergent because it is always increasing or decreasing based on the interaction of the underlying organizational conditions with the surrounding environment that includes social, technological, environmental, economic, and political forces.

Leadiators show who they are by their principled actions, not by their words or their titles.

The development of Creative Collaboration over time is a dynamic process because the power of collaboration comes from nine interconnected forces.

The leadiator role is to always point the organization toward TRUE NORTH, the continuing growth of its adaptive capacity. Then, the organization will be able to navigate change, uncertainty, and risk.

PART ONE FORMING

Joining together intentionally to collaborate

If you want to go fast, go alone.

If you want to go far, go together.

~ Proverb

Lesson One Thinking – the Force of Clarity

- Thinking Anew After a Civil War

- Improving Perspective to Think Anew

- Disciplined Thinking About the Structure of Collaboration

- Think About the Benefits of UNITING

- Think About the Common Barriers to UNITING

- Negative Attitudes (Mindsets) that Make UNITING Difficult

- Think About the Natural Opportunities for UNITING

- Think About How a Leadiator Stands in the Gap Between Reality and Possibility

Lesson Two Seeing – the Force of Perspective

- A New School Sees an Extended Community of Creative Collaboration

- Basic Behavioral Conditions for Creative Collaboration

- An Introduction to the Cornerstone Practices of Creative Collaboration

- The Architecture of Healthy, Collaborative Organizations

- Inquiry and Dialogue Generate Perspective to Chart the Course

- Three Universal Action Principles Improve Capacity to See Clearly

Lesson Three Belonging – the Force of Connection

- How Belonging Develops
- Healthy Organization Culture and the Capacity for Belonging
- Elements of a Healthy Organization Culture
- Psychological Safety Is the Connection Between Belonging and High Performance
- Leadiators Recognize That Trust Is a Verb
- Building Trust That Sustains Effort

Blueprint for Creative Collaboration

POSITIVE COLLABORATIVE FORCES
Generated by the cornerstone practices, action steps,
and *cultural characteristics**

Clarity   Perspective   Connection

Understanding   Moral Imagination   Leverage

Conviction   Reconciliation   Agility

SKILLSET

Cornerstone Practices

Values-Based Decision Making
Wise Planning   Principled Negotiation
Dialogue – the Foundational Practice

Designed **N**ecessary **A**ction Steps
that implement the practices

MINDSET
*Growth Mindset**

HEARTSET
*Integrity**
*Psychological Safety**

Lesson One THINKING

*The situation is piled high with difficulty
and we must rise to the occasion.
Because our case is new, we must think anew and act anew.*

~ Abraham Lincoln

The Force of Clarity

**Thinking is often rooted in unquestioned
attitudes and limiting beliefs.**

**A leadiator must think carefully and test assumptions in order to
positively shape the way individuals and teams understand how
to work well together.**

**The design of Creative Collaboration requires clear thinking about
challenges with the status quo.**

**There are five underlying conditions that must be cultivated to
grow a more collaborative organization.**

Abraham Lincoln's wise counsel from 160 years ago is timeless wisdom forged from a set of challenges in a crisis. It is not an understatement to characterize the intersection of a pandemic, global economic decline, climate change, and a social/political movement for racial justice as a crisis. Today's leadiators can only respond wisely in a rapidly changing landscape by moving beyond the thinking habits that produced the status quo. They must overcome predictable biases that can cloud individual and group thinking. These biases trick leaders into a false belief that they understand. **Too often, leaders believe they are thinking when, in fact, they are only rearranging their prejudices.**

Thinking anew breaks habits, overcomes biases, and stops recycling flawed assumptions that consciously and unconsciously reinforce the status quo. *With clear understanding of the importance of Creative Collaboration and its structure, leadiators can focus on practical action. UNITING has the power to generate fresh thinking by engaging diverse points of view.* Thoughtful steps can organize individuals into a team, teams into an organization, and organizations into alliances, coalitions and partnerships.

Clear thinking generates situational awareness of a changing landscape. This helps leadiators and teams identify threats and opportunities. With clarity about the situation and a vision of where WE want to go together, the organization can align and respond promptly, dynamically, and resourcefully.

In the introduction, you began to think anew about your organization's situation by using a design blueprint. Your organization needs to become an *all-terrain vehicle* that can carry everyone forward together. It needs to be built, maintained, and modified when necessary.

Learning Objectives

- Recognize thinking habits that have produced the organizational status quo.

- Overcome negative attitudes and limiting beliefs that could undermine the effort to think about, design, and build collaboration.

- Identify five underlying conditions that leadiators must cultivate to grow a more collaborative organization.

Thinking Anew After a Civil War

In 1996, my family hosted some emerging women leaders from Bosnia who came to New Mexico to gain peacemaking skills and build working relationships across ethnic lines (Muslim (Bosniac), Serb, Croat). They faced a huge challenge: how to rebuild a society shattered by civil war. One of these leaders, a Muslim school teacher named Jasminka Drino Krilic, saw her small city of Gornji Vakuf - Uskoplje reduced to rubble. The war also destroyed the social fabric of her community, dividing members of the major ethnic groups into polarized factions, unable to work together.

It was obvious that rebuilding a community required UNITING with collective effort. However, none of the existing leaders were leadiators. There was a lack of ability to bring people together due to the high level of distrust between these groups.

At the dining room table in our home, Jasminka shared the story of her journey to become a leadiator. It began with the recognition that her training and experience as a teacher provided her with a unique view of her community and its needs. She knew students and parents from all the ethnic groups. She understood the educational, social, and emotional needs of the young people. She could imagine using her positive relationships to bring the adults in the community together across the social divides to begin shared conversations about the process of UNITING to rebuild.

However, many of her attempts to mobilize the adults in the community failed to generate enough support. She discovered that the wounds were too deep and the trauma too great. The level of fear, grief, and hate formed a large barrier and there was a lack of understanding about how to join together.

So, she rethought her assumption that it was up to the adults to rebuild the community. Instead, she re-focused her thinking on the capacity and motivation of the young people. Perhaps she could build on her rapport and relationships with young people to bring them together to begin these conversations.

In this challenging situation, she recognized the need for something meaningful to draw the young people into collaboration with others from different ethnic groups. She needed something stronger than the legacy of fear, mistrust, and hate to attract the young people.

She began to talk with them individually, asking about their hopes and dreams. She found that the young people were interested. And, she learned three important things that they wanted: learn English; use computers; and use cameras and darkroom equipment. With this focus on the young people, she began to plant the seeds of a community of people who wanted to renew lives.

She also refined her thinking as she slowly attracted other adults who were teachers, translators, and professionals with knowledge to share. The idea of a Youth Center where young people from all the ethnic groups could learn and grow together emerged from this process of thinking together.

She moved forward with an idea of a Youth Center with resources that could motivate young people to come together. She began to think about the financial resources that would make it possible to renovate a ruined building and fill it with English teachers, computers, and photography equipment. She searched for funding and eventually found a church relief organization and a UN Development program to join with some local people to establish the Youth Center.

The Youth Center was a reality! However, when the young people from the different ethnic groups came into the center, the level of mistrust, fear, and anger kept the groups from talking and engaging with anyone outside their own group. They remained polarized and segregated from each other.

Again, the situation forced her to think anew about the challenges and the vision. Her initial vision was for a well-run youth center with adults in charge. She considered a different way to organize the youth center to fully engage the youth, not just as users, but as *owners* who accepted responsibility for the healthy operation of the center. Could more ownership and responsibility generate positive working relationships with young people from the other ethnic groups?

The beginning of the journey of Creative Collaboration often begins by asking better questions, to think, and think again about the challenges.

Jasminka shifted her thinking about "Who should run the Youth Center?" She conceived a board of directors structure composed of an equal number of Muslim, Serb, and Croat young people. This structure would also require that votes to approve action have consensus support from the entire board. The groups would be interdependent with a natural need to communicate and develop agreements together. The governance structure could become a strong foundation to respectfully build healthy relationships.

At this stage in her thinking, she arrived at the level of clarity needed to begin a journey of Creative Collaboration that became a bright light and catalyst of hope in a landscape of despair. This Youth Center continues to operate today as a model of an interethnic community that has inspired other youth centers in the region. There are still dedicated young people working there in line with its peacekeeping mission. They have taken over the management structure and are connected with other organizations in the country and the region. During the summer, many of them, now as adults, come to the Youth Center and volunteer to help the next generation. (1)

Improve Perspective to Think Anew

Before you can think clearly about building collaboration in an organization, it is necessary to take a step back. Then, you can reflect on the point of view where you now stand. With awareness from your point of view, you can carefully frame the practical opportunities and challenges of working together with others. Jasminka's journey shows that clear, positive thinking creates the structure necessary to generate skillful action.

Her story is also an example of the emergence of Creative Collaboration in the midst of extraordinarily challenging circumstances. The Holocaust survivor, Corrie Ten Boom, said "Worry does not empty tomorrow of its sorrow. It empties today of its strength." (2) To be creative requires strength. Jasminka didn't let the lack of resources, community hostility, and ethnic tension sap her will to face huge challenges. She kept thinking anew with a positive focus on possibilities.

All of us begin to build awareness that frames our thinking about collaboration in our family of origin. We continue to form our thinking with experiences: school; religious groups; clubs; sports teams; youth groups; military service; and teamwork on the job. The collective impact of all these experiences shapes the ways each one of us thinks, feels, and believes about working together.

Each of you has been on a life journey with many opportunities to observe, study, and learn about collaboration. These opportunities shape your point of view. Your point of view shapes your thinking and affects what you see and don't see.

For some, this journey may have never included a highly successful experience of collaboration. For others, the collaborative highlight of their lives may have been thirty years ago as a member of a school sports team that won a championship. Whether your personal experiences with collaboration have been negative or positive, these reference points from childhood, adolescence, or early adulthood may have little relevance to the important, challenging work of building unity among strong personalities on a sharply divided governing board or in a stressful day-to-day working environment. UNITING as a school sports team for a few hours a week for a few months is less complex than UNITING as a work team for 40 hours a week, year in and year out. Now, COVID-19 presents every organization with a new landscape and new challenges that will likely test every organization's capacity to think anew about UNITING virtually, and find ways to work together resourcefully.

In my work with adults in organizations, I often encounter problematic ways that leaders and participants view and think about the opportunities and challenges of working together. Often, there is a lack of ability to think anew about what Creative Collaboration is and how it could work in the organization.

The real needs for collaboration may be obscured by habitual patterns of framing and thinking about the ways to work better together. This framing only reproduces sloppy thinking, perpetuates mistaken beliefs, and reinforces negative attitudes about the practical, disciplined actions necessary to build and sustain collaboration. The beginning of the work to form a successful, collaborative effort involves ordinary, open-minded conversations to learn what is needed. These conversations will be shaped by people's thoughts, beliefs, assumptions, and attitudes about this thing called collaboration.

What is the structure of "thinking anew"?

Think of UNITING As a Generative Force. There are hundreds of best-selling books on collaboration and teamwork by championship coaches, leadership experts, and successful business CEOs. The need to understand the power of UNITING has many names. "Collective Impact." "ROI-Return on Investment." "Search for Excellence." "Wisdom of Teams." "Moving from Good to Great." "Creative Collaboration." "Learning Organization." "Team of Teams."

Now, more than ever, the importance of working well together is a critical issue. There will be continuing social, economic, and political impacts of a global pandemic on the operations of all sizes and types of organizations. Leaders must be able to rethink traditional structures and processes. In every sector (profit, nonprofit, government), leadiators must focus on the organization's value to those it exists to serve and how to generate it amidst the strong waves of change and uncertainty. A leader who guided a highly publicized turnaround of a major organization in crisis pointed to the essential variable to address.

"I came to see, in my time at IBM, that culture isn't just one aspect of the game. IT IS THE GAME. In the end, an organization is nothing more than the collective capacity of its people to create value."

~ Lou Gerstner, CEO, Author *Who Says Elephants Can't Dance: Inside IBM's Historic Turnaround* (3)

Lesson Three will explore the definition of an organization's culture and how leadiators can develop the overall character of an organization. Before examining the challenge to build collective capacity (culture), there is another element of this capacity to call out as essential. Every few years, IBM conducts a comprehensive global survey of the thinking of 1,500 CEOs from small, medium, and large organizations. This includes leaders of corporations, nonprofits, and government. In 2010, leaders ranked creativity as the most important quality to guide organization success. (4)

Every organization and every alliance, coalition, and partnership is looking for the *1+1 = 3 effect* by creatively aligning limited human and financial resources in a way that generates leverage for superior results. The tech industry has given us *10X* as the gold standard for innovation and breakthrough performance that improves results by ten times. With so much talk, so much need, so much interest, and so much effort, the results of these attempts to join and work together are often mediocre and sometimes terrible. Why?

According to a detailed survey by McKinsey and Company, a prominent international consulting firm, 80-90% of business mergers fail to successfully form a unified organization that achieves the stated goals of the merger. (5) Among the common reasons for these failures is the inability to turn the separate organizations into a united, integrated organization with a cohesive culture. Instead of becoming a creative expression that is more than the sum of its parts, the organization remains 1+1=2.

In 25 years of nonprofit consulting work with individual organizations and with alliances, coalitions, and other inter-organizational collaborations, I observed that there is often a large gap between how much people talk about the importance of collaboration and the reality that their practices demonstrate and achieve. I believe the reason for this gap between aspiration and performance is the absence of a robust, flexible structure that grows shared understanding (Mindset) with a common set of tools (Skillset) that focus whole-hearted effort (Heartset).

A structure helps close the gap because a common, practical language guides disciplined thinking, creativity, and determined action. *Leadiators can shape the thinking of others and influence the level of motivation and creativity people bring to the collaborative effort.*

The most common words used to describe working together that capture the significance of being unified in a common purpose are collaboration and teamwork. These words are used loosely to describe some degree of connected effort. People often draw upon irrelevant examples like famous sports teams or anecdotal past experiences. Collaboration generally means to work together with some degree of cooperation, teamwork, and partnership. However, this definition of collaboration doesn't measure up to the 21st century challenge of producing *1+1 = 3*, let alone "10X."

UNITING is a more powerful word that includes the capacity for collaboration plus deeper dimensions of shared commitment, cohesive relationships, and creativity that generate superior results. UNITING is an emergent, fluid state of being joined together in common purpose. This dynamic state requires strong connections through consensus, trust, respect, harmony, and solidarity. These connective elements provide strength that is more adaptive and therefore more sustainable than basic cooperation and teamwork.

Many organizations that talk about collaboration fail in the *walk* because they do not apply a common framework to shape the intentional effort necessary to sustain UNITING. They lack the strong connection and commitment necessary to stick together, resist forces of disunity, meet challenges, bridge differences, and move the mission forward.

In intra- and inter-organizational efforts when the spirit and reality of UNITING is present, the skillful, purposeful practice of Creative Collaboration becomes generative and sustainable over time. My experience is that UNITING can make possible what was previously thought to be impossible. At first, the journey may seem too difficult to succeed, but all journeys begin with steps and the will to move forward together.

Think Correctly About UNITING. It is necessary to address some common misconceptions before examining the structure for UNITING.

Just think and act like a sports team Lessons from successful sports teams do not easily transfer to organizational environments. Yet, they are often used to *cheerlead* and pump people up in poorly designed efforts at team-building with half-hearted follow through.

UNITING requires unanimity UNITING is not about conformity. It is not *groupthink* where people minimize differences to maintain pseudo-agreement. Diversity in seeing, thinking, and understanding adds quality and depth to a genuine unified effort. Constructive disagreement can be necessary and healthy. **UNITING doesn't require you be the same. It requires that you come together and stick together.**

"Kumbaya" Retreats, high quality team-building exercises, and other genuine, heart-felt moments of coming together can develop a heightened sense of connectedness and common purpose. However, a shared framework is essential to guide everyone and convert positive aware-ness and *we-feeling* into sustainable day-to-day behaviors amidst the often-pressured reality of organizational life. The positive, temporary experience is like a seed. Without the *water* from ongoing, structured conversations, the positive sense of *we* doesn't take root in the life of the organization. When the good feeling fades away, too often what remains is a cynical belief that future efforts to improve the ability to work together would be a naïve waste of time.

It's an impossible dream Many people have never had a solid experi-ence of the enduring power of organizational UNITING. Without a clear image of what UNITING looks like and how it can be developed, they are unlikely to be sufficiently motivated to engage in the practical work of building and sustaining unity.

This book is a flexible blueprint for leadiators and organizations to ef-fectively navigate in a rapidly changing landscape.

- This blueprint can be adapted to the particular context of any organization in any sector.

- It can be adapted to any size organization.

- It can be adapted to any team or group within an organization.

- It can be adapted to the work of independent organizations in coalitions, alliances, and partnerships.

- Leadiators and organizations can tailor these design principles to act with confidence and discipline.

- Adaptation is essential to unleash an organization's full poten-tial for UNITING.

Think About Connection and Cohesiveness Try this simple, physical metaphor to guide your thinking about UNITING and provide a founda-tion for the detailed design provided in these lessons. Think of the con-tinuum of working together effectively for a group of 5 to 15 people who have some reason to come together, e.g. a small organization, work team, leadership team, governing board, or neighborhood associ-ation. There are four stages.

Stage One - Contact Without Connection Take your two fists and put them together so the knuckles touch in an overlapping pattern. It is common in many organizations to regard this minimal degree of contact as a form of teamwork. Members of a working group come together periodically to confer. People in different organizational teams or divisions (silos) see each other at an all-hands meeting, hear an announcement by the leadership team, and provide feedback or ask questions. There is rhetoric about everyone being part of one, big team with little or no connective tissue in the working relationship. There is little, if any, trust because there are limited opportunities to experience each other over time. And, in many organizations this minimal level of real connection can quickly turn into division or active conflict (bump your fists lightly together).

Stage Two - Connection Without Cohesion Open your fists, hands flat with palms toward the floor, place the hands together with one on top of the other in front of you. The fingers overlap. Then, slide them apart until they are fully separated. Notice how little energy it takes to separate them. Many organizations believe they have functioning teamwork or, even collaboration, until stressful changes in operating conditions, e.g., a budget crisis, literally *pull* them apart into a competitive struggle for resources. At this stage, any trust that exists is superficial and there is no common framework that provides shared understanding of how to leverage the complementary strengths of individuals or teams by UNITING to make the whole greater than the sum of the parts.

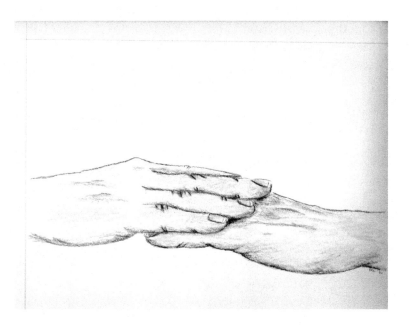

Stage Three - Connection With Cohesion Take your hands and firmly lace the fingers of the opposite hands together and give the fingers a squeeze. Now, pull the hands apart noticing the amount of effort required. This stage of collaboration represents the highest level that many organizations aspire to. There is meaningful communication and a solid, working-level of trust. There is capacity to work together cooperatively and creatively under most conditions. However, there is still vulnerability. High enough demands and stress can degrade the organization's capacity to work together.

Stage Four – Connection With Cohesion & Integration – Creative Collaboration Take your hands and firmly lace the fingers of the opposite hands together. Fold the hands and press the palms together. Lock the fingers and thumb of each hand onto the other. Then, use all your strength to try to pull the hands apart. At this stage, integrated working relationships have a high degree of trust, a sense of interdependence, and full creative engagement. There is a widely shared belief among employees that leaders and colleagues have their backs. The organization's mission, core values, and guiding principles are not just words. They bind the separate *fingers* of the organization together in unified strength.

Creative Collaboration requires more depth than typical understanding that effective working together equals basic cooperation and some degree of coordinated effort. Real strength requires connection, cohesion, and integration. This degree of UNITING to work together involves committed action.

- Treating each other as respected partners

- Standing shoulder-to-shoulder to face challenges

- Joining forces to solve hard problems

- Having each others' backs

- Actively seeking ways to become better together

Disciplined Thinking About the Structure of Creative Collaboration

With better perspective to think anew, an organization can become more disciplined. Discipline begins with an understanding that ***Creative Collaboration is a dynamic state of shared human potential rooted in five conditions that must be present***. The actions to develop each one of these conditions will be explored later.

- ***Consistent cooperative behavior*** develops out of participants' interactions over time. (Lessons Three and Four)

- Participants recognize their ***interdependence and shared purpose***. (Lesson Five)

- Participants have a collective determination to reach the same goal and a ***shared sense of ownership and responsibility*** for the work necessary to succeed. (Lesson Six)

- Important decisions enjoy broad support reflected in a ***meaningful consensus*** that the organization's goals and strategies are moving in the right direction. (Lesson Seven)

- Plans and decisions emerge from the **open, *constructive management of differences.*** (Lesson Eight)

UNITING is a practical, creative strategy to develop capacity inside an individual organization, department, or team, or in a partnership between organizations. UNITING needs to be viewed as a valuable asset that delivers immediate and ongoing returns on your investment. UNIT-ING is a *force-multiplier* that magnifies existing capacity to increase results by rapidly turning every success, challenge, or mistake into learning.

In good times, UNITING is the *high-octane fuel* that continuously generates trust. This naturally accelerates coordination and execution to move forward at what the author, Stephen M. R. Covey calls the "Speed of Trust." "Nothing is as fast as the speed of trust. Nothing is as fulfilling as a relationship of trust. Nothing is as profitable as the economics of trust. Nothing has more influence than a reputation of trust. Trust truly is the one thing that changes everything." (6)

It is pragmatic to recognize the game-changing, post-COVID-19 landscape of global vulnerability, uncertainty, and challenge. *In hard times of disruption, change, and uncertainty, UNITING is an all-weather plan B. It assures the capacity to respond effectively because the organization is already well aligned, able to adapt, and ready to pivot in a new direction when necessary.*

UNITING can have effects that seem magical, but it is not magic. It requires focused effort guided by clear thinking. UNITING only forms and sustains because leadiators (with and without formal authority) guide and inspire others to invest time, energy, and focused effort using a shared framework.

There are practical approaches that develop these five underlying conditions. Here are summaries that I will explore in more depth in later Lessons. Notice that these approaches interact and mutually reinforce each other. It is this synergistic relationship that can feel like magic.

Build Psychological Safety The process of UNITING over time requires full engagement and participation. Leadiators and managers must constructively manage differences. This means they must consistently act to develop and sustain a climate of basic respect, belonging, and trust that integrates diverse perspectives, talents, and contributions. This climate removes fear of embarrassment, ridicule, or punishment and promotes engaged cooperation and the flow of creative ideas. (Lesson Three)

Tap the Power of Purpose UNITING with purpose begins with a brief, clear, memorable statement of WHY the organization exists. In no more than 15 words, the mission statement lays the foundation for UNITING by bringing everyone together with a common reference point of orientation and motivation. Words matter! Purpose animates the heart and the will. Mission is a driving force for interdependence. (Lesson Five)

Use Vision to Pull the Organization Forward A common destination shows everyone the direction and provides an inspiring image of what it looks like to fulfill the mission. Consensus naturally emerges when purpose and destination are clearly aligned. Apple's founder, Steve Jobs said, "If you are passionate about what you do, you don't have to be pushed. The vision will pull you forward." (7) Vision orients and focuses the passion of purpose (the mission), cultivates a mindset of learning, and inspires innovation.

In Lesson Five you will find examples of organizations with permanent visions that are not reachable in a decade or a lifetime. To strengthen the *pull* of a distant vision on the current state, an organization can develop a more concrete, *horizon* vision of 2-3 years that points toward a visible destination that is bold and attainable. It this ability to imagine, see, and feel the destination that can pull an organization forward together.

Set Behavioral Guard Rails Clear core values and guiding action principles must be well-integrated into the organization's culture and practices to clarify shared expectations. These function as *guard rails that* set and maintain shared standards for the quality of the work, the way you treat those you serve, and the way you treat each other. Big values words like Teamwork, Integrity, Innovation, and Respect are critical for UNITING. However, these important words must not rest in a poster on the wall. They need succinct definitions, supported with specific commitments to take action. These commitments must transform the values into observable behaviors. Leadiators and managers must set the example and hold others accountable.

Values and principles are the ethical *heartbeat* of a healthy organization, encouraging every department and work team. Values are nouns.

Action Principles are the verbs that breathe life into the core values. These principles are more descriptive and indicate what the value looks like in action. Consistent, constructive behaviors are more specific commitments to act that align the organization with the core value and the action principle.

For example, INTEGRITY is a noun. An action principle that might implement INTEGRITY is "We will make our tracking and reporting transparent and accessible to the public." One specific, constructive behavior that implements this action principle might be, "Every quarter we will update our report on customer complaints and resolutions and post it on our public web site." (Lesson Five)

Be Accountable Accountability means everyone can be counted on to fulfill her commitments and own the results of her actions. This increases the organization's *response-ability*. When everyone in an organization connects to the major goals and wants to do his part, the sense of identity, belonging, and psychological safety matures into *esprit de corps* or spirit of the body. This palpable energy can be perceived in a well-run, collaborative organization. WE become stronger together. Everyone wants to do his part. (Lesson Six)

Think About the Benefits of UNITING

A leadiator needs a Mindset that regards the time and effort to cultivate UNITING as an investment in an asset of great value. This can provide an excellent return on investment (ROI). A leadiator uses these basic elements of a favorable ROI to enlist the support of others to spend time and money on the necessary shared effort.

- Accelerate organization progress in good times.

- Maintain the adaptive capacity to navigate change amidst uncertainty.

- Be resourceful and collectively ready to meet challenges and overcome difficulty in hard times.

With these elements in mind, a leadiator can engage and guide others in the focused development of UNITING.

Increase the Capacity to Respond For most organizations, the current and near future operating environment presents significant constraints (financial, material, time). However, two resources are abundant and waiting to be tapped: creativity and collaboration. Maximum leverage requires everyone to engage with a full effort.

> **Successful organizations fully leverage the resources they have, instead of worrying about the resources they don't have.**

Overcome Barriers to Success Poor coordination, miscommunication, unclear or unshared expectations, mistrust, lack of confidence in others, incivility, and disagreement will limit an organization's ability to achieve its goals. Without focused effort to establish and sustain a robust collaborative framework, these barriers are likely to prevent or diminish the capacity of individuals and teams to deliver their best, leading to mediocre or poor results.

Avoid Negative Consequences The inability to collaborate can lead to wasted time, low morale, lack of accountability, and costly turnover. In some cases, negative outcomes can threaten an organization's existence. At a minimum, the organization could lose valuable opportunities to excel and earn the trust and confidence of its stakeholders.

Design a System That Supports Collaboration At every level from senior leadership to front-line workers, the ability to work together well IS the foundation of a successful organization. Highly effective working relationships are not accidental. They begin by intentionally hiring people who are a good fit with the organization's mission, values, and culture. People are the heart of a system that can adapt to changing conditions, creatively respond to challenges, and fulfill the mission. An organization system must be intentionally designed, carefully built, and regularly maintained to deliver sustainable, positive results.

Think About the Common Barriers to UNITING

Creative Collaboration allows individual participants to retain power and influence but also requires sharing power with others and acknowledging their autonomy. Diversity and cultural differences must be openly embraced and respectfully addressed. The path to UNITING to accomplish a shared purpose can become rocky without attention to the process of integration. Human factors present leadiators with four types of recurring barriers to integration.

Politics There is a tendency to use power and seek to win or dominate at the expense of principle and relationship.

Personality characteristics There are negative habits, attitudes, and behaviors that may challenge and divide, e.g., the know-it-all, the judgmental gossip, the bully, the slacker, or "my way or the highway" stubbornness.

Preferences There are fixed ways to communicate and work together from prior experiences about "what works and what doesn't," e.g., a person with a military background who has a commitment to a chain of command hierarchy, but is now working in a civilian government agency with co-workers who prefer a more horizontal approach to communication.

Priorities There are motivations rooted in different guiding values and principles that create tension and conflict between members of the organization, e.g. a person who uses his commitment to the value of absolute honesty as ethical authority to be brutally candid even when this behavior reduces others to tears. (*It's their problem if they can't handle the truth!*)

These four barriers usually surface as personality clashes, poor communication, and turf issues. As a leadiator and advocate for collaboration, it is important to recognize the sources of discord. The rest of this book provides proven practices and skills to respond effectively. Watch for these patterns that call for a leadiator response.

Disagreeable disagreement Honest differences can coexist with collaboration. However, rancorous debate, personal attacks, and all forms of disrespect will generate a negative, polarized or toxic climate that can limit or destroy the capacity for collaboration.

Perception of Differences as Negative Differences come in many forms (age, gender, ethnicity, language, personality, working style, education level, values and principles, experience, sexual orientation, and ability). Diversity is reality and can become an organizational strength. The perception that others are like us supports a natural orientation toward collaboration. The perception of differences can inhibit the connection and rapport needed to collaborate. A negative attitude about differences can cause one person to make the other person the problem. *Differences require a healthy response to build understanding, bridge differences, and move beyond tolerance of differences to value, embrace, and tap the full power of diverse perspectives.*

Growing organization, team, or group size When the size of an organization increases beyond 10-15 members, the capacity or willingness to collaborate often decreases. When an existing organization with effective, established ways of working together adds new members, it may be challenging to sustain the same level of engagement and cooperation. Leadiators must be proactive to link people through forums for dialogue. In larger organizations with hundreds or thousands of members, UNITING requires an organizational architecture and widely distributed skillset to become a "Team of Teams." Each individual team can learn to collaborate well internally. Separate teams can use a set of structural connections and joint forums for dialogue to overcome the natural tendency to operate in separate, vertical *silos.* They can recognize their interdependence to fulfill a shared mission. (8)

Distributed or virtual work groups The post-COVID-19 world is likely to involve expanded use of technological options for work together across time and distance. Organizations must learn and become more skillful with this way of working. Software and webinars can help, but it takes much more to build and maintain virtual teams.

Thousands of years of evolutionary biology is not likely to be transformed by adopting a set of guidelines and attending a webinar together. Human beings have developed ways to communicate meaning and purpose, build trust in others, express our feelings, and address conflicts that rely on three-dimensional interaction and the ability to notice subtle cues in non- verbal behavior.

Limited opportunities for face-to-face, interpersonal communication will probably make it harder to develop trusting relationships. Relying solely or primarily on electronic and telephonic communication channels is a significant structural barrier that requires careful attention to build collaboration. Lesson Nine, Adapting, will address the new, virtual operations reality for many organizations.

Negative History Past negative experiences between specific individuals or with group dynamics within the organization may remain as an active source of resentment, non-cooperation, and unwillingness to communicate openly. This can be a major barrier to Creative Collaboration. Dialogue and Principled Negotiation are often necessary to clear the way. When uncooperative or hostile attitudes persist and related behaviors are severe, leadiators must address the issues so the situation does not become toxic to the organization's health and impair the capacity to fulfill its mission. Sometimes, mediation or facilitation by a skilled person is necessary to untangle the situation with Principled Negotiation in order to move forward. (Lesson Eight)

Negative Attitudes (Mindsets) That Make UNITING Difficult

There are attitudes that shape and distort the thinking of participants about what it means to work well together. These aspects of mindset are significant because attitude is where thinking meets behavior. A popular motivational slogan states, "Attitude determines altitude." Any one of these negative attitudes held by even one person in a group, can generate a downward spiral of morale and productivity. One person can decrease the ability of others to rise to higher levels of effectiveness in their work together. Leadiators must be vigilant and proactively engage negative attitudes to redirect them.

Simple communication behaviors that result from negative attitudes send social cues to other members of an organization, team, or group. These cues can interrupt the essential process of connecting to develop a sense of belonging which is the precursor to Creative Collaboration. Social science research on this dynamic refers to the negative power of one person in a group as a *bad apple* who can lower the morale of others and reduce group performance. (9)

Typical negative attitudes encountered in organizational life share a common tendency to avoid responsibility by placing it on others. Scapegoating is a typical way to shift responsibility to others. It is a psychological path-of-least-resistance because it frees the individual with the attitude from any responsibility to participate in the resolution of the issue.

A related concept from family therapy is the "identified patient." (10) When a family is struggling, members of the family can consciously or unconsciously collude to label one family member as the person who is "sick" or has the "problem." When he or she is *fixed* all will be well. *It's not my problem! He IS the problem.* However, if one member of a family is sick, the family may also be ailing. When there are problems in an organization, the system will never be examined as long as people think that one person or one group is the problem.

How many of these negative attitudes do you recognize from your experience?

Victim Entitlement There is a belief that an individual, group or the organization has transgressed in word or deed. As a result, the victim has the right to act as he or she wishes toward the alleged perpetrator. In other words, he deserves what he gets.

> *Typical behaviors* include noncooperation, speaking about others in critical ways, ignoring the other, passive aggressiveness, disrespectful behavior, or personal attacks.

Learned Helplessness There is a belief that one is without power and ability to influence the situation.

> *Typical behaviors* include low motivation, chronic complaining, unwillingness to make any effort beyond the bare minimum, making excuses, lack of initiative, or lack of creativity.

Arrogance/Superiority There is a sense that one is better than others based on seniority, experience, talent, education, training or some other personal characteristic. At an extreme level, an individual holds an exalted view of being correct that manifests as overbearing right-eousness and judgment toward others.

Typical behaviors include unwillingness to listen to others, bullying, refusal to cooperate with others, inability to receive ideas and feed-back, displaying contempt, or mocking others.

Terminal Cynicism Someone holds on to a fixed belief that the situation, the organization, or the system is completely hopeless. There is a belief that leaders and others are incompetent or self-serving with hidden agendas that drive their decisions.

Typical behaviors include sarcasm, low motivation, slacking, chronic complaining, gossip, or spreading rumors.

Crusader There is a sense of righteous indignation at past/present in-justice with the commitment to stand up and fight or resist (*us vs. them*) to correct real or perceived wrong.

Typical behaviors include chronic anger, being argumentative, mak-ing categorical accusations, habitual opposition, repeated use of formal and informal channels to complain, or lobbying others to join a *crusade* of chronic dissatisfaction.

Naive Optimism There is a belief that everything is OK or will work out. *Don't worry. We all just need to get along.*

Typical behaviors include accommodating or allowing others' abu-sive or disrespectful behavior to go unchecked, unwilling to get in-volved in direct discussion of issues, or lack of interest in working for change.

Underdog There is a belief in subordinate status or inadequacy leading to a pattern of deference and submission to those of higher status (for-mal or informal).

Typical behaviors include resentful, sullen acceptance of the way things are, malicious compliance with authority, passivity, passive-aggressiveness, pessimism about the future, or unwillingness to take risks.

Any of these attitudes can be connected to problems with the organi-zation's operations, leadership, and culture. However, it is important to recognize that attitudes, even with some basis in reality, can circulate through an organization like a toxic virus. Healthy organizations pay conscious attention to the positive climate necessary to support mission success. Then, they can respond to problems by learning, correcting problems, and improving policies, procedures, and processes. Organizational culture and health are malleable and can be positively shaped toward Creative Collaboration.

Leadiators must be proactive to address negativity and promote positivity. They can encourage constructive responses to the environmental conditions and situational dynamics that foster negative attitudes. Creative Collaboration requires an environment where everyone becomes willing to accept responsibility and be accountable for his or her attitude and behavior before assigning any responsibility to others.

Think About the Natural Opportunities for UNITING

Entire organizations, departments and small work teams, boards of directors, family businesses, and communities all move through natural phases of development. During these transitions, it is common to reach a place where the organization experiences a limit to the capacity to fulfill the mission and achieve its goals. Healthy organizations use natural transitions for UNITING to increase organization capacity.

Lay a solid foundation for new relationships and initiatives Formation of a new organization, team, or partnership, the beginning of a major project, and the election of a new board of directors represent opportunities. Synchronize expectations, accelerate progress with a common framework, develop a shared language, and clarify roles and responsibilities.

Integrate new members into an existing group It is not always easy to bring in new people without some loss of effectiveness. Different work styles, unclear expectations, inadequate training, or lack of orientation can slow down the integration process and limit productive engagement. Conscious onboarding orients new people to the collaborative process. With a strong start, they can rapidly integrate into the culture of the organization. This effort becomes a wise investment that can generate future performance.

Improve the current level of performance It is easy for an organization to become complacent, lose the edge necessary to excel, or settle into patterns that produce marginal results. A complacent or stuck organization can use the Creative Collaboration blueprint to shift into inquiry and learning. Break limiting patterns to discover the upper limit of what is possible.

Forge a new partnership or a strategic alliance between organizations Leaders in all sectors from local to global recognize that external partnering is a key strategy to leverage additional resources for improved performance. Satya Nadella, Microsoft's visionary CEO, highlighted the extraordinary value of partnerships. "Our partners help us see around corners." (11) In a rapidly changing operational environment, an organization becomes smarter by joining together with others in common cause. Creative Collaboration is a powerful strategy to increase collective intelligence.

Evolve from silos to internal partnerships What is true for external partnerships is also true for separate departments and divisions within the organization. Groups are often separated in *silos* or *stovepipes* to a degree that keeps them from working well together and creating synergy.

Change dysfunctional dynamics When an organization falls into unhealthy patterns of behavior, the blueprint can guide a well-designed effort to positively shift the status quo. There is a broad spectrum of negativity from borderline tension and noncooperation that impair performance to polarization and toxic relations that destroy the ability to work together. It is easy to overlook or deny negative attitudes and behaviors when they are less severe. However, it is usually much easier to correct dysfunctions when the problems are small. Don't wait until a treatable symptom becomes an irreversible illness. Like a human body, an organization is a social body. Polarization and toxic dynamics can become a chronic or terminal disease.

Think About How a Leadiator Stands in the Gap Between Reality and Possibility

A leadiator who wants to help an organization adapt to change through Creative Collaboration needs a Mindset that accepts ambiguity, acknowledges uncertainty, and manages anxiety. Jasminka stood in the tragic gap between her community's divided present and her vision of a united future. Standing and facing the challenges courageously, she provided a critical example of Mindset, Heartset, and Skillset. When a leadiator shows the way, others can gain confidence and capacity to remain positive, become more resourceful, and mobilize creative, pragmatic efforts to move toward possibility.

Figure 3 shows this gap where every leadiator must stand between reality and possibility. Meaningful change requires the courage to stand in this gap, realistically accepting WHAT IS and persevering to generate WHAT COULD BE. It is critical to avoid predictable, negative patterns of thinking and feeling that tend to pull a leadiator and others out of the action. Leadiators inspire confidence and show others the way when they display positive, pragmatic thinking that guides whole-hearted engagement.

Figure 3

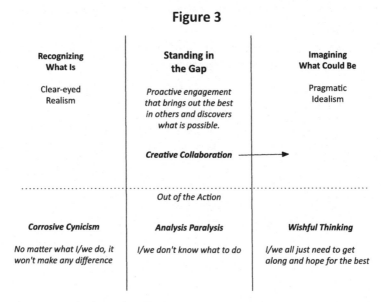

Recognizing What Is	Standing in the Gap	Imagining What Could Be
Clear-eyed Realism	*Proactive engagement that brings out the best in others and discovers what is possible.*	Pragmatic Idealism
	Creative Collaboration ⟶	
	Out of the Action	
Corrosive Cynicism	**Analysis Paralysis**	**Wishful Thinking**
No matter what I/we do, it won't make any difference	*I/we don't know what to do*	*I/we all just need to get along and hope for the best*

A leadiator can help individuals, teams, and a whole organization think anew by convening the right people to begin a dialogue. Open, honest inquiry and deep listening can break through old thinking habits and move beyond biased viewpoints.

Inquiry Into Action

- *In your organization or community, where is there a need for people to begin UNITING?*
- *Where are the natural opportunities in the organization's work together to build more capacity for Creative Collaboration?*
- *What potential benefits could your organization receive from an investment of time and effort to develop Creative Collaboration?*
- *Where do you stand in the gap as a current or potential leadiator who can step up to guide people toward Creative Collaboration?*
- *What are barriers in the gap between **what is** and **what could be** that must be navigated?*
- *Who are your natural allies inside the organization to engage?*
- *How can you reach out to them and begin a conversation about working better together?*
- *Are there external partners that could increase the organization's capacity to fulfill the mission?*

The Core Ideas of Lesson One

There are five underlying conditions that must be cultivated to grow a more collaborative organization.

UNITING doesn't require you to be the same. It requires that you come together and stick together.

With clear understanding of the importance of Creative Collaboration and its structure, leadiators can focus on practical action steps.

Leadiators can shape the thinking of others and influence the level of motivation people bring to the collaborative effort. UNITING has the power to generate fresh thinking.

In intra- and inter-organizational efforts where the spirit and reality of UNITING is present, the skillful, purposeful practices of Creative Collaboration become generative and sustainable over time.

In challenging times of disruption, change, and uncertainty, UNITING is an all-weather plan B. It assures the capacity to respond effectively because the organization is already well aligned, able to adapt, and ready to pivot in a new direction when necessary.

Blueprint for Creative Collaboration

POSITIVE COLLABORATIVE FORCES

Generated by the cornerstone practices, action steps,
and *cultural characteristics* *

Clarity   **Perspective**   Connection

Understanding   Moral Imagination   Leverage

Conviction   Reconciliation   Agility

SKILLSET

Cornerstone Practices

Values-Based Decision Making
Wise Planning   Principled Negotiation
Dialogue – the Foundational Practice

Designed **N**ecessary **A**ction Steps
that implement the practices

MINDSET
Growth Mindset *

HEARTSET
Integrity *
Psychological Safety *

Lesson Two SEEING

Nature works with five polymers. Only five polymers.
In the natural world, life builds from the bottom up,
and it builds in resilience and multiple uses.

~ **Janine Benyus** *Biomimicry: Innovation Inspired by Nature*

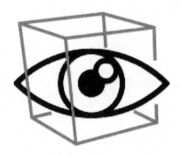

The Force of Perspective

Leadiators help others see the importance of four cornerstone
practices that build sustainable, Creative Collaboration.

Leadiators lead by example and show others how
to use the four cornerstone practices.

These practices develop three cultural
characteristics that everyone can perceive in a
cohesive, collaborative organization.

Leadiators must guard against biases and attitudes that cloud
perspective in order to clearly see the way forward.

By actively seeking other perspectives,
leadiators fill in the gaps and see more clearly.

In this lesson, you will see how organizations can use seven *polymers* to build sustainable Creative Collaboration from the bottom up.

Three Cultural characteristics

- Integrity

- Psychological Safety

- Growth Mindset

Four Cornerstone practices

- Dialogue

- Values-Based Decision Making

- Wise Planning

- Principled Negotiation

Instead of habitually reaching for familiar solutions to address the problems in an organization that limit the ability to work together, you will see how an integrated understanding of the structure of these characteristics and practices (polymers) builds the organizational *vehicle*. The organization becomes more resourceful to meet today's challenges with capacity to navigate the changing landscape ahead.

A vision is essential to orient and unite others. Vision provides a bigger perspective. With a vision a leadiator can recognize collaborative possibilities and engage others in practical discussions to design and align as a collaborative organization. A leadiator plays a critical role to encourage others to shift the negative thinking patterns described in Lesson One. It may not be easy for people to recognize limiting beliefs, mistaken assumptions, and negative attitudes. However, when the big picture vision includes what is to be accomplished as an organization, there is an invitation to align and begin to feel a sense of belonging. Individuals can begin to see and connect the dots of their particular work with the work of others as the larger goals of the organization become visible. They can understand their place in the blueprint for success.

Learning Objectives

- Use the *four cornerstone practices as the building blocks* for sustainable, Creative Collaboration.

- Recognize that *three cultural characteristics are the glue* of a cohesive organization capable of Creative Collaboration.

- Become aware of biases in perception to more *clearly see issues, barriers, and choices,* instead of only seeking evidence that supports existing beliefs.

A New School Sees Itself as an Extended Community of Creative Collaboration

In 1999, the public education landscape in Santa Fe, New Mexico had no shortage of committed administrators and dedicated teachers, but there were not very many organizational bright spots. From 2000 to 2005, I had a unique opportunity to observe the birth and development of a remarkable public school, deeply committed to build a new organization from the bottom up with Creative Collaboration.

As a member of the governing board, a parent of a student who completed grades 7-12, the chairperson of the fundraising campaign to build a new building as its permanent home, and a consultant who advised its leadership on planning, I had a full view of the inner workings of the school as well as its public image. I watched the *3-D printing* of a collaborative organization, layer by layer. I saw exactly how Creative Collaboration began in the imagination, formed, and developed. I saw the developmental challenges the school and its leadership faced. I saw how they overcame these challenges and succeeded. The name of this school is Monte del Sol (MdS).

Community is what made MdS unique. This word was at the heart of the mission and vision of the school. The purpose of MdS was to become a vibrant, safe, and accepting learning community where students could answer the question, *Where/How do I fit in the world?* This is a question about SEEING connections and relationships. This question integrates the students with their families and the surrounding community. The question invites visualization.

The center of the building and the symbolic center of the shared life of MdS was a large, open room with high ceilings hung with flags of countries from around the world. It was called the "gathering space." This area was used for regular scheduled activities and for announcements and updates like most schools. What distinguished MdS from other schools was the practice of convening and connecting by gathering as a large group to see, hear, and experience each other *as a community*.

At these times, the gathering space fulfilled its most essential function as a place to speak, listen, and witness each other. It was a place to talk about controversies and engage the community as a whole in problem solving around tough issues. It was a place to celebrate and share victories. It was a place where every student, teacher, and administrator could see and feel themselves as part of a community. A common question asked to open the floor to any student, teacher, or administrator who wished to speak was, "Who's got an inspirational story or something great to share?" The process of gathering demonstrated the power of diverse perspectives and respectful listening. Students and staff used the space to be grateful for good deeds, to challenge the community to do better, to speak about the world outside the school, and to embrace members of the community who were hurting.

The deep commitment to build a strong school organization of students, parents, faculty, and administration as a community grew and extended into a dynamic relationship with the larger Santa Fe community. MdS's robust mentorship program was a major learning initiative that set it apart from most other public schools. Each school year, the school recruited and matched hundreds of community volunteers with individual students for a yearlong project. They used each student's interests as the central design element. The mentorship subjects ran the gamut from ultra-advanced intellectual study of polymer chemistry to work with a master blacksmith to create an iron sculpture.

This collaboration between a network of mentors and the school became the *secret sauce* in the success of MdS. Two years worth of mentorship credit were required to graduate. The mentorship experience acted as an educational *force multiplier*, because it enhanced the students experience and it accelerated their learning.

Connection The work with a mentor became a unique portal for each student to enter the broader community. It connected students through direct experiences that reached the heart, mind, and spirit. Possible answers to "Where is my place in the world?" emerged from a series of dialogues (student-school, student-mentor, and mentor-school). These dialogues created a sense of ownership and personal responsibility that increased student engagement and enhanced learning. Students experienced adults in the community as teachers, learners, and allies.

Growth The mentorship gave students a template so they could see, feel, and understand collaborative, life-long learning as a way of being. This growth was a direct result of the student's choice of the area of interest to explore.

Motivation The mentorship was the one thing that kept many students fully engaged in school. For some, the mentorship shaped the course of their lives after graduation as a springboard to continue to pursue a deep, authentic interest. Years later, stories abound of graduates engaged in work they began through the mentorship program. For others, the mentorship was an opportunity to learn about something that was more fantasy than deep interest and *get it out of their system*. They became able to see their real interests with greater clarity.

Inspiration Students had the opportunity to learn and grow as individuals. Then, in the annual mentorship festival, each student entered the spotlight to creatively present her work and document her learning. Members of the extended community (parents, students, faculty, mentors, administrators, donors, and community supporters) could see, hear, and witness the experience in multi-media presentations and stories. This festival was an inspiring, shared celebration of the gift of students' growth and development. This positive display of the fruits of collaboration was inspiring and UNITING.

Learning For adolescents, examples are usually far more powerful sources of learning than pep talks from adults. Students who were unmotivated about the value of a mentorship became inspired by the stories of their peers. One non-academic learner, a student who came to the school unsuccessful in traditional settings, was transformed by his mentorship in auto mechanics. He stated that he never understood how much reading, analyzing, and thinking went into fixing cars. Teachers developed greater understanding of the unique interests and capacity of their students. Mentors developed a passionate connection with the education of the city's youth.

Service The example of generous, heart-felt investment of time and talent by the volunteer mentors set up a virtuous cycle of community generosity. New mentors were influenced to join the volunteer talent pool and participate. Time donated by mentors encouraged donors to match their generosity with financial support. The larger community also saw firsthand the interest and determination of the students and this view positively shifted public opinion about teenagers.

Financial Resources The author, Muriel Rukeyser said, "The universe is made of stories not of atoms." (1) As a fundraiser for MdS, I found that the sincere testimonial of a student was a powerful way to motivate foundations and major individual donors to become collaborative partners and invest in the school's future. When potential donors could see and hear the students speaking from the heart about the power of their learning, they often wanted to invest and become a part of the MdS community.

Basic Behavioral Conditions for Collaboration

Collaboration only emerges and is sustained through constructive, predictable behavior that creates a psychologically safe space. MdS's work to build community, inside the school and in the surrounding community, highlights four of the basic behavioral conditions that must be present for collaboration to flourish.

Sense of interdependence Repeated connections through community interactions fostered the recognition of WE. The daily gatherings in the common space, the mentorship festival, the integration of community mentors as a part of the school, and funding partnerships with foundations and donors strengthened the shared understanding that WE are more resourceful together.

Respect for differences The community helped students discover what inspired them through relationships and find their unique *formula* for learning. Students received direct, personal recognition for their gifts and their efforts, strengthening identity and a sense of belonging. Consistent listening to all stakeholders' perspectives modeled respect and built positive working relationships.

Shared responsibility Students became architects of their own learning. They felt liberated from the *four walls* of school and were blessed by the heart-felt service of hundreds of community mentors who assumed significant responsibility to educate and guide the next generation.

Consensus support for key decisions A sense of belonging and ownership grew and strengthened the shared direction. Behind the scenes, important decisions about curriculum, school policy, and fundraising included robust opportunities for students, teachers, parents, and community stakeholders to question, engage, contribute, and understand.

An Introduction to the Cornerstone Practices of Creative Collaboration

These predictable behavioral conditions must be developed and maintained over time through disciplined practice of four skills. They are some of the structural *polymers* that sustain collaboration. To construct something strong and beautiful, it is necessary to learn to work diligently with the available tools and materials. The following skillset of practices are the structural *cornerstones* of a solid foundation.

Dialogue accelerates learning This practice is the gold standard for high quality learning conversation that reinforces all the other practices. Dialogue is formed from the root words *dia* and *logos*. Its essence is the exchange of meaning through the word. When issues are important and participants have strong opinions laden with emotion, the exchange can easily drift from a win-learn understanding to a divisive, win-lose debate over positions. Debate can weaken the bonds of respect and consensus necessary for UNITING and moving forward together.

Debate is about who has the best answer. Dialogue is about better questions that enhance what we can learn and understand together. Reliable dialogue among collaborative partners respectfully and creatively taps diverse perspectives, supports honest engagement to examine issues, and cultivates collective wisdom. Figure 4 on page 67 positions dialogue as the foundation for all the other cornerstone skills and cultural characteristics that support and shape a healthy organization.

Action Steps shift debate to Dialogue.

Go deep to understand Resist the urge to argue with or characterize the views of others. Model what you want from others and speak with the intention to clarify what has meaning and importance for you. (*I want you to see this through my eyes and experience AND I want to understand why it is so important to you.*)

Keep your eyes on the prize The highest good in a challenging conversation often lies beyond agreement or disagreement. The focus must remain on learning. Listen attentively with the primary goal to learn rather than find a weakness in the other's position, argue for what you already believe, or settle for a quick solution.

Emphasize discovery questions Ask open and honest questions (*How did you reach that conclusion? What matters most to you?*) that invite others to clarify their views and increase your understanding. Continue to return to questions that deepen the learning conversation. (*What else can you share that will help me see this from your perspective?*)

Lesson Four, LEARNING, presents an expanded set of action steps that implement the cornerstone practice of dialogue. **Dialogue is the fundamental means of learning in healthy organizations.**

Wise Planning leverages effort To be sustainable, collaboration needs an integrated plan that sharpens everyone's focus on the shared vision and coordinates a full, efficient, and effective effort to get there.

Many organizations plan. Some organizations plan strategically. Few organizations plan wisely. Wisdom in planning develops because several key elements combine.

- Excellent understanding of the current and near-future operating environment (strategic thinking)

- Alignment of strategic choices with guiding values and principles (ethical intelligence)

- Common sense choices pragmatically focus the effort (discernment)

Wise Planning naturally integrates strategic priorities with the mission and guiding principles. This builds the ethical and structural integrity of the organization. *A wise plan becomes a living blueprint that increases the organization's discipline to orient toward results, act in alignment, and adapt to change.*

The plan is *alive* because the organization uses it actively, revises and updates it as necessary, learns from setbacks, and celebrates progress together. This practice strengthens collaboration by choreographing shared responsibility, confirming interdependence with shared purpose, and maintaining alignment to build momentum toward the shared vision.

Action Steps generate Wise Planning.

Lead from the heart Discuss, define, and describe the guiding values and action principles that will orient your work together.

Track clear measures of success Formulate meaningful outcome measures that the organization tracks to assess the results of the collective efforts.

Work from a one-page blueprint Complex multipage documents fail to keep everyone focused. Create a clear visual summary of the plan that everyone can refer to with mission, vision, values, goals and measures. Schedule regular review sessions to assess, modify, and course correct.

Lesson Six, ALIGNING, presents an expanded set of action steps that implement the cornerstone practice of wise planning.

Make Values-based Decisions to move forward together Collaborative organizations navigate by making key decisions that address inevitable challenges and skillfully maneuver through a changing operational landscape. Key decisions deliver superior results because they are formed deliberately.

- Reflect clear thinking from multiple perspectives.

- Communicate integrity to all stakeholders.

- Earn trust and build confidence in the organization's character and direction.

- Enhance leadership credibility for future decisions.

Key decisions must sincerely balance and reconcile the needs and concerns of internal and external stakeholders. This earns the consensus support of others. When leadiators credibly communicate key decisions, they strengthen the organization because organizational stakeholders remain linked, aware, and supportive.

Action Steps that generate better, stronger decisions

Think stakeholders Always create a visual stakeholder map that reminds the decision maker(s) of those affected by the decision.

Give voice to what matters Inquire and learn what is important to stakeholders (group or individual) before examining options.

Be transparent about consequences and risks Assure accountability by explaining the reasoning for the decision to those affected, including the likely downside.

Lesson Seven, NAVIGATING, presents an expanded set of action steps that implement this cornerstone practice of values-based decision making.

Stick together with Principled Negotiation Leadiators must negotiate many things. Beyond an agreement or resolution of a specific issue, leadiators also *negotiate* with others to gain their acceptance, understanding, and support. They *negotiate* difficult situations. With this broader understanding of negotiation, leadiators must be willing and able to fearlessly address diverse opinions, disagreement, or conflict that could create division. From frontline work teams to the senior leadership team, everyone must develop this capacity. Leaders and managers must provide positive examples. Without their proactive engagement it is not possible to seek understanding and bridge differences. Without agreements that honorably reconcile diverse needs and interests, UNITING is out of reach. Working relationships often lack respect and multiple perspectives cannot be tapped for collective intelligence.

Dialogue is the superior means to understand different perspectives. Principled Negotiation is the superior means to engage and reconcile differences. All other forms of negotiation inherently or explicitly favor power over principle and tactics over transparency. Negotiation based on power and positional arguments to reach a compromise may be acceptable in some types of organizational transactions. However, this approach is inadequate to build and strengthen collaboration. A leadiator must act, and be perceived as acting, based upon principles, particularly when using power and authority over others. *A leadiator must guide the effort to sincerely and vigorously seek fair solutions that address diverse needs and gain sincere acceptance from all sides.*

This practice requires more skill than traditional, power-based negotiation because it is both *hard-headed* (pragmatic and concerned about a good outcome for the individual) and *soft-hearted* (empathetic and concerned about a good result for others). When a leadiator engages differences instead of smoothing them over, she can seek agreement that balances concern for outcome with concern for the relationship. Then, there is an opportunity to rise above a half-hearted, watered-down, or reluctant compromise. The way a leadiator negotiates must affirm interdependence and maintain respect, always seeking a positive outcome for the organization, its employees, and its stakeholders.

Action Steps that generate Principled Negotiation

Peel the artichoke When others put forward preferred positions or demands, get to the *heart* of the matter by peeling back the layers with deep listening. Respectfully ask WHY this matters to them, repeating as necessary to focus on meaning. (*I am not yet clear about WHY you are opposed to this idea? Would you say more about your concerns?*)

Be respectfully tenacious Acknowledge disagreement and continue to search for options that could provide some satisfaction to all sides. Collaboration requires will and patient effort. (*We seem to be stuck. However, this is too important to just kick the can down the road or settle for a half-baked solution that may not satisfy any one. I respect your concern. Please tell me again how this could work better for you.*)

Measure twice, cut once Before making an agreement, test each person's satisfaction level against what they have said matters to them. Resentful acceptance is likely to undermine collaboration. (*We may not like this outcome, but it needs to work well enough that everyone will support it and move on. Are you sure that you can accept this AND commit to make it work?*)

Lesson Eight, BRIDGING, presents an expanded set of action steps that implement the cornerstone practice of Principled Negotiation.

The Architecture of Healthy, Collaborative Organizations

In all sectors (private-for-profit, nonprofit, and government), there are healthy organizations that consistently perform at a high level. The pyramid in Figure 4 represents strength, stability, and health. There are three vital signs that show how healthy an organization is.

Figure 4

Superior Results The organization fully delivers on its mission. For a nonprofit it is beneficial services and positive impact with the issues it exists to address. For a corporation, it is profitability along with levels of quality, customer service, and other stated business priorities. Some corporations also elevate social and environmental goals alongside business priorities, e.g. People, Planet, and Profit. For a government entity, effective delivery of services, earning the public's trust, and protecting the public interest are usually at the heart of the mission.

Ethical Reputation Employees, partners, community stakeholders, clients and customers, funders, and investors have confidence in the ethical character, trustworthiness, and credibility of the organization and its leadership.

Adaptive Capacity The organization is well integrated and strong. It works together with coordination and efficiency as a whole and within each division, department, and team. Collective capacity enables aligned, agile creative responses to changes in the operating environment and challenging situations.

In order to consistently deliver mission results at a high level, an organization must build and maintain health through the disciplined use of the four cornerstone practices described on pages 61-66. Each of the cornerstone practices must be implemented with designed necessary action steps. These action steps become predictable, constructive behaviors that fill out the skillset of the organization and its teams. The behaviors develop and sustain a working environment with three cultural characteristics that continuously generate results, reputation, and adaptive capacity.

Integrity is a characteristic of individuals with ethics and courage to face difficulties. Integrity generates a high level of trust that is the essential *glue* that holds relationships and organizations together. Trust must always be earned and re-earned. Hard-won trust can be lost through one careless action or omission. Once lost it is harder to rebuild. Every day, ethical leadiators earn trust with words and deeds that consistently demonstrate character, credibility, and accountability. Firm belief in the integrity of the organization and its leaders generates health and inspires confidence.

Psychological Safety transforms the full potential of individuals and individual teams into a collective enterprise capable of creative efforts that produce results. Safety enables a climate where strong bonds of belonging and connection form. Individuals become willing to speak up, take risks, contribute their talents, and share their ideas. Safety only develops when the behavioral norm of mutual respect is rock-solid.

Participants bring important history from experiences in the social environment outside the organization, previous encounters within the organization, and previous jobs. Experiences can be positive or negative. Organizations are part of a social environment and must face the challenge of historic and current trends of discrimination and injustice that shape perceptions about fairness and the level of safety to speak up inside the organization right now. Mutual respect is a powerful start, but it is not enough. In addition, when differences or conflict arise, leadiators and staff need the cornerstone practices of Dialogue and Principled Negotiation to learn from each other and build agreements that restore peace, maintain unity, and build Psychological Safety.

Growth Mindset is a simple and powerful framework to view the work together as a never-ending journey of learning that will improve results. When people are open to discovery, there is less defensiveness about mistakes and more willingness to be vulnerable, acknowledge doubt and uncertainty, and ask for help. An organization with this shared mindset is able to squeeze lessons out of everything, including mistakes. The learning velocity of the organization accelerates.

When a Growth Mindset is the norm, teams within organizations naturally unify to creatively address inevitable change and emerging challenges. At every level from senior leadership to a small work team, people share perspectives and listen with interest to others. There is a connected synergy among the individuals and teams that compose the organization as a whole. By learning together, they produce more as a whole than the sum of the parts. This shared, positive orientation can only develop and sustain with careful definition of the structure of individual accountability throughout the organization. Everyone needs to accept responsibility for a fair share of the total responsibility.

Leadership at all levels supports an organization's development, beginning with the formal leaders with titles and authority to lead. Then, it is important to also recognize another form of authentic leadership that frequently exists within middle management and at the team level of organizations. Without a big title or much formal authority, these *leadiators* demonstrate leadership through their example of dedication to the well being of the organization and their willingness to influence others to act for necessary change.

Formal leaders and others who lead can guide the ongoing effort to build and maintain health by adopting and consistently using the four cornerstone practices (Dialogue, Wise Planning, Values-Based Decision

Making, and Principled Negotiation) that develop the three cultural characteristics (Psychological Safety, Integrity, and a Growth Mindset).

Like snowflakes and human fingerprints, there is uniqueness to the way each organization expresses the emerging state of UNITING in Creative Collaboration. Project ECHO's development of a worldwide, technology-intensive network to reach one billion people (described in the introduction) looks very different from Monte del Sol's high-touch mentorship network to educate and inspire 300 students in a small city (described earlier in this lesson). And yet, the fundamental practices at the core of their success are the same. The practices are universal.

The practices must become more than a checklist. UNITING by design requires conscious effort and skill to sustain collaboration amidst change. In order for leaders to become leadiators, they must develop the Mindset, Heartset, and Skillset to resourcefully implement the cornerstone practices.

Inquiry and Dialogue Generate Perspective to Chart the Course

The work over time to build Creative Collaboration is filled with decisions about how to come together, learn together, work together, and stay together. These decisions are aided or impaired by the perspective of leadiators.

Asking the right questions and listening well to others builds a better perspective. Leadiators must ask questions that continually identify and assess the choices to move forward together. *How do we leverage limited financial resources? Who do we link with as strategic partners? How do we develop innovative ways to reach underserved parts of our community?*

Open, honest questions invite others to be thinking partners. The cornerstone practices (Dialogue, Wise Planning, Values-based Decision Making, and Principled Negotiation) are all designed to include others. This is principled because it is respectful and equitable to include people. It is also pragmatic because inclusion of diverse viewpoints forms a more complete perspective that taps collective intelligence and usually produces better decisions and results.

The wisdom of the ages from cultures around the world may seem cliched and out-of-date. And yet, these common sayings align with the leading edge of neuroscience about how we SEE, behave, and choose. Consider a few examples.

- "He couldn't see the forest for the trees."

- "What you hear about may be false. What you see is true."

- "Seeing is believing."

- "A bird in the hand is worth two in the bush."

- "We see the world, not the way it is, but the way we are."

Now move to the understanding of information age experts about seeing.

- "Point of view is worth 80 IQ points." Alan Kay, computer pioneer (2)

- "What You See Is All There Is." Daniel Kahneman, leading neuroscientist (3)

The difference of 80 IQ points is the difference between average and genius. The smarter and better educated someone is, the easier it to assume that one sees everything clearly and has the situation figured out. However, you can't know what you don't see.

Neuroscience is the interdisciplinary study of the brain, perception, cognition, and decision making. This field has exploded with significant developments that help us understand how perspective influences the capacity to learn and work together to make decisions. Daniel Kahneman is one of the leading researchers of modern neuroscience who won the Nobel Prize for Economics. As Kahneman summarizes, you only SEE what you can SEE. You don't know what you might be missing that is outside of your perception.

In his best-selling book, *Thinking Fast and Slow*, he describes the two dimensions of the brain that we use in decision making as System 1 and System 2. System 1 is the *fast* brain, located in the instinctive, emotional centers of the brain. It is the oldest part of our biology that scans and *decides* immediately. System 2 is the *slow* brain located in the neocortex and the upper brain. We use it to reason and work more deliberately to consider what to do. To bring System 2 online, a slower pace is necessary. Seeking and listening to others' perspectives engages this part of the brain.

Kahneman developed the acronym WYSIATI (**W**hat **Y**ou **S**ee **I**s **A**ll **T**here **I**s) to label the common human tendency to make flawed judgments based on a limited perspective, unaware of what one does not see. *A leadiator can help the organization and its teams become more effective collaborators by avoiding common biases and attitudes that produce limited perspective, flawed judgment, and poor results.* The action steps provided after each bias or attitude develop dialogue habits that shine a bright, clear light on the issue, improve perspective, and generate the extra 80 *IQ points* to act with more clarity, creativity, and wisdom. (4)

Framing Bias The way you state (frame) a question, problem, or decision affects the way you respond. Ultimately, it is likely to affect the soundness of the decision. Frames are powerful because they highlight or exclude experience, values, training, people, options, and relevant information. One of the most common framing errors is to see a decision as an either/or choice instead of both/and, or multiple options. *Should we close the program or keep it going?* A more inclusive frame that includes additional alternatives could be, *What should we do with the program?* This frames includes, close or keep open along with keep open with modifications, keep open for another 90 days and close if there is no improvement, spin off into a separate company, sell to another organization, or _____.

Problems can also be framed poorly. As the pioneer educator, John Dewey, said, "A problem well-defined is a problem half solved." (5) For example, a problem might be narrowly framed as a performance problem of a single work team. This frame eliminates consideration of systemic issues that may be a large part of the problem. If so, any solution is likely to fail to fix the problem and the work team will continue to struggle in a poorly functioning system.

Action Step *Frame Intentionally* Take time to develop a frame that is expansive enough to hold all the relevant issues. Remember that what you see depends upon where you stand. Use people who stand in different points of view to help frame the issue or define the problem. To get to a better answer, frame a better question.

Loss Aversion We tend to attach greater weight to loss of something we already have than to the possible gain of something we do not yet have. Fear of loss is a powerful, emotional response that may prevent a reasoned evaluation that consciously weighs losses and gains. There is a tendency to underweight the upside and overweight the downside.

> **Action Step** *Shine a Light on the Downside* Take time to mindfully identify and evaluate potential losses and gains for all stakeholders. A possible loss deserves to be weighed differently from a probable one. Actively consider how to mitigate potential losses.

Judgmental Overconfidence This is the tendency to overestimate the accuracy of your assumptions and predictions about future events and consequences. There is a failure to acknowledge that you may only have part of the information. Acknowledging this leads to more thoughtful consideration of the importance of uncertainties and unknowns.

Confirmation Bias This is the tendency to only look for evidence, information, and opinion that supports one's existing position, idea, or proposed solution. Disconfirming information and alternate views are either unseen, actively ignored, or summarily dismissed without any consideration.

> **Action Step** *Speak As an Angel of Reality* Commit to a process that provides enough time and psychological safety for participants to speak honestly. Empower every participant to be an *angel of reality* and ask pointed questions that test assumptions, surface missing information, fill in blind spots, and calibrate levels of confidence. Phrases like *devil's advocate* or *critical evaluator* refer to speaking up against something and they don't necessarily imply a sincere, positive contribution. A person who speaks up when it is challenging to do so and adds a missing perspective should be viewed as a benevolent presence instead of a critic. In some cases, an *angel of reality* can be a guardian angel who saves the organization from an

expensive mistake or extraordinary hardship.

Mental Accounting There is a tendency to keep different psychological accounts for valuing and comparing things. A person may be willing to spend hours driving to different stores to save $50 on an item and make a five-minute decision to spend thousands on a cruise by accounting for the expenditures differently. A corporation may cut the health benefits of its employees while lavishing millions on a golden parachute retirement plan for its senior executives.

> **Action Step** *Balance the Mental Accounting* Ask stakeholders how they value and listen to their *logic* to account for value. When a leadiator accepts the challenge to acknowledge and discuss alternate ways to evaluate, this can develop a more balanced discussion and a more principled outcome.

Denial This common state is a refusal to accept things as they are. The emotional and intellectual investment in an unrealistic perspective as the *Truth* prevents a step back to consider other perspectives, look again, and see reality more clearly. This bias eliminates the need to acknowledge painful costs or consequences for others. Instead, the individual or group that is in denial remains comfortable with a false belief that negative impacts are or will be minimal. Comfort with an idealized picture is more important than the truth.

> **Action Step** *Do a 360 degree walk around* Before flying a plane, a pilot does a 360 degree walk around to visually inspect everything. The same should be done with any important problem, issue, or decision. Think of a successful conclusion as *flying the plane* and arriving at the intended destination. Before you *take off* to implement a solution or make a key decision, enter into a dialogue to receive feedback from those who have other perspectives and stakeholders who will be affected by the decision. With a more complete picture from different points of view, you reduce the risks of denying some part of reality that should be considered before you take action. You become better informed so you can arrive at your intended destination.

Sunk Cost Fallacy There is a tendency to want to continue to invest resources in an activity when you focus on what has already been *sunk* into the effort. If you terminate the activity, this means that everything you already invested is *lost*. A decision maker may spend even more to avoid *losing* what has already been invested. (See Loss Aversion) The continued investment avoids the immediate psychological pain of loss or the loss of face in the eyes of others. This flawed thinking is a fallacy that keeps projects going when they have outlived their usefulness. More money goes down the drain with programs that don't work. Expensive court battles continue. Wars that make no sense drag on and more lives are lost.

> **Action Step** *Use the Windshield Instead of the Rear View Mirror* Ask the questions, *What is the best use of our resources (time, money, effort) now? If we stop investing in this project, what better alternatives might we fund?* and *What am I most afraid of losing if this is over?* An organization culture that sees mistakes as opportunities to learn, asks the question, *What lessons can inform future efforts?* Valuable lessons for the future can turn sunk cost losses into long term gains.

Three Universal Action Principles Improve Organizational Capacity to See Clearly

In addition to these specific action steps, there are three overarching principles that can guide a leadiator's efforts to see more clearly in the ongoing effort to build a healthy, collaborative organization. These principles are universal because people of all socioeconomic and education levels are subject to the same errors of thinking and perceiving. (6)

Always seek perspective Perceptions influence judgment. Stress test your perspective by asking for feedback and proactively seek the diverse perspectives of others.

Proceed with deliberate speed Excess speed can *kill* clear thinking. People are less rational and more prone to manipulation than they think. When you drive fast at night, your headlights only show you what is right ahead and you may not have time to avoid an accident. Slow the pace enough to look ahead and look around to make more conscious choices. When you practice with deliberate speed you retrain your instincts to use positive habits of discernment. Then, in a situation when you don't have time to slow down, these habits will serve you well so you are not reactive or impulsive.

See mistakes as opportunities to learn Some organizations press forward to the next project, decision, or strategic plan and continue to make the same kinds of mistakes. Some organizations see others make costly mistakes and fail to learn. Wisdom comes from the willingness to take time to examine your mistakes and the mistakes of others. Then, lessons learned can become part of the organization's intellectual capital. Excellent organizations often have a structured way to convene, engage diverse perspectives, and *audit* key decisions and major projects. Candid, non-defensive discussions of challenges and mistakes become standard operating procedure in order to learn together and grow. (Lesson Nine)

When a leadiator sincerely engages diverse perspectives and actively includes others, this encourages the organization to use dialogue to tap the power of collective intelligence to make better-informed decisions and improve the next project.

Without reflective space, decision makers are prone to the common patterns of bias and flawed thinking described above. Deliberate, step-by-step dialogue builds a natural space where reflection and learning grow. An effective process acknowledges strong emotions but does not let them *run the show*. Calm (System 2) thinking together lets reason balance emotion (System 1) and opens a quiet space for wise intuition to emerge. (7)

Intuition is a remarkable human capacity. It can provide a message of moral conscience. It can be a source of common sense. It can generate creative insight. For some it *speaks* with a body sensation like a gut feeling or a knowing in the heart. For others, it may be a flash of insight, a dream, or a still, small voice. A little space can pay a big dividend when an individual or a group becomes able to reflect and see more clearly to make an important decision with little time.

A leadiator can help individuals, teams, and a whole organization deepen the dialogue to SEE the status quo and stand in the gap between What Is and What Could Be.

Figure 5

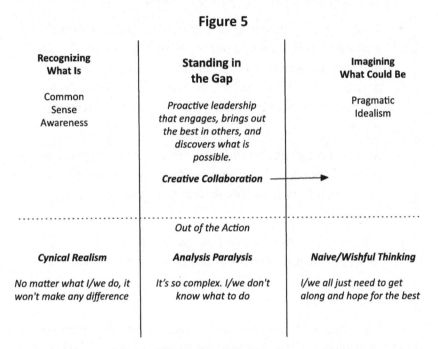

Open, honest inquiry and deep listening can help people come together with shared understanding of the value of the four cornerstone practices and the three cultural characteristics in an organization's current situation. The answers to these questions will guide you.

Inquiry Into Action

- *In your community or organization, where do you see the greatest needs for people to come together and work together? How do others see these needs?*

- *Many organizations are so busy doing that they rarely step back, reflect, and examine where they want to go and how to get there together. Where do you see a gap between your organization's "What Is" and "What Could Be"? What are others' perspectives about the gap? (Figure 4)*

- *As a current or potential leader, what steps can you see yourself taking to become a leadiator who can stand in the gap and guide people forward to build Creative Collaboration?*

- *What barriers to Creative Collaboration do you see that must be navigated to cross the gap between "What Is" and "What Could Be"? What are others' perspectives about the barriers?*

- *In the habits of your organization, what examples have you seen of some of the biases and attitudes (pages 72-75) that limit the perspective available to work together and solve problems? How can you apply any of the recommended action steps to improve perspective?*

- *Do you see examples to follow in your organization of the cornerstone practices of Dialogue, Values-Based Decision Making, Wise Planning, and Principled Negotiation? Who do you see that already uses these practices?*

The Core Ideas of Lesson Two

A vision is essential to orient and unite others.

*Dialogue is the fundamental means of
learning in healthy organizations.*

*Like snowflakes and human fingerprints, there is uniqueness
to the way each organization expresses the emerging state
of UNITING in Creative Collaboration.*

*A leadiator can help the organization and its teams become more
effective collaborators by avoiding common biases and attitudes that
produce limited perspective, flawed judgment, and poor results.*

*A leadiator can help individuals, teams, and a whole organization
deepen the dialogue to SEE the status quo and stand in the gap
between What Is and What Could Be.*

Blueprint for Creative Collaboration

POSITIVE COLLABORATIVE FORCES
Generated by the cornerstone practices, action steps,
and *cultural characteristics**

Clarity   Perspective   **Connection**

Understanding   Moral Imagination   Leverage

Conviction   Reconciliation   Agility

SKILLSET

Cornerstone Practices

Values-Based Decision Making
Wise Planning   Principled Negotiation
Dialogue – the Foundational Practice

Designed **N**ecessary **A**ction Steps
that implement the practices

MINDSET
Growth Mindset*

HEARTSET
Integrity*
Psychological Safety*

Lesson Three BELONGING

*Trust is the glue of life. It's the most essential ingredient
in the connective tissue that sustains the social health
of the organizational body. It must be built every day.
It's the foundational principle that holds all relationships.*

~Stephen R. Covey *First Things First*

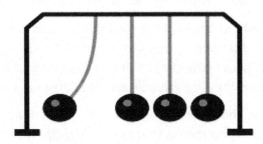

The Force of Connection

*An organization's culture can be a powerful, positive force that
increases collective capacity to produce superior results.*

*A leadiator must intentionally shape a healthy organization
culture with a sense of belonging and trust that connects
everyone to the work and to each other.*

Belonging and trust require a climate of psychological safety.

*Leaders and managers develop psychological safety through their
consistent, day-to-day interactions.*

*A leadiator is always seeking opportunities to make deposits in
the trust account so it is available when necessary.*

Organizations and their component divisions, departments, teams, and groups are social *bodies*. Each person is a *cell* in this body and groups of *cells* have particular functions to fulfill parts of the overall mission as teams, divisions, or departments. Like a healthy human body, a healthy organization needs a design that integrates the functions, engaging everyone in the right place.

This lesson centers on the need for healthy, connective *tissue* to integrate all the human *cells* so they function well together.

Integrated, healthy engagement requires more than rules, compliance, evaluation, and discipline. It requires a sense of authentic connection. People need to know how they fit in and how they fit together. They also need to know they are valuable and that their work matters.

Belonging is not about sacrificing to fit in as an anonymous cog in a mechanism. **Belonging means that people identify with the mission of the organization and with each other.** Individuals and teams know they are respected and valuable. They have the authority, willingness, and skills to make full, creative contributions to the organization's capacity to reach shared goals.

Leadiators must prioritize the development of a trustworthy organizational culture. A healthy culture is a set of habits and norms, usually unwritten, that mold predictable, positive behaviors. These behaviors form the *connective tissue* of trust and belonging.

Learning Objectives

- Recognize the design elements of organization culture to promote belonging and trust over time.

- Develop psychological safety as a cultural characteristic to align everyone, build trust, and increase belonging.

- Take practical steps and seize opportunities to build a trustworthy environment.

How Belonging Develops

By all accounts and measures of performance, the U.S.S. Benfold was an organization with many problems. The Benfold is a modern guided missile frigate in the US Navy, a floating organization and a community of 310 people. In 1997, the Benfold had disciplinary issues, safety and readiness deficiencies, and a negative reputation. Experienced sailors often wanted to transfer or leave the service, resulting in a less experienced, poorly trained crew. Previous leaders had not been able to improve the situation.

The hierarchy and command structure of a Navy ship is absolute, and yet the problems persisted. There was leadership, but there was not yet a leader who could guide the Benfold through its problems to become a high performance organization. Then, a new captain took charge. Michael Abrashoff was trained in the same command and control methods as his predecessors. However, he recognized that the situation called for a different leadership approach. Leader and crew needed to join together to transform the culture of the ship from disempowerment to creative engagement and from alienation to belonging. The crew of the Benfold needed a leadiator who could bridge the divide between leadership and crew.

Over a period of a few months, this leadiator did something unusual for a Navy captain. He arranged to meet individually with all the sailors on the ship and listen to their responses to three questions.

- *What do you like most about this ship?*

- *What do you like least?*

- *What is one thing you would change if you could?*

He took all the improvement ideas he gathered and began to implement the most promising ones that were within budget and Navy regulations. Captain Abrashoff announced changes over the loudspeaker to everyone and gave credit to the crewmember who suggested the idea. Then he asked for more ideas, expressing that he needed the crew's help to improve the ship. He did not give up his authority, he grew it by shifting his approach from command and control to listen and learn. Instead of leader as *know-it-all* giving directions from on high, he became leader as *learn-it-all* working side-by-side.

This approach communicated respect, vulnerability, and a commitment to genuine partnership. A positive, steady signal of belonging continuously encouraged a new mindset among the ship's crew. The ship was no longer an unfortunate work assignment to be endured, but a home where people belonged and felt valued. It became a place where everyone's ideas mattered and anyone's idea might make a difference. The crewmembers had the power, as partners and co-creators, to work alongside the captain and his leadership team, to contribute, innovate, and change the ship for the better.

Any organization can intentionally establish an environment with belonging signals that begin on the first day a new arrival sets foot inside the door. On the Benfold, the captain created a "new arrival" program designed around the principle that a new, 18 year-old recruit is someone's son or daughter. Therefore, treat him or her like you would want your son or daughter treated. The new "welcome aboard" program choreographed details of arrival and settling in that were filled with *belonging cues* to forge a sense of respect, dignity, and connection. Each arrival also received a "running mate" for the first five days to guide the acclimatization process and provide formal and informal knowledge about the reality of ship, its culture, and the work. Everyone was made to feel "at home."

Captain Abrashoff authored a book about the experience with a title that sums up the essence of belonging: *It's Your Ship.* Where you belong, you *own*. You care for what belongs to you and what you belong to. (1)

This mindset generated a culture that turned the USS Benfold into an award-winning ship with the best combat readiness, best gunnery record, and highest morale in the fleet. Instead of losing valuable trained crew at the rate of 35% per year, the Benfold achieved a 100% re-enlistment rate. The catalyst was a leadiator who listened and learned to forge a sense of belonging to connect everyone.

Healthy Organization Culture and the Capacity for Belonging

Organizational health and culture are deeply interrelated. *The culture of an organization is its basic personality expressed in the essential ways its people interact and work. These essential ways develop into self-sustaining patterns of behavior that determine how things are done and how well they are done.* Therefore, an organization's culture is directly tied to its mission performance. Despite this close connection between culture and performance, many organizations ignore culture's significance.

There is a parable that describes how people take for granted the importance of the environment where they function. "There are these two young fish swimming along, and they happen to meet an older fish swimming the other way, who nods at them and says, *"Morning, boys. How's the water?* The two young fish swim on for a bit, and then eventually one of them looks over at the other and says, *What the hell is water?*" (2) Many leaders take for granted the obvious influences on behavior of the invisible cultural environment where people *swim* everyday.

Leadiators must recognize the importance of organization culture for the entire organization as well as sub cultures of specific departments, divisions, or work teams inside a larger organization. There can be significant variation within an organization when the nature of work is unique, e.g. marketing and sales is quite different than factory floor production; a museum curatorial team functions differently than the security team; the field personnel who fix underground water mains for a city water department have different backgrounds than the members of the customer service team who deal with billing.

Culture can be difficult to see and talk about. A specific culture is often not so easy to describe because an organization's culture continually renews itself and evolves, affected by leadership shifts of personality and style, changing circumstances, and adopted strategies. However, wise reflection and focused work can strengthen an organization's culture and generate significant value in mission performance for several reasons.

- Culture has sources of emotional energy and influence that can be tapped to accelerate needed action.

- When the force of the culture and strategic priorities are well-aligned, people's positive feelings help propel progress.

- Improving collective morale (*esprit de corps*) increases emotionalcommitment to the mission.

You can observe all three of these performance-enhancing dimensions of a positive culture shift in the Benfold's dramatic turnaround. The captain's approach shifted the environment and tapped into a reservoir of dormant positive potential. The culture came into alignment with the critical priorities of a navy warship that turned the ship into an excellent performer. Finally, the positive emotion and the progress molded a new sense of collective identity around "our ship."

Organizations are powerful social, economic, and cultural forces in our interconnected world. This recognition has generated ongoing research on the nature of healthy and unhealthy organizational cultures. This research offers principles and practical approaches that can generate effective change. Particularly in the private sector, the relentless search for marginal improvements in economic performance and case studies of major success turn-arounds deliver a shelf full of recommendations about organizational culture and how it can change. (3)

Here are five core questions that offer your organization a sound framework for dialogue about intentional work to strengthen the organizational culture. As a leadiator or change agent interested in your organization's healthy development, these questions will help you assess your unique organizational context with its challenges. Then, you have an opportunity to design meaningful responses. The example from the Benfold's experience is in parentheses.

- What is the clear, shared **vision** that the change will move us towards? (Become the best ship in the fleet)

- What **key behaviors** must we shift to support and sustain the change? (Dialogue between crew and captain, respectful listening, continuous development of constructive ideas for improvement, regular updates for everyone on projects, welcoming new crewmembers aboard in a personal way to connect them from the beginning)

- How can we **involve others** in order to deepen and widen the effort? (Regular requests for new ideas, giving credit to crew for ideas, using experienced crew as "running mates" to integrate new crew members from day one)

- What are the early small-scale results we can use to **build momentum** toward larger scale change? (Celebrating progress together, using the language of "we" and "our" success, identifying lessons learned)

- What are the **barriers** that block desired change that must be cleared away? (lack of belonging and trust, divide between crew and leadership, low morale disciplinary problems, high level of turnover with experienced personnel)

Elements of a Healthy Organization Culture

Healthy organizations succeed because they can respond effectively to setbacks, challenges, and change. This ability to respond is called *adaptive capacity*. It is not an add-on or a refined skill that comes from skills training. It grows from the inside out starting with the organization's core identity.

The mission statement confirms WHY the organization exists. With the USS Benfold, the bottom line of its mission as a warship was combat readiness. This didn't change. However, a new captain guided a change in the ship's culture with clearly articulated core beliefs and values to define WHO WE ARE as we deliver this mission. The Benfold became everyone's ship as listening, teamwork, and innovation became part of its cultural *DNA*.

In Figure 6, a circle image of an organization shows the three layers of structure that grow the adaptive capacity to respond. The inner core of an organization is its identity formed by two elements.

- Mission/purpose

- Core values and guiding principles that set the standards for behavior expected of leaders, managers, and employees internally, and externally with the people and organizations it serves, and with its community partners

People need to understand to what they belong and with whom they belong. This positive sense of identity is continually reinforced and confirmed with day-to-day behaviors that are predictable, constructive, and well aligned with aspirational statements of purpose and values. If people come to work every day without a realistic expectation of consistent, fair, respectful treatment by leaders and co-workers, they cannot trust and they cannot develop a sense of belonging.

Too many organizations stop with the big words of Mission and Core Values in the center of the circle. They talk about what is important, but they don't consistently walk the talk. The second layer of predictable, constructive behavior requires clarity about expectations and discipline. The captain's listening tour with all the sailors could have ended as a feel-good public relations exercise. He needed to keep listening and showing that he was paying attention to their ideas and concerns.

When the day-to-day walk aligns with the aspirational talk, the organization has a foundation to build a healthy culture with six major characteristics that generate and sustain enduring capacity for adaptive response: Integrity; Psychological Safety; Growth Mindset; Agility; Perseverance; and Innovation. All the characteristics are briefly defined in Figure 7. Lesson Two described the first three of these characteristics on page 68-69. They play a primary role to generate the rest. Agility, Perseverance, and Innovation will be covered in Lesson 9 – Adapting.

Figure 6

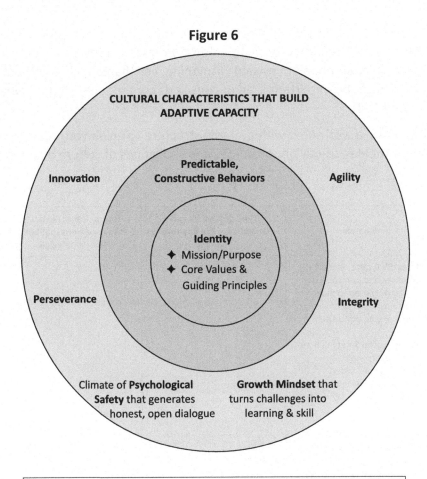

CULTURAL CHARACTERISTICS THAT BUILD ADAPTIVE CAPACITY

Innovation

Agility

Predictable, Constructive Behaviors

Identity
✦ Mission/Purpose
✦ Core Values & Guiding Principles

Perseverance

Integrity

Climate of **Psychological Safety** that generates honest, open dialogue

Growth Mindset that turns challenges into learning & skill

> **There are leaders with titles and authority, and there are those who lead by building the important elements of a healthy organization that can adapt and navigate change.**

Everyone has a role to sustain a healthy culture. However, it starts with a leadiator who is accountable and provides a positive example of the values and daily behaviors needed from everyone. Then, the leadiator must be proactive and cultivate the underlying organizational conditions that develop the necessary behaviors. This inevitably requires training, coaching, and holding others accountable. It is critically important that managers at all levels reinforce these important characteristics. Unlike senior leaders, managers are always close to the day-to-day experience of the employees where they can correct undesirable behavior and reinforce positive cultural norms. In Principle-Centered Leadership, Stephen Covey said, "Anything less than a conscious commitment to the important is an unconscious commitment to the unimportant." (4)

Figure 7 is a worksheet with a simple structure to guide your reflection about the day-to-day opportunities and challenges of culture building.

Figure 7

Elements	How do leaders and managers set the day-to-day example	How do leaders establish the conditions that build everyone's skills
Integrity A clear statement of values and principles that are actively used to make key decisions, guide behaviour, and shape an ethical culture		
Psychological Safety Climate where everyone's contributions matter, everyone is willing to speak up, and no one's dignity is at risk		
Growth Mindset Shared belief that we all can continue to learn and develop by turning mistakes and challenges into lessons		
Agility Structural capacity to rapidly come together, assess, and shift direction to adapt to change and better fulfil the mission		
Innovation Individual and collective ability to reimagine and turn creative ideas into practical solutions		
Perseverance Strong connection to mission plus *can do* attitude to tackle challengers		

Psychological Safety Is the Connection Between Belonging and High Performance

Jobs at Google are highly sought after so they have a strong pool of talented people to choose from. It is an organization obsessed with the use of data and analytics to achieve excellence. Starting in 2012, Google spent millions of dollars on a strategic initiative called Project Aristotle to find the answer to a critical question. "What is the *formula* for a high performing team?" The ultimate goal was to identify the most important replicable elements of its highest performing teams that could be developed by less successful teams in their 50,000+ employee organization.

This initiative examined the latest neuroscience, studied best practices from other organizations, and applied the most sophisticated human resources surveys and personality instruments. The study tapped the advice of leading experts on organization behavior, and used Google's unlimited analytical capacity to test every variable they could identify as a potential contributor to the performance of their best teams. Here is what they discovered:

- The mix of personalities, skills, experience level, and backgrounds did NOT matter much.

- The right norms (traditions, behavioral standards, and unwritten rules) for treatment of each other distinguished the best-performing teams from the rest.

Two key behaviors of the best teams were (1) giving each person a fair opportunity to talk and contribute, and (2) the social sensitivity to read voice tone, expressions, and nonverbal cues to understand others' feelings, i.e. emotional intelligence. In the time of a pandemic as many organizations have moved to virtual operations, this critical element of human behavior will challenge leadiators and organizational designers to recognize the impact on collaboration when we can't see the face behind the mask or we are meeting online with limited opportunities to establish rapport and build working relations. This challenge will be addressed directly in Lesson Nine - Adapting.

Other behaviors like having clear goals and a team culture of dependability mattered, but Google's data indicated that one factor is by far the most important. **PSYCHOLOGICAL SAFETY is essential.** (5) When you distill Psychological Safety to its essence you arrive at interpersonal trust and mutual respect that support interpersonal risk taking and creativity, i.e., a strong sense of connection and belonging.

Google's conclusions were directly influenced by the extensive organization research of Amy Edmondson, whose books on *Teaming* and *The Fearless Organization* lay out her definitive recommendations to increase Psychological Safety that improves team performance. (6)

Google's conclusions may seem like human relations 101. However, in our brave new technological world, it is useful to have an endorsement from the ultimate data geeks proposing *the gold standard of 21st century team performance: the enduring power of trusting, respectful human relationships.*

As an organization consultant, I have walked into hundreds of businesses, nonprofits, and government agencies to assess challenges and propose solutions. Edmondson's extensive research and Google's practical validation of her findings strongly align with my experience. Once a leadiator cracks the belonging code to generate a high level of trust and respect, the organization's latent potential to collaborate emerges. With Creative Collaboration, health grows and results improve.

Therefore, every organization and every team needs an ongoing answer to the foundational question to improve the capacity to work together. *How do we develop and maintain interpersonal trust and mutual respect?*

The foundational practice of DIALOGUE is the only form of communication that will reliably produce the predictable norms of behavior that answer this question. Organizations cannot reach the gold standard of performance without consistent, respectful learning conversations that produce new levels of understanding AND build trust. DIALOGUE is the primary focus of Lesson 4 - Learning.

Google was looking for a *formula* to build more successful teams. Instead, they found a superordinate principle in the research of Amy Edmondson. Her leading-edge work on the nature of teaming in the knowledge economy of this century demonstrates that high performance requires innovation and the full contribution by all members of the team. **The team environment must provide a sense of psychological safety that supports everyone's willingness and ability to engage, offer ideas, express concerns, challenge the status quo, and admit mistakes.** (7)

Paying attention to the level of safety in an environment (family, neighborhood, classroom, social group) is deeply wired into us. Human beings develop the social awareness to scan environments for safety beginning in childhood. If people in the organization believe that they could be subject to embarrassment, humiliation, disapproval, exclusion, or punishment, this belief can trigger the drive to remain safe and limit risk-taking participation. This drive for self-preservation will predictably silence some voices and reduce the possibilities for learning and growth for individuals, teams, and the organization. (8)

The job description of leaders and managers must include the responsibility to establish and sustain a psychologically safe environment. This responsibility requires consistent daily behavior to send belonging signals that encourage and value everyone's full participation. (9)

The mindset of a leadiator has two characteristics that enable the capacity to fulfill this responsibility.

- Able to recognize the indicators of the presence/absence of psychological safety

- Awareness of the importance of being a leader or manager with strength (confidence and conviction) balanced with flexibility to remain open and willing to consider others' ideas, concerns, questions, and opinions

The heartset of a leadiator connects with others.

- Caring about each person's ability to find her voice and express her honest views

93

- Empathy for people with prior negative experiences who may need additional support, encouragement, and skills to overcome their reluctance to take risks in group settings

Everyone, from the janitor to the president, can make a meaningful contribution to a psychologically safe environment. However, a leadiator has a critical responsibility to set the stage for everyone else to play his part. Each person has a duty to cultivate the kind of environment that enables others in the organization to work together well and fulfill the mission. The worksheet in Figure 8 and the Action Steps on page 102 will guide you to explore practical ways to develop Psychological Safety.

- *What is your assessment of the warning signs that may indicate a lack of safety in your organization?*

- *What practices can you adopt to increase the level of safety in the environment?*

- *How will you begin to increase the level of psychological safety?*

Figure 8

WARNING SIGNS	ACTION PRINCIPLES THAT BUILD SAFETY	HOW CAN WE IMPROVE OUR PRACTICES?
Holding mistakes against people	Demonstrate engagement through consistent, positive communication	
Inability to bring up problems and tough issues	Seek understanding and remove barriers to understanding in conversation	
Rejection for being different		
Unsafe to take risks	Actively include everyone	
Difficult to ask others for help	Demonstrate flexibility to listen and learn from others while also showing confidence and conviction	
Lack of confidence that others will not undermine you		
Concern that others do not value and utilize your skills and talents	Use a transparent decision-making process that seeks diverse perspectives	

Action Steps to Lay the Foundation of Respect

Pay attention and connect respectfully with team members

- Remove distractions and give your undivided attention to the person in front of you

- Maintain positive non-verbals (eye contact, orientation toward the speaker)

- Use simple statements of acknowledgement that show your interest and provide the space for others to express themselves (*I see what you mean. Please go on.*)

Establish no frills respect as the bedrock of the organization

- Always use common courtesy toward everyone, particularly when you disagree or dislike someone.

- Provide a fair hearing to others when you disagree so you can agree to disagree without damage to the working relationship.

- Make sure the *door* remains open with people you don't like. Closed doors and lack of communication generate mistrust.

Cultivate respectful, effective meeting dynamics

- Keep team discussions professional, not personal, by insisting on simple respect, avoiding side conversations, and stopping interruptions.

- Make it a point to seek participation from the quiet members of the group.

- Do not allow one or two strong, outspoken personalities to take over a meeting. (see the Guidelines for Meeting Dialogue on Page 124 in Lesson Four.)

Action Steps to Build on a Foundation of Respect

Seek understanding and remove barriers to understanding

- *Loop back* your understanding of what was said and check with the speaker to make sure you understood. (*It sounds like 3 things are important to you. 1. 2. 3. Is that right?*)

- Ask open questions that invite others to share their concerns, opinions, and ideas (*How do you see this issue?*)

- Shift the focus of discussion to the positive side of the issue to keep the issue productively discussable without defensiveness. (*We seem to clearly disagree, about _____. Let's look at other aspects of this to see what we can learn from each other's perspective.*)

Use a transparent decision-making approach that seeks diverse perspectives

- Actively think about who the stakeholders are and what matters to them.

- Invite full participation by people with diverse perspectives and acknowledge differing views.

- As the decision-maker, ask others to advocate for their guiding values and preferred solution BEFORE you indicate any preference.

Demonstrate flexibility while showing confidence and conviction

- Consistently encourage the team to push back and challenge your perspective. (*What do you think I am missing that needs to be examined further?*)

- Admit mistakes to show vulnerability and identify lessons learned. (*You were right to point this out. I made a mistake. The policy needs to remain in place and everyone needs to follow it consistently to prevent something like this from happening.*)

- Model risk-taking and encourage others to take risks. (*We have to be able to take intelligent risks. When we do, we can learn and keep improving.*)

Leadiators Recognize That Trust Is a Verb

Important missions and difficult challenges require people to come to-gether, address their differences, and contribute time, effort, and re-sources to reach a goal. In order to motivate and organize shared effort toward a common goal, it is not possible to exaggerate the importance of trust. Eric Schmidt, the leader of an organization on the cutting edge of technological change reaffirms the enduring power of trust. "In a net-worked world, trust is the most valuable currency." (10)

Individuals and groups need to work well together to accomplish more than they could separately. Individuals must trust and rely upon leaders and coworkers to keep promises and remain accountable to fulfill their commitments. With trust, everyone can take the shortest, most direct route to the desired outcome.

Trust assumes positive intent. Mistakes don't become barriers. They be-come opportunities to learn from and move on. Mistrust fosters judg-ments about incompetence and suspicion of negative intent that get in the way of effective working relationships. Trust enables productivity, efficiency, and creativity.

The most common words used to explain trust are the nouns confi-dence, competence, and reliability. However, the best way to under-stand trust is as an active principle, a verb instead of a noun. You know from your own experience that trust is not static. It is dynamic. Trust takes time to build and it can be destroyed in a moment. Trust can also regrow again after it has been broken.

Begin to build trust by thinking and speaking about the existing trust level in any situation using this simple continuum.

- Deep Mistrust (active hostility or fear – *I distrust him, com-pletely!*)

- Lack of Trust (neutral, absence – *I don't yet trust her.*)

- Uncertain/Doubtful (maybe, tentative – *I am not sure whether to trust him.*)

- Working Level of Trust (functional, not high – *I trust her to a point.*)

- Full Trust (high, unconditional – *I trust him completely.*)

You can't jump levels. Trust can only be built starting from where the relationship is now, one person at a time, one interaction at a time.

The need for a leader to ask others to trust him and follow whole-heartedly may arise without warning in a crisis. The need for new teams to come together and collaborate quickly may test the levels of trust that are present. Therefore, it is important to seize opportunities to *deposit* trust in a relationship savings account as a *currency*. Then, this *currency* is available, ready to draw upon when you want or need help, no-questions-asked. When someone trusts you, he or she will take a leap of faith on your idea or on a risk you want to take.

Trust also enables the skillful practice of Principled Negotiation that is essential to successfully manage differences. When differences present a barrier to effective collaboration, the path forward is a search for negotiated agreement or understanding. Principled Negotiation is a good faith, trust-based, and trust-building practice that protects collaborative relationships. (see Lesson Eight)

Most of us have experience with some people who could not be trusted or betrayed our trust. Those types of experiences may make us skeptical about the limits of trust or its practicality in the organization. However, there are clear examples of historic adversaries who eventually found ways to build some degree of trust, end conflict, reach agreements, make peace, and establish alliances, coalitions, and communities that work together. For example, after fighting two world wars against each other, France and Germany are now major partners in the European Union.

Trust building is challenging because it takes willingness, patience, commitment, and skill. In decades of mediation experience, I have personally witnessed husbands and wives forgive affairs, reconcile, and move forward. I have watched estranged siblings and a parent in a successful family business overcome serious legal and financial misconduct and agree on a plan to unify the family enterprise. I have facilitated conversations that shifted a racially polarized government agency into a more peaceful, respectful workplace. All of these required the willingness to build trust and patient effort over time.

The work to build Creative Collaboration depends upon a common sense understanding of the universal pillars of a durable, trusting relationship.

- Respect (treating others with dignity, fairness)

- Honesty (truth-telling, sincerity)

- Predictable, positive behavior (reliability, keeping commitments)

Don't take trust for granted. You never know when a leader or an organization will need the currency of trust to spend. Keep trust on deposit. Even when things are going well, it is an excellent time build trust using some combination of these behavioral strategies. They are the *verbs* that express your trustworthy intentions toward others through your positive actions.

Action Steps to Build Trust

Promote Effective Communication Increase the quantity and quality of interpersonal communication. Suspicion and fear thrive in the absence of open channels of communication. Take time to check out perceptions. Confirm that messages have been received and interpreted correctly. Create forums and opportunities for direct communication. In the reality of a pandemic, identify a psychologically safe communication channel where everyone can see others' faces. Use a facilitator or mediator when needed.

Be Honest Even in the most cynical, settings where mistrust is expected, experienced observers know that it is fundamental to preserve credibility by being honest and trustworthy. Be direct and transparent. Do not exaggerate.

Offer Unconditional, No Frills Respect Send a steady signal that EVERY-ONE has a human right to receive common courtesy and civility. This is *no frills* respect. Unlike *RESPECT* that must be earned through one's competence and character, no frills respect does not imply approval or admiration of someone.

Be Reliable and Predictable Reliability means keeping your word and your commitments. Follow through. When you say you will do something, make sure it happens. If you cannot, let the person know at the earliest opportunity. Predictability = NO SURPRISES! People usually dislike surprises more than bad news. If there is going to be a change, let others know in advance. Follow the ACBD principle (Always Consult Before Deciding.) Even when it is your decision, check with others to hear their input whenever it is possible. (11)

Admit Mistakes and Acknowledge Risks Fess up about omissions or things that could have been done better. Be candid about uncertainties or risks instead of overselling or pretending that the situation is without risk or doubt.

Acknowledge Emotional Data A strong individual or group feeling in response to an action or event may be connected to their sense of identity. To deny, criticize or ignore how people feel can be taken as a message of disrespect and deeply offend. When others communicate strong feelings, let them know that you have heard them and received their point of view. This is different than agreeing with them.

Try Confidence-Building Measures When there is little trust, don't overload the situation by working toward agreements that require trust or risk-taking. Find *doables.* These are lower risk activities that allow people to experience each other while working together side-by-side. These activities can build confidence that more ambitious agreements are possible.

Take Symbolic Action Consider ways to signal an individual or members of a group that you are willing to act positively without preconditions or the assurance of anything in return, e.g. a modest unilateral concession, a conciliatory gesture, delegation of some authority, or a public apology.

Deal with Problematic Conduct Treat difficult or bad behavior as a joint problem, not a crime. Separate the people from the problem by focusing on the behavior, not the person. Find a good time and place to discuss the behavior so there is less risk that the other person could lose face or feel exposed and become defensive.

Inquiry Into Action – Building Trust

Find the right time and place to talk candidly and positively about ways to strengthen the working relationship by addressing trust directly. Before you come to the conversation, review the action steps for trust building and pick a few that you believe are relevant. Use mutual language that assumes responsibility and does not *point the finger* of blame. Start a dialogue with these open-ended questions.

- *I want our working relationship to grow in mutual benefit. How can we increase the trust level between us?*

- *What can I do to earn your trust?*

- *Are there aspects of our work, where we need to become more confident and able to rely on each other?*

- *What ideas do you have for us to begin to build trust?*

- *Where in our current working relationship is the trust level high?*

- *What has helped us build this trust? Are there ways that we can extend this into other areas?*

Inquiry Into Action - Assessing Psychological Safety in Your Organization

Here are some discussion questions to begin to frame and assess the Psychological Safety of your team's environment.

- *Are mistakes held against people in the organization?*

- *Can team members bring up problems and tough issues?*

- *When problems and tough issues come up, can they be fully discussed with candor and respect?*

- *Do people ever reject or exclude others for being different?*

- *How easy is it to take a risk?*

- *Is it easy or difficult to ask other team members for help?*

- *Are you confident that no one on this team would deliberately act in a way that undermines your efforts?*

- *In your work with all the other team members, are your unique skills and talents valued and utilized? Do you think this is true for everyone?*

- *How do your leaders assess their capacity to build a psychologically safe environment? See Appendix 1.*

The Core Ideas of Lesson Three

Belonging means that people identify with the mission of the organization and with each other.

The culture of an organization is its basic personality expressed in the essential ways its people interact and work. These essential ways develop into self-sustaining patterns of behavior that determine how things are done and how well they are done.

There are leaders with titles and authority, and there are those who lead by building the elements of a healthy organization that can adapt and navigate change.

Psychological Safety is essential for organization health.

The gold standard of 21st century team performance is the enduring power of trusting, respectful human relationships.

The team environment must provide a sense of psychological safety that supports everyone's willingness and ability to engage, offer ideas, express concerns, challenge the status quo, and admit mistakes.

The job description of leaders and managers must include the responsibility to establish and sustain a psychologically safe environment. This responsibility requires consistent daily behaviors that send belonging signals to encourage and value everyone's full participation.

With a sound collaborative structure and positive working relationships, an organization can be a place where people feel a sense of belonging and trust in each other.

PART TWO BECOMING

Growing full capacity to work together

Vision is not enough. It must be combined with venture.
It is not enough to stare up the steps, we must step up the stairs.

~ Vaclav Havel *First President of the Czech Republic*

Lesson Four LEARNING – the Force of Understanding

- A Learning Organization in Action

- Dialogue Is the Gold Standard to Generate Learning Through Understanding

- Dialogue is the Foundation of All the Cornerstone Practices

- Leadiators Are Architects of Positive Conversation Space

- The Design of Dialogue

- Raise the Standard for Professional Communication Behavior

- A Growth Mindset Accelerates Learning

Lesson Five ENVISIONING – the Force of Moral Imagination

- A Small Organization with a Large Imagination for a Better World

- Mission (the WHY) Drives Purposeful Action

- Develop a Memorable Mission Statement

- Deepen the Organization's Ethical Roots with Core Values and Guiding Principles

- Two Large Organizations Use Core Values and Guiding Principles to Unite

- Moral Imagination Is the Renewable Energy Source that Sustains Action

- Vision Pulls the Organization Forward

Lesson Six ALIGNING – the Force of Leverage

- A Dying Town Comes Alive

- The Elements of Wise Planning

- Wise Planning Is an Investment

- Strategic Planning Often Fails to Be Wise

- Wise Planning by Design

- Map the Operating Environment

- Strategies That Increase Adaptability

- Commit to Stretch Goals, S.M.A.R.T. Objectives, and Concrete Action Steps

Blueprint for Creative Collaboration

POSITIVE COLLABORATIVE FORCES
Generated by the cornerstone practices, action steps,
and *cultural characteristics**

Clarity   Perspective   Connection

Understanding   Moral Imagination   Leverage

Conviction   Reconciliation   Agility

SKILLSET

Cornerstone Practices

Values-Based Decision Making
Wise Planning   Principled Negotiation
Dialogue – the Foundational Practice

Designed **N**ecessary **A**ction Steps
that implement the practices

MINDSET
***Growth Mindset**

HEARTSET
*Integrity**
*Psychological Safety**

Lesson Four LEARNING

When we change the conversation, we change the future.

~Juanita Brown, *The World Café*

The Force of Understanding

Leadiators must actively cultivate the cornerstone practice of dialogue and use its skillset for all important conversations.

An organization must be able to constructively discuss and understand every important issue, no matter how difficult.

Differences and diverse perspectives are valuable sources of learning, creativity, and innovation that generate understanding.

A growth mindset and the practice of dialogue turn mistakes into lessons that accelerate learning velocity.

How much an organization can accomplish working together is directly proportional to its capacity to learn. How much can each person learn from others? How quickly can he or she do so? How can teams learn together? How effectively can an organization circulate the force of learning throughout the organization? Every lesson learned builds more capacity to adapt and succeed.

Lesson Four centers on the leadiator's duty to set an example and actively promote the habits of constructive conversational engagement that are foundational to the collaboration mindset, heartset, and skillset. Only dialogue is predictably able to open minds and hearts, harness the power of diverse perspectives, and develop collective intelligence and wisdom.

Debate and argument have become 20th century conversational dinosaurs because personalities, power, privilege, and politics shrink the learning space. In a rapidly changing operating environment, an organization must not miss opportunities to learn from diverse perspectives and adapt.

The organization must become a dialogical community of practice like Project ECHO (page 4) where respectful, learning exchanges are the norm. Then, the flow of ideas becomes powerful, moving vertically and horizontally, back and forth across levels and boundaries. *The skillful collision of ideas requires enough supporting structure (Lesson 5 - Envisioning and Lesson 6 - Aligning) to turn promising ideas into innovations that enable the organization to adapt and thrive (Lesson 9 - Adapting).*

Dialogue is not a soft skill. It is rigorous, open-minded inquiry coupled with deep listening, always seeking learning through understanding. Only consistent, deep listening builds respectful working relationships and sustains collaboration over time. In this lesson, you will learn about a powerful development from the positive psychology movement called a Growth Mindset that turbocharges learning by turning every mistake or failure from a negative loss into positive learning.

Learning Objectives

- Apply the dialogue skills of open inquiry, straight talk, and engaged listening to co-create a conversational learning zone and address every key issue

- Identify the mindset barriers that block learning

- Recognize the practical behaviors that leadiators use to reinforce a Growth Mindset and power up organizational learning velocity

A Learning Organization in Action

In Lesson Two - Seeing, I introduced you to Monte del Sol (MdS), a school that saw itself as part of an interdependent web of community. With this understanding, the school was able to think *outside the box* of the physical school building and leverage the community as a much greater resource to deliver transformative learning experiences to students. You already have read about MdS's devotion to mentorship as a pillar of learning. Now I want to take you more deeply into its organizational DNA for learning.

Tony Gerlicz, the head of the school, rejected the traditional title of principal. Instead, he reframed how he and everyone else spoke about him and thought about him. The sign outside his office said, HEAD LEARNER. This inclusive frame placed him side-by-side with everyone else in the extended school community. However, as a true leadiator, he also showed the way to others with two practices that were critically important to facilitate and open up the learning process for everyone. First, he was candid about what he didn't know and he regularly asked others for help and ideas. When a leadiator acknowledges interdependence, this signal opens up channels of possibility for everyone to be a learner. Second, he demonstrated his vulnerability to the teachers and students. The words, *I don't know. I will find out and get back to you*, should come naturally to a leadiator.

These words send a powerful, positive message that learning never stops for anyone. If the Head Learner became emotional about a topic when speaking publicly, he let everyone see this emotion. When he made mistakes and experienced his limitations, he often acknowledged this publicly. He accepted and demonstrated his own humanity as a leader. In my experience, this openness and honesty is not so common among leaders. These attributes provide the fertile soil in which dialogue can grow and collaborative learning thrives.

In Lesson Six - Aligning, I will discuss further the critical role of consistent, authentic, and constructive messaging from leadiators and leadership teams as a *steady signal* necessary to keep creative collaboration on course. MdS had this element in abundance. The Head Learner, who was always learning, admitting mistakes, and circulating lessons learned, attracted a remarkable collection of talented teachers who embodied the same authentic spirit of life-long learning.

Consider your own adolescent experience or your experience as a parent or relative observing young people moving through the passage of adolescence into young adulthood. Middle school and high school students are frequently critical of adults and have well calibrated radar for hypocrisy. When adults are *preaching* the importance of learning, it is obvious to young people when they are not sincerely practicing what they are preaching.

MdS students saw the Head Learner and the teachers offer daily examples of continuous learning. One noteworthy example was my son's mathematics teacher. This was not an easy job. My son, though intelligent and capable in all subjects, had a negative attitude about mathematics. He thought it was irrelevant and without practical value in his life. However, his mathematics teacher was a *polymath*, a person with expertise in multiple domains. Besides mathematics, he was accomplished in Greek, Latin, plumbing, world religions, and meditation. He captivated my son with his joy of learning and reframed his understanding of mathematics as interesting and valuable. My son went on to become a college honors graduate in biochemistry and took many upper level mathematics classes.

My son's story was common at MdS because the learning *DNA* was so well integrated throughout the school culture. The core belief of MdS was that great learning doesn't come from external rules and test scores, but from internal motivation and an environment that encourages exploration, honesty, questions, and community. The teachers' inner fire to learn ignited similar fires in their students through learning conversations. There was a shared understanding among teachers that they needed to engage students in a dialogue to become partners in learning.

Dialogue Is the Gold Standard to Generate Learning Through Understanding

Most conversations about important topics are not dialogues. This is particularly true when conflict and tension arise within an organization, within a group setting or between individuals. The most common form of communication amidst differences is debate. The word, debate, conveys its essential nature. The root of the word is the French verb *debattere*, meaning to beat upon. Debate assumes a win-lose outcome and often focuses on attacking or beating down the arguments and positions of the other side.

It is possible to maintain a climate of healthy, civil debate that remains constructive and productive. Debate in a team can reveal new angles of understanding and solutions to a problem. However, there is an inherent tendency in the dynamics of any debate toward argument about who is right and who is wrong. In a moment, argument can morph into adversarial communication that lowers the psychological safety of the climate, decreases the willingness of some to share their ideas and concerns, and shuts down the search for new possibilities.

Dialogue is learning conversation that unites instead of divides. Dialogue builds collaboration and enables people to maximize learning together. The word is formed from the root words *dia* and *logos,* that indicate the exchange of meaning through the word. The purpose that guides a dialogical exchange is a higher quality conversation of reasoning, learning, and understanding. These intentional actions raise the level.

- Respectfully engage different perspectives.
- Develop greater individual and shared understanding.
- Clarify what is most important.

- Forge connections between people and ideas.

- Generate possibilities.

- Build the conversational muscle for the next important conversation.

Organizations consciously committed to the practice of dialogue are not yet commonplace. Debate behavior is the default conversation mode that assumes a winner and a loser. Dialogue requires discipline to avoid predictable argument and debate behavior that may only reproduce the same level of understanding that already exists.

Alfred Mehrabian was a social scientist who conducted pioneering research in communication that resulted in a *rule* about the meaning that comes from different forms of communication. His work posits that only 7 percent of meaning comes from the actual words spoken. 38 percent comes from voice tone (attitude, confidence, emotional content implying judgment, respect or disrespect, etc.) and 55 per cent comes from other non-verbals (body language, particularly facial expression). (1) The safety requirements during the pandemic have moved much organizational communication to video calls, voice calls, and digital messages. The communication limitations of these platforms will tax the capacity of groups to communicate effectively, assure understanding, build trust, and bridge differences. These challenges make a debate approach as a cultural norm in an organization even more risky.

Good decisions depend on clear discussion and full understanding of the situation, stakeholders, values, options, and risks. Debate-oriented argument, poor listening, and conflict behaviors tend to produce *noise.* This can interfere with the clear communication necessary to harness the power of diverse perspectives that increase understanding and respect. Only dialogue predictably communicates enough respect to support collaboration.

Dialogue is the Foundation of All the Cornerstone Practices

The first cornerstone practice of a healthy organization is Dialogue that balances advocacy and candor with inquiry and listening. This balance is critical to support Psychological Safety, introduced in Lesson Three.

Without enough safety, clarity and full understanding are likely to be compromised.

Dialogue requires more skill than debate and is a better path to the truth because the process encourages minds to remain open. Dialogue is an emotionally intelligent practice that strengthens relationships and maintains respectful listening. Governing boards of profit and nonprofit organizations, management groups of all types and sizes across sectors, work groups, and project groups are all *teams*. Any member of any form of team can be a leadiator who, by example, models behavior norms that create psychological safety through dialogue. The power of example is usually more powerful than any words.

MINDSET

Neither agreeing with nor liking someone is necessary Approach each encounter with a mind ready to learn. Assume that the other members of the team have something new and valuable to contribute to your comprehension and then stretch your mind to find out what that is.

None of us has the whole truth Be aware of the tendency to try to confirm what you already believe or find a weakness in the other position. Orient your focus toward meaning. Seek to comprehend the facets of meaning that emerge within the team. Believe that diverse perspectives will enrich the quality of the dialogue.

HEARTSET

Pay attention to the voice of the heart Listen for the *voice of the heart* as well as the mind—yours and others'. Tune into the language, tone, and the unspoken feelings beneath the words. Listen to others as you would listen for the themes played by various instruments in an orchestra and the way they relate to each other. It's the relationship that makes the music. In dialogue, it's the quality of the exchange that makes the collective meaning. This goes well beyond the literal meaning of the spoken words.

Observe, rather than identify with your judgments Notice when you are holding a strong judgment about the person and what is being said. Judgment closes the mind and the heart. If you can't re-center to become open to the other(s), bring the concern into the dialogue, *I do not* understand the practicality of your idea given our limited resources. Can you give me an example so I can see it from your perspective? Examine the observations and assumptions. Find ways to describe the judgment honestly in a firm, calm manner or let it go.

SKILLSET

Respond, don't react Responding is the basic principle for dialogue. Dialogue requires space. Take a step back, reflect, and then respond rather than react automatically or defensively. Balance advocacy (asserting your opinion or position) *Here's how I see this issue…..* with inquiry (seeking clarification and understanding) *Since I see this very differently, help me understand how you reached the opposite conclusion.* When advocating, do not impose your opinion, simply offer it as such. *I feel strongly that we have to move forward now and cannot risk further delay. Here's why I believe this…..* Then return to inquiry that seeks further clarification and a deeper level of understanding, not the exposure of weakness. *Is there an example that you can offer to illustrate how this would work?*

Recognize and name patterns In your responses do not argue, analyze, rescue, nit-pick or give advice. Instead, look for patterns and connections among the diverse views. *We don't seem to have any common ground yet. However, I do hear a pattern in all the comments so far. Everyone has affirmed the basic nature of the problem and seems to agree that we cannot accept the status quo. Is this right?* Keep potential solutions on the table in order to go deeper and learn together. *Yes, I see what you are suggesting AND I think we need to look at this from other angles to make sure we solve this at the right level.*

Leadiators Are Architects of Positive Conversation Space

There are four primary modes of organizational conversation that lie on a spectrum of increasing quality towards understanding, learning, and improved collaboration.

Argument (Terrible quality) is non-listening with the primary intent to dominate and win. There is little, if any, concern for others' views. Speaking and reacting quickly usually precludes understanding. Too often, the arguer has the tragic combination of a fixed agenda and a closed mind. As described in Lesson Two, confirmation bias causes an arguer to only seek information and perspective that supports what he already believes. Argument is often motivated by a sense of one's status and expertise that manifests in a sense of entitlement, anger, or defensiveness.

Adversarial Debate (Poor quality) emphasizes disagreement and listens for opportunities to prevail as right, prove another wrong, embarrass someone, or show off. This form of conversation has spread like a virus through the mass media (talk shows, news shows, sitcoms, movies, blogs...) and other public exchanges that affect conversation in organizations, neighborhoods, and families. At its most toxic, communication becomes calculated or even *weaponized* to harm others in order to advance a selfish agenda at the expense of the greater good.

Principled (Healthy) Debate (Fair quality) is listening from your own position with respect and some degree of objectivity. While openly committed to one's separate interests, there is also a genuine interest in the truth and learning. There is shared willingness to acknowledge legitimate interests held by individuals and groups on the other *side* of the issue.

Dialogue (High quality) is listening with the mind and the heart (empathy), willing to be changed by what you hear and learn. The purpose of dialogue is a higher shared level of understanding while also communicating your own preferences, needs, and concerns. Increased understanding is the superordinate goal above who is right. In the context of a problem to be solved or an issue to be addressed, there is a commitment to develop ideas and seek an outcome that benefits everyone. Dialogue is the only conversation mode that is designed to encourage creative collaboration because it offers range and depth. (2) (See Figure 9)

In my experience, healthy organizations often settle for principled debate as the norm, because they are not willing to make the investment in dialogue. A commitment to dialogue as a practice requires enough time and space to intentionally convene people with diverse perspectives. In our time-pressured operating environments, the default mode for most important conversations is efficiency at the expense of creativity and wisdom.

Figure 9

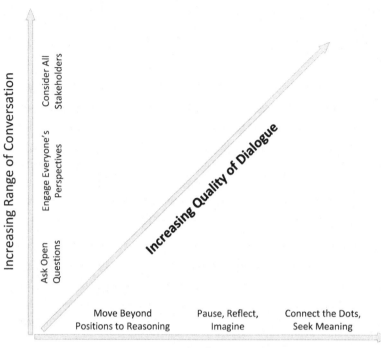

Increasing Depth of Conversation

Organizations tend to settle into limited habits of debate because they lack commitment to the development of critical skills. Organizations with rigid hierarchies preserve the status quo through limits on forums where leaders, managers, and employees engage at a level *table* where all voices matter. Like any form of skill, dialogue improves with deliberate practice. These skills build the quality of the exchange and constructively navigate any tension or disagreement. A skilled, dialogical conversation progresses through three phases.

- *Diversification* – Opening the scope of the conversation to hear and understand diverse perspectives

- *Emergence* – Patiently refining individual and shared understanding and beginning to identify possibilities for action

- *Convergence* – Coming to shared understanding of the path forward and next steps, either by a consensus process or another principled decision-making approach. (see Lesson Seven)

Even a principled, skilled debate conversation is likely to shortchange the diversification and emergence phases. Premature focus on already formed positions marshals the reasoning to support the *right* answer or preferred outcome.

It may also help to use a slightly different perspective by dividing the dialogue space on important topics into two parts. First, focus on the **Problem Space**. As the educator, John Dewey, has said, "A problem properly stated is half solved." (3) The participants deliberately and thoroughly pull apart the topic needing clarification and resolution to develop a clearer understanding of the issue and its dimensions. *How do these issues touch people and groups? What are the underlying interests of these people and groups?* Interests come from what people need and what they value. *How do we frame the problem we want to resolve?*

Then, focus on the **Solution Space**. Intelligent resolution or forward movement from the conversation comes from the creative examination of options. It is here where dialogue shines particularly brightly because the psychological safety generated by openness, respect, and listening frees participants to ideate and share spontaneously.

- *What if....?*
- *How have others...?*
- *Would it be possible to....?*
- *How might we.....?*

You will find more examples of these kinds of open questions that invite creative ideas on page 121. After generating a robust set of possibilities, participants can move on to assess the options and settle on a solution using the cornerstone practices of Values-Based Decision Making (Lesson Seven) or Principled Negotiation (Lesson Eight).

The Design of Dialogue

Dialogue creates a safe, stable *container*. Imagine directors in a boardroom facing a critical question about the strategic direction of the organization. Imagine a project team facing a major deadline, falling behind on schedule, and examining divergent ideas about what to do. Imagine a senior leadership team with a remarkable business opportunity that also has a high degree of risk, weighing the wisest course of action.

Imagine an emergency command center in the midst of a public health crisis making recommendations about the deployment of limited life-saving equipment like ventilators.

In environments like these, skillful means are necessary to develop a quality conversation. There are three critical qualities that enable an environment of dialogue that can transform differences and difficulties into understanding and agreement.

- Participants engage with a **purpose** that is honest and positive.

- There is enough **courage** to act, face differences openly, admit mistakes, and acknowledge not-knowing.

- Even if the going becomes difficult, there is a firm commitment to **no frills respect**. Disagreements remain principled, not personal.

While purpose, courage, and respect lay the foundation for dialogue, three skills are the primary building blocks of the conversation along with enough silent spaces to encourage reflection, sustain a sense of calm, and create room for the quieter voices to enter the conversation. (See Figure 10)

Listening Presence Grow the ability to fully understand others and demonstrate that you understood what they communicated.

- Keep your focused attention on their message that includes words, tone, body language, emotion, and meaning.

- In your own words summarize and share your understanding of their message. Then, pause and wait to hear from them if your understanding is correct. *Let me make sure that I understood. From your perspective, what happened was _____. Is that right? (pause)* or *I heard three things that are priorities for you. Did I miss anything? (pause)* Your summary and the response you receive is called *looping*. The exchange completes a *loop* of understanding that grows clarity and also demonstrates respect.

- Use brief encouraging responses to invite others to continue to express their views while you continue to listen and seek understanding. *OK. Please go on. Uh-huh (head nodding) I see.....* (followed by silence)

Open Questions Use positive inquiry to draw others into dialogue, learn from them, and explore the issue and the possibilities. A question becomes more open when it invites the other person to answer in her own way.

- *What do you think about this issue?*

- *What can you tell me that will help me see this from your point of view?*

- *What if….? How might we….? How have others resolved problems like this?*

- *What ideas do you have about this situation?*

- *Is there anything else you can tell me that might change my mind about this decision?*

- There is a time to pin people down on an issue or nail down a factual matter. However, open questions are necessary to increase the breadth and depth of the conversation. Closed questions tend to narrow the conversation.

  - Asking for Yes/No answers. *Were you in the meeting the entire time when this happened?*

  - Seeking facts. *What does the contract say about delays in the schedule and notice?*

  - Leading others. *Isn't it true that you left the meeting before you heard his response?*

(In Appendix 3, page 310, you will find a list of open questions that can energize a dialogue in any group.)

Straight Talk Candid, civil expression firmly informs others where you stand, what you believe, why you believe something, what you value most, and what you want.

- Set boundaries about what is acceptable and unacceptable. *The situation isn't acceptable. It needs to change right now. Here's why_____.*

- When you say NO, deliver your message without aggression and with respect. *I am not going to support your proposal. What is most important to me about our work is the principle of fairness* to all employees across all wage levels in all departments. I believe that your proposal weakens this principle. However, if you modify the provision about _____, I am willing to reconsider and join you in putting this forward.

- Avoid niceness and placating at the expense of honesty. *I am willing to continue our conversation and talk about the issues and your concerns. I will not sit here and listen to profanity and personal attacks.*

- Create the conditions for subordinates and others who may be reluctant to speak up honestly and openly. (See Lesson 3, Belonging, and the specific guidelines for practices to increase Psychological Safety)

Figure 10

In the Creative Collaboration blueprint, the cornerstone practice of dialogue supports the other three practices: Wise Planning; Principled Negotiation; and Values Based Decision Making. Dialogue directly generates three core characteristics that were introduced in Lesson Two (Psychological Safety, Growth Mindset, and Integrity). With more specific action steps for dialogue that are integrated throughout the book, you will build your capacity to collaborate.

Start important meetings with leadership teams and work teams using the following guidelines. I include them with the agenda and materials I give to everyone before the meeting. In a live meeting, they are posted on the wall on a flip chart for reference. In a virtual meeting, they can be shared on a screen. I find that it helps to have participants take turns and go around the *table* one at a time to speak them aloud. These simple steps increase everyone's awareness of positive conversational norms to create and sustain a climate that generates understanding and maintains constructive working relationships.

These guidelines will help you and your organization break the destructive habit of speaking in serial monologues. Typically when someone is speaking in a strong exchange of views about an important issue, others are not listening very carefully. They are waiting to speak, mentally critiquing the speaker's idea, waiting to make a point, and rehearsing their message. All of these habits of debate undermine the listening-rich exchange of meaning that powers a dialogue to explore new territories of understanding and possibility.

Adopt a Listen/Learn Mindset Listen with the intent to learn rather than confirm what you already believe or find a weakness in another's position.

Air Traffic Control Only one person talks at a time. Do not cut others off and avoid 'cross-talk.'

Don't Beat Around the Bush Speak directly, calmly, and honestly to what you believe is important.

R.E.S.P.E.C.T. Speak respectfully at all times, especially when the issue is tough.

Share the Back Story When you have a strong position, share it AND describe the reasoning that led you to your opinion, recommendation, or conclusion.

Leave Some Oxygen for Others Be brief and share the air time so others have a full opportunity to speak.

Candor Without Aggression Express disagreement directly and honestly. Avoid making any personal attack or negatively characterizing the motives, beliefs, or ideas of others.

Connect the Dots Link ideas and highlight common threads or areas of possible agreement.

Question to Discover and Understand Ask open and honest questions that invite others to clarify their views and increase your understanding of their goals, needs, and concerns.

Raise the Standard for Professional Communication Behavior

The term professionalism is a useful way to frame shared expectations about communication in the workplace. After decades of work in environments with highly educated personnel (law firms, medical practices, hospitals, scientific laboratories filled with scientists and engineers, and universities) I observe that most people want to think of themselves as *professionals*.

However, high levels of professional education and training do not necessarily include the capacity to communicate skillfully and respectfully with others. I will use an example with which I have a great deal of experience: the way doctors communicate with lower status workers in hospital settings. With their domain expertise, highly developed intellects, and the relentless pressure to deliver service and manage risks, doctors are subject to being unable or unwilling to listen well. They can come across as brusque, rude, or arrogant. This is probably not true of most doctors. However, even a few doctors who communicate in this way can create difficulties in health care team environments. Within a hierarchy of status and authority, critical problem solving requires that everyone speak up when they see a problem. (4)

One way some organizations *raise the bar* of shared expectations for professional communication is with a team agreement. A team or workgroup within the organization can make a written commitment to specific guidelines. (See Figure 11) This commitment must be strong enough to grow a consistent conversational space that makes constructive discussion possible for every important issue, no matter how challenging. Here is an example of the type of agreement that can clarify the behaviors to practice and the behaviors to avoid. Can you imagine making this agreement? If so, can you imagine asking others to join you on a work team, leadership team, or board?

Figure 11

Our Commitment to Professional Communication

Our day-to-day words and actions must consistently align with our identity as people of integrity and professional ethics. Leaders and managers have a professional duty to practice respectful, effective communication skills, provide a positive role model to others, and develop a positive work environment that will sustain our capacity to work together with respect and trust.

Poor interpersonal communication practices are unprofessional and will limit our ability to fulfill the mission and reach our goals. Follow these guidelines to improve the work environment for everyone.

Professional Behaviors to Practice	Unprofessional Behaviors to Avoid
✓Ask open questions to learn others' knowledge, experience, and views	✗Cutting off others or discouraging them from making a contribution
✓Listen carefully to respect and understand other perspectives	✗Attacking, belittling or minimizing the ideas and concerns of others
✓Treat others who disagree with you as valuable professional partners	✗Unwillingness to listen to others or seek guidance from others
✓If you disagree, actively explore the thinking of those who disagree with you	✗Arrogance and self-righteousness in tone, body language, or attitude
✓Assert your point of view, idea, or proposal clearly and succinctly, with firmness and respect	✗Dominating conversations and leaving little room for the contributions of others
✓Clarify your position by sharing the reasoning and data that support it	✗Being defensive or argumentative
✓Speak up when you have concerns or differences about important issues	✗Disrespect in any form (rudeness, discourtesy, incivility)
✓Keep your ego in check to remain committed to the project's needs above your preferences	✗Remaining silent when something important needs to be addressed, discussed, or corrected
✓Examine your assumptions by asking others to help you test them	✗Failing to hold others (including other leaders) accountable for unprofessional behavior
✓Express appreciation for the contributions of others, particularly when they challenge you	✗Complaining to others about the behavior of another leader or manager instead of addressing the issue openly and directly with that person

126

A Growth Mindset Accelerates Learning

All organizations that want to excel need to carefully evaluate the collective attitude and perspective that exists in the organizational environment. You began to reflect upon this in Lesson Three in the consideration of your organization's culture. Mindset is a focused way to deepen the understanding of culture. It is fundamentally important to what does or doesn't take place. ***Mindset frames what is seen, recognized, and acknowledged, and, what isn't. Powerful limiting beliefs about what is possible or impossible are embedded in mindset.*** A popular proverb sums this up. "Whether you think you can or think you can't, you are right."(5)

In 1990, the movement toward a modern understanding of healthy, successful organizations leapt forward. Peter Senge and others launched a powerful framework that linked the nature of an organization as a system with the evolutionary imperative to learn and develop. The "Learning Organization" movement has continued to mature into a widely recognized set of thinking and behavioral tools that promote systems thinking and build organizations with the capacity for continuous learning. (6)

Additional well-developed principles have emerged from recent decades of research and practice in the field of positive psychology. Many of these principles link to an understanding about the human brain's capacity for change. This characteristic is called "experience-dependent neuroplasticity." (7) In essence, the repeated stimulation of positive experiences can grow new neural connections in the brain. A catchphrase attributed to one of the pioneers in neuropsychology distills this principle. "Neurons that fire together wire together." (8)

As organizations seek performance advantages, some of these principles are being embraced to inform their efforts toward excellence in the way people learn together and *wire and fire* together. One of the most promising developments is a Growth Mindset. It is a powerful framework for organizations that must continually learn and adapt.

In the 1970's, researchers and educators identified that the way children thought about and viewed challenges, failure, and mistakes affected their ultimate ability to learn and succeed. From this basic understanding about learning in childhood, the term *Growth Mindset* describes a robust framework that has become the leading edge of the learning organization movement. This orientation toward mistakes has now become an attribute of a healthy culture that encourages lifelong adult learning, continuous organization improvement, and increased organizational capacity to adapt to challenges and change.

Carol Dweck, Ph.D. is a leading researcher and the author of *Mindset: the New Psychology of Success*. She connects the dots for CEOs and organizational change agents. Studies of organizational environments validate the linkage between the prevailing *mindset* and worker satisfaction, perceptions of the organization culture, levels of collaboration, supervisors' attitudes toward employees, and ethical behavior. (9)

People with a Growth Mindset embrace challenges, commit to learning, and treat the opportunity to develop new skills as a call to action. An organization fosters a culture with a Growth Mindset that demonstrates five consistent behaviors.

- Working together in collaboration
- Openly sharing information
- Actively seeking and embracing feedback
- Honestly admitting and discussing errors in order to learn
- Taking smart risks in order to innovate

To return to the story that opened this lesson, all of these behaviors were in active day-to-day practice at Monte del Sol. The school building and the surrounding community became a fertile garden of learning possibilities. You can use this framework for a learning organization to actively assess and develop your organization's collective capacity to embrace change and respond to challenges, learn from each other, improve, adapt, and navigate forward.

As I mentioned in the introduction, the case examples in this book will not emphasize large organizations in order to illustrate the opportunities and challenges to design and build collaboration in the communities where most of us work and live. However, it is useful to examine the challenges to build collaboration at a much larger scale in order to reduce skepticism about the feasibility of organizational transformation.

Microsoft is one of the world's largest technology organizations. When he arrived in 2012, as the new CEO, Satya Nadella, a computer scientist from India, seemed an unlikely choice for the job and an unlikely leadiator. In the brutally competitive, high-velocity environment of the technology giants, Microsoft was falling behind its rivals and faced huge challenges, struggling to adapt and grow.

As a long-time Microsoft insider and manager, Nadella knew its culture well. Microsoft was ultra-competitive with people trying to progress by proving themselves smarter than others. Strong silos limited lateral, interdisciplinary communication. Microsoft's past success and its international prominence led to a pride in its intelligence and status that affected its interest and willingness to partner with others. In Nadella's words, it was a culture of *know-it-alls*. He believed that the only path forward required a radical shift in the entire worldwide, 120,000+ employee enterprise. How?

He envisioned a transformed Microsoft with increased adaptive capacity leading the industry through extraordinary performance by hitting *refresh*. In order to refresh, cultural habits needed to shift from internal competition and silos to an environment marked by two fundamental characteristics: empathy and collaboration. Only through strong connection and synergy throughout Microsoft could the fully engaged energies and talents of all employees be harnessed to thrive amidst change. Nadella also believed that an internal environment of learning and collaboration would be critical to enable successful collaboration with strong, external partners that could become invaluable allies because their outside perspectives "help you see around corners" in a dynamic operating environment. He imagined a cultural shift in mindset from *know-it-alls* to *learn-it-alls*. (10)

He described his leadership approach simply and powerfully: "Anything is possible for a company when its culture is about listening, learning, and harnessing individual passions and talents to the company's mission." (11)

Satya Nadella's example of leadership is not just another high-profile story about an elite, corporate giant with a charismatic, new leader. It is prophetic in these times because it places a Growth Mindset, learning capacity, and learning velocity at the center of a design for organization health and success.

The waves of change are not only affecting Microsoft's operations. They are arriving with varying degrees of intensity in the operations of non-profits, businesses, and government agencies everywhere. Since February, 2020, the convergence of global waves have inundated the operating environment of every sector. A pandemic, a movement for racial justice, extreme weather patterns, and a worldwide economic power down, challenge all organizations to learn and adapt.

Nadella's leadership is a bold AND practical example that can be implemented in any organization to transform its culture. (12) Leadiators in every business, nonprofit, or government agency can emerge to inspire the organization to better understand its mission space, come together, learn together, and rise together. Every organization is responding to a call to action in order to face new challenges. Instead of being *know-it-alls* leaders, managers, and staff need to become *learn-it-alls*.

Every organization must learn how to consistently excel in the delivery of the mission. Organizational capacity to deliver superior results as it fulfills its mission depends upon healthy functioning. Organizational health and culture are deeply interrelated. The culture of an organization is its basic personality expressed in the essential ways its people interact and work. These self-sustaining patterns of behavior determine how well things are done. As presented in Lesson Three, do not underestimate the power of organization culture to expand or limit what is possible. An observation attributed to many veteran observers of organizational development makes the point: "Culture EATS strategy for breakfast!" In other words, an organization's culture determines its capacity. (13)

Nadella's actions demonstrate an understanding that a large organization culture is not easy to change. However, culture is malleable and can be renewed and evolve, affected by shifts in leadership, changing circumstances, and adopted strategies. In a small nonprofit organization, the department of a city government, or a family business with ten to fifty employees, the values, personality, and behaviors of a leadiator, are often the primary source of the culture of the organization. Therefore, a leadiator's shift to *download* Growth Mindset *software* can catalyze continuous movement toward learning. Instead of being a CEO, Executive Director, or principal, a leadiator can become the *Head Learner.* In larger, more complex organizations, the individual leader's style and personality cannot determine the organization's culture. Instead, the leader must act as a facilitator of evolution over time using the collective values, beliefs, and principles of leaders and employees rooted in history, purpose, strategy, management style, and the operating environment.

The evolution of a Growth Mindset can change behavioral habits that only reinforce the status quo tendency to accept the existing level of knowledge and understanding.

Actions that Promote a Fixed Mindset of Know-It-Alls

- People are judged and *star* workers are highly valued. Intelligence and talent are seen as fixed traits

- There is less openness about mistakes, questions, concerns, and problems, e.g., a *cover yourself* atmosphere where people keep years of emails to protect themselves, just in case.

- Hierarchical structures, silos, and relationship status limit the flow of information and there is less openness to feedback and constructive criticism

- Those in positions of authority focus more on their power to reaffirm their authority, protect their status, and hold back high-performing employees because they feel threatened.

- Employee learning and development is not carefully structured and designed

- Commitment to the organization by leaders and employees is uneven and, if it exists, it is often to the team, program, or department.

- Formal and informal acknowledgement focuses on output instead of effort.

- Risk-taking is not encouraged as necessary for learning and innovation.

- In hiring, the organization focuses on talent demonstrated by credentials and past accomplishments. (14)

Actions that Develop a Growth Mindset of Learn-It-Alls

- People consistently receive support to develop. Capacity is seen as learnable through practice and effort.

- When mistakes happen, they are openly admitted, discussed, and transformed into learning.

- There are open channels of growth-promoting feedback (constructive criticism) in all directions (up, down, across silos).

- Those in positions of authority focus more on the well-being of employees and see and treat employees as collaborators, as a team.

- There is an active program to engage employees and help them develop on the job (apprenticeships, coaching sessions, workshops).

- There is a high level of employee commitment to the organization (the organization has our back).

- The organization focuses more on effort than output.

- The organization supports risk taking and fosters innovation.

- In hiring, the organization emphasizes potential capacity and passion for learning more than credentials and past accomplishments. (15)

Inquiry Into Action - Here are some questions for personal reflection and group discussion. They will guide your development as a learning organization with the cornerstone practice of dialogue and the cultural practice of a growth mindset.

- *How skilled is your team with dialogue? See Appendix 2.*

- *What can you do to introduce the action guidelines of dialogue into your group/team meetings? See Appendix 3.*

- *Does your organization need an agreement about its approach to conversations that matter? If so, can you use the professionalism model from this lesson to develop your own guidelines?*

- *How many of the listed barrier conditions and behaviors that promote a fixed mindset are present in your organization?*

- *How many of the actions and conditions that promote a Growth Mindset are present in your organization?*

The Core Ideas of Lesson Four

Differences and diverse perspectives are valuable sources of learning, creativity, and innovation.

Dialogue is the gold standard for learning conversation for UNITING instead of dividing.

Dialogue is not a soft skill. It is rigorous, open-minded inquiry coupled with deep listening that always seeks learning through understanding.

The skillful collision of ideas in dialogue requires enough supporting structure to turn the most promising ideas into innovations that enable the organization to adapt and thrive.

Mindset frames what is seen, recognized, and addressed, and what isn't. Powerful limiting beliefs about what is possible or impossible are embedded in mindset.

A growth mindset accelerates learning velocity.

Blueprint for Creative Collaboration

POSITIVE COLLABORATIVE FORCES

Generated by the cornerstone practices, action steps,
and *cultural characteristics**

Clarity   Perspective   Connection

Understanding   *Moral Imagination*   Leverage

Conviction   Reconciliation   Agility

SKILLSET

Cornerstone Practices

Values-Based Decision Making
Wise Planning   Principled Negotiation
Dialogue – the Foundational Practice

Designed Necessary *Action Steps*
that implement the practices

MINDSET
*Growth Mindset**

HEARTSET
*Integrity**
*Psychological Safety**

Lesson Five ENVISIONING

A vision is not just a picture of what could be;
it is an appeal to our better selves,
a call to become something more.

~ Rosabeth Moss Kanter
The Challenge of Organizational Change

The Force of Moral Imagination

The organization's core values and guiding principles form the
ethical heart of a healthy organization.

Moral imagination integrates these important words with the
mission to envision a destination,
UNITING the organization for the journey.

A compelling vision is a powerful call to action that can pull everyone together and focus collective effort on the journey toward a reachable horizon or far beyond. A positive vision directs everyone and provides purpose. The ethical character of the vision can summon forth the better selves of individuals, a team, and an organization.

A healthy organization brings ethical awareness into the reality of key decisions and choices. How does the vision align with the organization's mission and a shared understanding of its guiding values and principles? The full, positive power of a vision comes from the exercise of moral imagination. This is the capacity to imagine beyond the present moment and envision the creation of something new. Then, with an affirmative perspective on what could be, make choices that align with what is good and right to do.

Moral imagination is an expression of our better selves. It melds mindset, heartset, and skillset into a powerful force that generates individual and collective effort to overcome the limitations and challenges of present reality. It does this by holding the image of what is right, good, and true as a beacon to guide everyone's steps forward together.

The power of moral imagination comes from genuine roots in core values that begin with big words like Excellence, Integrity, Equity, Diversity, and Customer Service. These words have been used, misused, and overused by organizations to identify their aspirations and the image they want to project to others about their character, commitment, and ethics. However, in many cases these positive declarations of big values words lack strong roots.

It is one thing to make a declaration. It is another for leaders to be an example and make sure everyone understands what the values mean and knows how to convert them into daily practice. Only practice infuses values with meaning that resonates in the heart, strengthens the will, and inspires sustained effort. When an organization's vision of what it wants to accomplish integrates well with its core values, the vision has the power to pull people forward together toward the desired end state.

Moral imagination stretches the shared sense of what is possible, UNIT-ING diverse people to work together, and sustaining commitment for the long haul. Moral imagination is a force that generates hope. You have already been introduced to living examples of this force in earlier lessons.

- Young people come together after a civil war to bridge a divide of ethnic hatred.

- A new school becomes a beacon of learning with a spirit of community partnership.

- A navy warship transforms from a rigid hierarchy into a creative community of belonging.

- A worldwide health network unites to bring quality health-care to a billion underserved people.

In the lessons to come, there are more examples of the power of the moral imagination.

- A new generation of women leaders will help bring peace to a conflicted region of the planet.

- A dying city will become economically vital.

- Two large health care organizations will merge to become a large, complex, organization while maintaining high, ethical standards.

- A worker without authority or power will show a segregated organization the path away from racial prejudice and towards inclusion.

Learning Objectives

- Articulate a clear memorable statement of purpose to drive the work forward. (the WHY)

- Define guiding values and action principles that infuse the collaborative work with meaning and moral character.

- Harness the power of moral imagination to frame a vision that strengthens hearts, focuses minds, and inspires skillful, collective efforts.

A Small Organization With a Large Imagination for a Better World

The Middle East has a long, troubled history and a current reality that is deeply polarized and violent. Seemingly irreconcilable differences in Israel and Palestine continue to defy all efforts to make progress toward peace. Tomorrow's Women (TW) is a small nonprofit organization that envisions a peaceful Israel and Palestine and a path that will lead there. This vision has motivated a sustained effort since 2003 to imagine beyond the large barriers to peace and develop the leadiators necessary to guide future generations toward peace. TW is an inspired example of Margaret Mead's words, "Never forget that a few committed citizens can change the world. Indeed, it is the only thing that ever has." (1)

Even a seemingly impossible vision far in the future can energize the heart and focus the mind of people to skillfully work together in creative collaboration. When the vision is noble and moral, it can pull people out of cynicism to capture the individual and collective imagination with hope for better days. Hope becomes a power source that motivates sustained, practical action, even against the odds. Hope is not soft and idealistic. It is muscular and practical. As the social entrepreneur, Paul Hawken, has stated, "The most unrealistic person in the world is the cynic, not the dreamer. Hope only makes sense when it doesn't make sense to be hopeful." (2)

TW recognizes that, for now, peace in the Middle East is impossible, given current societal attitudes and political leadership in the region. Therefore, its mission centers on the hearts and minds of young women as an opening of possibility, a new force for peace. TW's young women leaders, staff, board, donors, and volunteers are a vision community that imagines the emergence of a new generation of women leaders with powerful skills, positive relationships with the *other side*, and the moral imagination to see a better future. Their website states, *"Tomorrow's Women* trains young Palestinian and Israeli women to partner as leaders by transforming anger and prejudice to mutual respect, facilitating an understanding of the other, and inspiring action to promote equality, peace, and justice for all." (3)

Many people wish the world could be different, more peaceful and just. However, a true vision is different than a dream or a wish disconnected from the present difficulties. A true vision is inspired by moral imagination and embraces deeply held values. It connects with empathy to the painful reality that cries out for change. Moral imagination combines a tender heart and a muscular will that refuses to accept the status quo and points toward committed, principled action. This is the inner fire of purpose that can sustain individual and collective will to persevere on what Nelson Mandela called "the long walk to freedom." (4)

TW is a *greenhouse* to grow moral leadership. These young women choose to come and cultivate their capacity to become collaborative leaders and peacemakers. With ongoing support and skills development, they become the seeds of positive possibilities in a barren landscape of mistrust, fear, and anger.

A summer camp setting far away from the conflict provides a safe space so these young women can learn to share their stories and speak their deep truths to the *other*. They also learn to speak and listen in a different way that creates the possibility for heart-to-heart communication. The wisdom that guides TW's approach is simple: *If you don't work on peace inwardly, you can't work on peace outwardly.*

After the summer camp experience, TW coordinates a network of friendship, support, and mentorship to support the young women as they transition back to their homes. Then, they must set off on the long journey to peace. On they way, they must overcome the barrier of physical segregation that does not allow one side to know the other in any real way. They must have the courage and perseverance to face the inevitable challenges of peace building in a challenging environment. Most of us face challenges in our organizations and com-munities that are far less complex and require far less courage to address. We can learn much from these young women.

TW's approach has a simple, powerful design with a few action principles. These principles are universal and will help any organization on the long journey toward a vision of a better future.

- **MINDSET** Open the mind a little bit to accept that there is much to learn from others who see the world differently.

- **HEARTSET** Develop the capacity to be self-reflective, non-judgmental, and non-reactive.

- **SKILLSET** Continue to step back from the situation and seek a clearer and bigger perspective through open communication, listening, and speaking authentically.

A strong, clear vision is a critical piece of the architecture of creative collaboration. The moral imagination of a better future inspires and lifts the heart, activates the force of will to act over time, develops grit to overcome obstacles, and builds courage to engage others in an ongoing dialogue to bridge differences and find common ground.

Mission (the WHY) Drives Purposeful Action

Before articulating a vision that provides the destination for the shared journey, it is essential to clarify and strengthen the mission of the organization. The mission and vision are deeply interconnected. When both are clear, they form a set of dynamic *bookends* that serve as a motivational framework.

A mission is a short, powerful declaration of the organization's enduring purpose. It is the essential WHY, the reason for the organization's existence. This brief, clear meaningful statement is the motivational *glue* that bonds people together. It is also a public promise to internal and external stakeholders. Often with service providing organizations or collaborative alliances of independent organizations, the mission is framed as a short combination statement of WHAT we will provide and WHY it will matter to those who will be served.

The importance of WHY has been well developed in the popular culture in many business books investigating the basis of success over time. One of the best known is, Simon Sinek's TED Talk, How Great Leaders

Inspire Action with over 50 million views. He has since expanded his talk into a best-selling book, *Start With Why*. (5)

A meaningful mission is not just a well-drafted set of words or a *check-the-box* statement posted on an organization's website. It is the foundation of a set of elements that form the organization's identity and provide a blueprint for success.

- Statement of core values and guiding principles

- Vision of success

- Set of major goals that define the hard work necessary to fulfill the mission and realize the vision.

My long-time collaborator and co-author, Joan McIver Gibson, and I unpacked the layer of values and meaning in key decisions in our book, *A Field Guide to Good Decisions: Values in Action*. (6) WHY usually has its roots in the core values that guide choices and motivate action. I will explore values and principles later in this lesson on page 146, and then address goals as part of Wise Planning in Lesson Six.

A vision differs from a mission in that it describes a picture of future success when the organization fulfills the mission. The vision provides direction to set the course toward a point on the future horizon.

A clear, powerful, memorable mission statement offers four potential benefits.

- Unite the organization.

- Provide a useful point of reference to make major decisions that integrate short-term objectives with big goals

- Energize action by clearly communicating the essential meaning of the organization's work

- Attract outside stakeholders to align and provide necessary support

Develop a Memorable Mission Statement

Sometimes members of boards of directors and leadership teams balk when I bring up the subject of their mission statement and whether to review it or not. This response often has its roots in a prior experience to draft or redraft a mission statement in a small group. Too often, attempts to write a mission statement devolve into a tedious exercise that feels like a form of grammatical periodontal surgery.

There are ways to painlessly develop a well-crafted, useful mission statement. The answers to some of these questions will help you focus the conversation to craft a powerful, useful mission statement.

- *What is our fundamental purpose?*

- *What is unique or distinctive about us?*

- *Why do we exist?*

- *Who do we exist to serve?*

- *What do they want or need from us that is important?*

- *How should we respond to our clients, customers, users, and other key stakeholders?*

- *What are our guiding values?*

These answers give you the raw material. However, like digging up ore that has to be sifted well to find the *gold*, you can't pack all of this into a mission statement. Use the following criteria to sift the raw material of your answers to find the greatest value. Then, shape it into a powerful statement of your organization's purpose.

Essence Think....and think again about what is most important and essential that provides the motivating direction. Ask 'WHY?' several times to get to the heart of your purpose.

Length A mission statement should be brief (10-15 words), but it needs to be long enough to reach the target audience(s) AND contain the emphasis (guidance) needed to help clarify priorities and illuminate tough choices. Consider this simple structure to keep the mission statement short and memorable: Our mission is to _____ so that _____.

If there are other things that are important to state about your work and how you do it, you can often keep the mission lean and powerful by adding a separate set of bullet points that describe the programmatic ways the organization carries out the mission. Place these HOWs below the mission with a transitional phrase like, "We carry out our mission by.........."

Tone Find the right tone for the audience. Avoid language that is too lofty or ponderous to be taken seriously. The language should be clear and inspiring, more poetry than dry, pro forma prose. Think of it like the classic Japanese verse form, the haiku. It uses a limited number of words to express what is essential while conveying expansive meaning.

Audience Understanding Consider whether to present the mission as the lead *headline* alongside other key statements such as vision, key values and action principles, and other major commitments. Some audiences can benefit from understanding the overall design blueprint that conveys the organization's clarity about WHY?, WHERE?, AND HOW? This is an approach many of my organization clients use.

Here are some examples of well-drafted mission statements:

- TED *Spreading ideas*
  (a 21st century knowledge organization about leading edge thinking)

- The Nature Conservancy *To conserve the lands and water on which all life depends*
  (an organization that protects and preserves natural resources)

- Museum of International Folk Art *To foster understanding of the traditional arts to illuminate human creativity and shape a humane world*
  (a public museum that preserves and presents the work of traditional artists)

- Heifer International *To work with communities to end hunger and poverty and care for the Earth*
  (an international nonprofit that addresses the basic needs of people)

- Center for Independent Living of North Central Florida *To empower people with disabilities to achieve their goals for independence*
  (a community-based advocacy organization for people with disabilities)

- Positive Energy Solar *To be New Mexico's most trusted and reliable partner for sustainable energy solutions*
  (a regional solar energy company)

Once you have a brief, powerful mission, give further thought to the deployment of the mission internally and externally. A well-drafted mission can serve without revision for years. However, it is a good practice to intentionally review and confirm the mission statement once a year as part of your wise planning (Lesson 6). Underscore the mission's practical value as a conscious reference point for all other planning activities. Ask leaders and managers to reaffirm the mission or address the need for changes.

Deepen the Organization's Ethical Roots With a Statement of Core Values and Guiding Principles

A clear, memorable statement of the organization's mission calls people into action. The statement of core values and guiding principles transforms the mission into ethical, virtuous action. Values are aspirational and express standards the organization commits to at all times. They are usually stated as a set of 5-7 big nouns, e.g. "Integrity," "Excellence," "Fairness," and "Innovation." These important words need clear definitions. A values statement is a set of promises about the organization at its best. This promise can only be fulfilled when there is shared understanding of their meaning joined with the capacity and will to put the big words into practice.

The stakes are high when an organization makes a public commitment to big values words. A declaration is necessary, but it is not sufficient. There are quite a few prominent examples of organizations with shocking conduct in policies, practices, and products that harmed people and betrayed the promise of their commitment to noble values like Integrity, Respect, and Quality. The names Enron, Wells Fargo, and Volkswagen are just a few high profile examples.

Failed commitment to big values words is not limited to giant corporations. It is not uncommon in small or medium size businesses, non-profits, and government agencies. Therefore, every leadiator must be a guardian of the organization's ethics. This role requires faithful demonstration of the organization's standards. Then, the leadiator must actively orient and reinforce the faithful practice of the organization's values statement, i.e. *walk the talk*. The values statement is the *talk*. The faithful practices are the day-to-day *walk*.

In Lesson Seven you will receive a structured decision making process that places values at the center of every key decision. This process is a cornerstone practice that demonstrates accountability to an organization's values declaration. Decisions that *walk the talk* earn credibility and trust from an organization's employees, volunteers, customers, clients, funders, investors, collaborators, and community stakeholders.

Values matter and they affect the way we see the world. This values mechanism exists alongside another mechanism to quickly make choices and then rationalize and package the explanation afterwards. (7) Each of us has a set of values, operative in all of our key decisions. We develop these values through our experience and the influence of important people, situations, and institutions. When faced with a difficult choice, we call upon this larger set of values (often automatically and unconsciously) to apply them to the particular issue we need to address.

A leadiator can show an organization how to put values into practice. The values statement becomes a tenacious commitment to a set of conscious standards for individual and collective accountability. This level of commitment requires a set of action principles that clarify specific behaviors that must be practiced regularly to live the big words. These principles describe how people will treat each other inside the organization, how employees will serve clients or customers, and how the organization will engage with suppliers, strategic partners, and community stakeholders.

When organizations fully commit to turn values into principled action, they build a powerful, virtuous set of habits that stamp Integrity into the culture and connect everyone to the vision. Here is an example of a carefully drafted set of organization core values and principles framed as commitments to act.

Two Large Organizations Use Core Values and Guiding Principles to Unite

For over a decade I had the opportunity to work with two corporations as they merged different cultures, histories, and core values into a unified organization. You will learn more about this work in Lesson Seven. For now, it is enough to describe Centura Health in the late 1990s as a complex regional healthcare organization with more than 15,000 employees in multiple independent operating units in different locations. Their work to build a common culture began with a common set of core values and guiding principles. (8)

RESPECT positive regard for the dignity of all persons

In our daily work with each other, we will:

- Encourage and value the contributions of each person, and make each feel supported and empowered

- Listen well, communicate openly and honestly, and encourage others to do the same

- Treat others as we would like to be treated ourselves, relating so well with them that they actively seek to associate with us

INTEGRITY honesty, directness, and respect for commitments made

In all of our interactions, we will:

- Foster trust by being truthful, empathetic, and consistent
- Be authentic and courageous, aligning what we are thinking, saying, feeling, and doing
- Be responsible for and follow through on the commitments we make

STEWARDSHIP respectful use of natural, human and financial resources

In managing the natural, human, and financial resources to which we have been entrusted, we will:

- Seek ways to appropriately utilize resources, allowing us to become more effective and productive
- Act responsibly, taking only those actions that align with our mission
- Be accountable to the organization and to each other for our actions and the outcomes they produce

IMAGINATION creativity in all we do

In our shared effort to fulfill our mission, we will:

- Look beyond the challenges of the present and envision what is possible
- Cultivate and reward innovation and risk taking
- Embrace continuous learning and positive technological advancement

EXCELLENCE striving to exceed the quality, customer service and cost performance expectations of our customers

In every job at every level of our operations, we will:

- Put forth our personal and professional best, providing the highest quality of service of which we are capable

- Commit ourselves to continuous improvement, seeking to set the recognized performance standards within our industry

- Deliver a superior experience for all of our customers, sensing their needs and exceeding their expectations

Each big word has a short, clear definition followed by three principles that guide action. Each principle begins with a verb. All of the principles are framed as shared commitments.

This strong, clear statement of values and principles provided the organization with an ethical reference point AND it was only a beginning. In a new, merged organization, the statement required additional planning to shape and align the new organization's culture. This kind of a statement reflects the moral imagination about *our best selves*. It is also a promise to employees, patients and their families, and community partners. In the Centura example, this merged organization was not yet a unified organization. How would they walk the talk?

Centura's leaders recognized that each key decision at every level of the organization offered a visible opportunity to be act in alignment with this statement. This included the board of directors, the corporate leadership, the leadership team of each operating division, and smaller department management teams. In order to take advantage of these opportunities, everyone needed to know how to take this statement of values and principles and apply it to important decisions.

For over a decade during this new organization's development, my partner, Joan McIver Gibson and I, designed and implemented a practical process to put these values into action. We trained hundreds of leaders and managers at every level from the executive suite, to leadership teams of operating divisions, to frontline managers. Everyone learned to follow a simple, disciplined decision-making process called "Values in Action" or VIA, which in Latin means the way.

This process delivered on the promises made with several of their core values and action principles:

- ***Respect*** Listen well, communicate openly and honestly, and encourage others to do the same. (The process promotes dialogue instead of debate to open the communication channel for maximum learning that strengthens working relationships.)

- **Stewardship** Act responsibly, taking only those actions that align with our mission. (The process brings the mission, values, and principles from the frame on the wall and puts them in the middle of the table to invite advocacy for strong alignment.)

- **Stewardship** Be accountable to the organization and to each other for our actions and the outcomes they produce. (The process requires transparent communication to be accountable to affected stakeholders.)

- **Integrity** Be authentic and courageous, aligning what we are thinking, saying, feeling, and doing. (The process encourages each everyone to share the air time so each participant has an opportunity to speak directly, advocate for importance, and be heard.)

- **Integrity** Foster trust by being truthful, empathetic, and consistent. (The process elicits sincerity instead of posturing, and understanding instead of division.)

In Lesson Seven, you will learn how a deliberate decision-making process can help any organization put values into practical action. Instead of quickly choosing and then rationalizing the reasoning, a sound process grows stronger decisions that are rooted in values.

In my work with other organizations after this period with Centura, I discovered the importance of one more step to move the statement of values and principles into action. It is necessary to identify a set of key supporting behaviors that implement the action principles. Some organizations also identify problematic behaviors that detract from the positive expression of the values and principles. For example, a key supporting behavior under RESPECT (encourage contributions) could be: *Design regular meeting formats that make time for people to speak and offer ideas.* An example of a detracting behavior to avoid could be: *Avoid backbiting (speaking negatively about someone to others when they are not present).* These behavioral standards act like guardrails to shape the organization culture to keep everyone on the road heading in the same direction. High performing, collaborative organizations integrate these behavioral expectations when they onboard new employees, promote managers, recruit leaders, and evaluate the performance of leaders, managers, and employees.

Moral Imagination Is the Renewable Energy Source that Powers Action

In the spring of 2020 in the midst of the social unrest about issues of police brutality and racism in the US and many other countries, more than a dozen daily messages arrived in my inbox from banks, software providers, an insurance company, airlines, and many nonprofit organizations. Each one made some form of public declaration about the commitment to social justice, addressing police violence, standing against racial discrimination, and increasing diversity and inclusion in their organization practices. These declarations were all well worded and sounded sincere. Some also acknowledged the necessity to follow through with meaningful action to *walk the talk*.

All moral statements to address problems and envision a better world should be questioned. Too often, the sincere and positive declarations of an organization's position on a challenging issue and its good intentions lack the commitment necessary to work for a better future. Think about an organization as a tree. A vision statement is a description of the fruit that will be produced by a healthy tree. A vision declaration is only a small tree. Leaders and organizations may say all the right words about the desired fruit, but the harvest may fail because the roots of the organization's commitment are not planted deeply enough.

The life force of a tree that will produce abundant fruit comes from its deep roots. The roots are the organization's purpose (mission), core values, and guiding principles discussed earlier in this lesson. When an organization is driven by positive purpose and aligned with values and principles that build an ethical culture, it engages a renewable energy source, moral imagination.

Moral imagination is the capacity to recognize turning points and possibilities in the midst of the current reality, no matter how challenging the conditions. It often requires that a leadiator become a trailblazer. The organization must work together to build a new path and create

what does not yet exist. The journey is powered by a shared conviction about the rightness of the mission and the strength of the vision to pull everyone forward.

Many of the vision examples included below have this quality, e.g. Tomorrow's Women does not have a clear path forward. The organization has the moral imagination to *see* the non-existent, constructive processes that must take root amidst the day-to-day challenges of political polarization and violence. Only with a long view and patience can a new generation of leadiators cultivate the seeds and grow new possibilities.

In *The Moral Imagination: the Art and Soul of Building Peace*, veteran peace-builder, John Paul Lederach, describes the fundamental capacities of moral imagination. (9)

Focus on connectedness Able to see yourself (and your organization) in a web of relationships that includes leaders, managers, employees, community stakeholders, adversaries, and even enemies. Move beyond isolation, separation, and division to search for new forms of meaning. Difficult problems in communities may need historic adversaries to come into alliance and work together. ***Find ways to engage, deeply listen, see through their eyes, and understand.***

Rely on uncommon sense Embrace complexity. Recognize systemic forces. Hold the tension of contradictions, conflicting position, and divergent ideas. Discover new perspectives, possibilities, and surprising capacities. ***Replace either/or thinking with both/and. Reframe from challenge to opportunity.***

Challenge assumptions Open up spaces where creativity and innovation can emerge. Respectfully challenge the status quo. ***Build new forums for better conversations that involve people who are not yet talking with each other.***

Venture Out Take risks and step out onto unknown ground without assurance of safety or success. ***To be moral, there must be sincerity and the will to persevere and engage over time.***

Rooted in mission, values, and principles, it is possible to activate moral imagination that "is an appeal to our better selves." (10) Once activated, moral imagination generates power and collective will to work together, creatively and collaboratively. This power source is critical in a time of disruptive change, uncertainty, and anxiety. "Some people see things as they are, and say why. I dream of things that never were, and say why not." Robert F. Kennedy. (11)

Vision Pulls the Organization Forward

Mission provides purpose, focus, and motivational drive. Vision provides a destination at the horizon or beyond to chart the organization's course. Vision is a key success differentiator for organizations because it inspires, organizes, and sustains effort over time. Through the strength of a positive vision, the organization develops the capabilities to shape the future. A vision must be clear and compelling so it attracts others who share it and agree to support it.

Steve Jobs said, "If you are working on something you really care about, you don't have to be pushed. The vision will *pull* you." (12) In order to engage this positive force for an organization's success, you have to get the level of difficulty in the vision right. I regularly work with organizations that have a permanent or enduring vision to change the world. The vision lies far beyond the visible horizon. It may be so expansive that fulfillment is beyond the lifetime of all the people now working together. Here are some examples of permanent visions.

> Tomorrow's Women "a world in which our young women will lead their people to a time when justice, human rights and peace will prevail in Israel and Palestine."

> The New Mexico Coalition Against Domestic Violence "Homes of Peace Everywhere."

> The World Health Organization "a world in which all peoples attain the highest possible level of health."

> The International Folk Art Market "a world that values the dignity and humanity of the handmade, honors timeless cultural traditions, and supports the work of artists serving as entrepreneurs and catalysts for positive social change."

I honor the beautiful, aspirational power of each one of these noble statements to change the world. However, I have found that the power of a large, enduring vision can be magnified when it is aligned with a

154

bold and realistic vision that people can imagine and *see* at the limit of the visible horizon. For most organizations operating in a time of so much social, economic, and environmental change, it is hard to see too far ahead.

Therefore, I recommend a horizon vision of two-three years in the future so all levels of the organization and its stakeholders have direct line-of-sight to the place they want to arrive in their work together. This is far enough away to imagine changes that increase the organization's capacity and mission effectiveness. It is near enough to be relevant to the lives of the people who must do the work. This proximity can inspire a sense of possibility that pulls at their hearts.

Figure 12

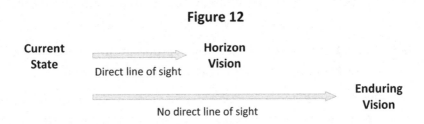

Another refinement strengthens the envisioning process. At the visible horizon, what are specific images of how the organization works differently and how the results of the work are different? Like a *mosaic*, these more detailed images of progress with financial resources, human resources, service delivery, and operational excellence can be put together to provide a unified picture of the desired future state. Specific images turn the planning into a story about a journey toward a destination. This narrative of where the organization wants to go together directs the work that will be necessary and shapes the path forward.

Consider a recent example of a mosaic vision at the visible horizon. The Center for Independent Living (CIL) is a regional organization in north central Florida. CIL is a part of a statewide and nationwide network of independent organizations with a common purpose to serve people with disabilities. While it serves people across all socio-economic groups, its 16-county region is largely rural and many of the people they serve are low income. They call the people they serve consumers.

CIL's enduring vision is: "a *World in which everyone can live with dignity, safety, and possibility."* They wanted this noble, distant vision to pull strongly against the inertia of the status quo. Therefore, CIL came up with a mosaic description of six images that captured their vision of success as a stronger, healthier organization at a three-year horizon. (13)

"On December 31, 2022, these statements will be true.

- We are recognized and respected as the leading disability service organization throughout our 16 counties.

- We are a diverse, unified team that excels in our communications between leaders, staff, programs and offices.

- Our high-quality, consumer-driven programs develop strong advocates who are actively engaged in their communities.

- Our outreach and marketing increased our volunteers, collaborators, donors, and sponsors to fully support all programs in meeting the needs of our consumers.

- We consistently deliver value to consumers through our highly organized and efficient services.

- Our dedicated and knowledgeable staff continually improves their skills through ongoing professional development opportunities to better serve our consumers and the community."

This more specific, mosaic vision builds capacity to stretch the organization toward a bold, realistic horizon. This stretch inspires the wise planning necessary to set meaningful goals and objectives. Well-framed goals and objectives align and focus the effort into practical action. Well-coordinated effort leverages the organization's human and material resources for maximum impact. Lesson Six describes the design of wise planning to guide this effort.

CIL has a long journey ahead AND it needs the organization's consumers, leaders, employees, volunteers, donors, and community partners to align with a common story of where they are going together. With this common story, CIL's internal and external stakeholders can assess progress, celebrate victories, and learn from mistakes and challenges.

A healthy organization becomes a *vision community*. Tomorrow's Women and CIL in this lesson, Monte del Sol School in Lessons Three and Four, and Project ECHO in the Introduction are all examples of organizational communities shaped by bold visions. The vision becomes a focal point for the ongoing work to build and maintain organization health. The elements of the blueprint for Creative Collaboration can also be seen in a healthy organization structure oriented toward a shared vision.

Figure 13

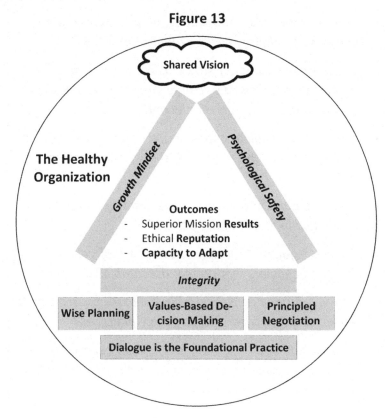

Inquiry Into Action These questions will guide personal reflection and group discussion as your organization envisions better days with an integrated statement of Purpose (Mission), Principles (Core Values and Guiding Principles), and Possibility (Vision).

- *What is your organization's essential purpose?*

- *How can you express it simply and powerfully so it is clear, memorable, and draws the right people to your cause to drive the work forward?*

- *What are the values that you want employees and those you serve to identify as the organization's DNA?*

- *Are these values better stated as compact phrases or as a single word followed by a brief definition, e.g., RESPECT - positive regard for the dignity of all people?*

- *What are the guiding action principles that are necessary to breathe life into the values and shape your organization's culture?*

- *Do these guiding principles have a set of concrete supporting behaviors that are desirable?*

- *Do these guiding principles have a set of concrete detracting behaviors that are not acceptable?*

- *How well do your employees believe that the organization's leaders and managers are living these principles?*

- *How well do your external stakeholders believe that the organization's leaders, managers, and employees are living these principles?*

The Core Ideas of Lesson Five

A mission is a short, powerful declaration of the organization's enduring purpose. It is the essential WHY, the reason for the organization's existence.

The organization's core values and guiding principles form the ethical heart of a healthy organization.

A compelling vision is a powerful call to action that can pull everyone together and focus collective effort on the journey toward a reachable horizon or far beyond.

The full, positive power of a vision comes from the exercise of moral imagination. This is the capacity to imagine beyond the present moment and envision the creation of something new.

Moral imagination is a force that generates hope.

Blueprint for Creative Collaboration

POSITIVE COLLABORATIVE FORCES
Generated by the cornerstone practices, action steps, and *cultural characteristics* *

Clarity   Perspective   Connection

Understanding   Moral Imagination   *Leverage*

Conviction   Reconciliation   Agility

SKILLSET

Cornerstone Practices

Values-Based Decision Making
Wise Planning   Principled Negotiation
Dialogue – the Foundational Practice

Designed **N**ecessary **A**ction Steps
that implement the practices

MINDSET
Growth Mindset *

HEARTSET
Integrity *
Psychological Safety *

Lesson Six ALIGNING

Vision without action is merely a dream.
Action without vision just passes the time.
Vision with action can change the world.

~ Joel Barker *Futurist*

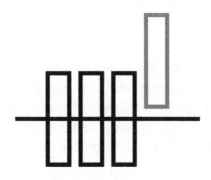

The Force of Leverage

Amidst change and uncertainty, Wise Planning
sets the course and direction
toward a shared vision of success.

Wise Planning is an ongoing dialogue that turns collective
intelligence into practical, well-coordinated actions.

Aligned, focused effort generates
leverage to fulfill the mission and improve results.

Stick together. Learn from mistakes. Assess progress.

Celebrate successes. Adapt to challenges.

The pace of change in every organization's operating environment will quickly make any fixed plan irrelevant. The waves of change in the current landscape (pandemic, racial justice, climate change, global economic vulnerability) are likely to challenge every organization with difficult choices. In these big waves, the organization is like a boat that needs direction to keep its bow oriented. All hands need to be on deck, well trained, and ready to act. Without wise planning an organization is adrift without clear orientation as the waves crash upon it. When the boat has direction and movement, it can maneuver to navigate the waves of change.

Wise planning creates a flexible blueprint that does not attempt to predict the future. Wisdom comes from the integration of purpose, enduring core values, and guiding principles with practical strategies. The organization consciously uses its values and principles to align and leverage precious human and material resources.

A well-structured planning process continues to direct the organization's focused attention on the path forward. Diverse viewpoints from key contributors provide a wide-angle perspective to take in the big picture and also zoom in to recognize critical details. At its best, planning generates practical wisdom through a set of ongoing conversations that assess progress, examine changing conditions, and guide adaptation to change. The organization becomes stronger because it moves steadily forward in unity, and gains momentum.

Learning Objectives

- Apply a disciplined, Wise Planning approach to align and unify the organization, increase leverage, and improve results.

- Realistically assess the value that Wise Planning can deliver to your organization that justifies the time, effort, and resources necessary.

- Recognize and avoid common mistakes that undermine the value of planning.

A Dying Town Comes Alive

In 1995, Howard, South Dakota, in Miner County, was declining like hundreds of other small, rural towns. Year by year, for decades, its population shrank as the farm and industrial job base withered. Young people graduated from high school and moved away, never to return. Compared to other cities in the region its demographic ratios (the most elderly, the highest outmigration of young people) painted a dire portrait of its future at the end of ninety years of decline. (1)

When a small city in a rural area is caught in a downward cycle of decline in economic and social health, there are no obvious answers. This is a complex, systemic problem. Many factors contribute to the lack of vibrancy of a community and the region that surrounds it. If asked individually, it is highly likely that the overwhelming majority of any small city or town's residents would express concern and support for some action to improve the future of their community. In my experience, it is often the case that leaders become paralyzed by the complexity and incorrectly assume that a complex problem requires a complex solution.

I have provided leadership training for more than 20 years to an organization called the Municipal Officials Leadership Institute. During this time, I have spoken with hundreds of city councilors and mayors from cities, towns, and even tiny villages in rural areas that face issues just like Howard, South Dakota. I engaged them in dialogue about subjects including wise planning, building collaboration, bridging differences, and making critical decisions.

Howard's situation was complex and baffling until a planning process unique in the town's history began that aligned young and old in a common cause. It all started in a high school business class. Students commented about a book examining the economic decline of rural communities in the region, and observed that this seemed to be the inevitable future of Howard.

Creative Collaboration requires alignment of people who share reasons to join together.

- A purpose to pursue

- A cause to promote

- An unmet need to address

- A difficult situation to face

- A problem to solve

In Howard, South Dakota, the seed of Creative Collaboration and wise planning was planted with a strong, open-ended question that embraced all of these requirements. "How could we change this?" As they began to examine this question, the students began to align themselves into a planning process founded on dialogue. Pragmatic reflection on the reality of the situation is the foundation of all wise planning. The first step was to establish a learning exchange with registered voters using a survey to gain perspective and better understand the situation.

In a situation like this one, many of the inputs necessary to rebuild a healthy local economy require action and decisions by others.

- Major economic investment

- New entrepreneurs

- In-migration of new residents

The survey responses revealed an important pattern: half of the residents were shopping outside the county in bigger cities. This pattern presented an opportunity to build collaboration among residents that the students identified as extremely promising.

The initial planning momentum necessary to align, build, and energize collaboration with others needed to clearly focus on strategies and resources within the control of willing participants. Momentum and hope needed to be built. The students were willing participants without the necessary resources. However, within the control of every resident in Miner County was the location where they chose to spend their money.

Their teacher encouraged the students to take action and present their ideas to the community. The leadership strata of the communities of

Miner County (city councilors, school board members, and county commissioners) gathered in the high school gym. According to their teacher, the adults recognized and responded to the students' sincerity and their emotional investment in the future of their community. The students marshaled the information and presented one simple, compelling, and actionable idea: if residents changed their habits and spent only 10% more of their disposable income in Miner County, the local economy could receive a $7 million economic boost.

The students carefully framed and presented the problem, the situation, and a possible solution in a way that dramatically increased the clarity with which others could understand the collaborative opportunity to carry out a public campaign. *Keep Miner $$ in Miner County.* This meeting was a catalyst that generated momentum. More people began to see the path forward, recognized their part in a solution, and chose to align to increase the leverage to make positive change.

Within one year, the actual increase in money spent in Miner County was $15.6 million and the city's sales tax revenue increased by 41%. A diverse, creative collaboration was steadily on the move with more resources, further increasing the leverage. The availability of resources generated more planning ideas for community improvement and community building activities. The dramatic *rebirth* of a dying rural community became a powerful story that attracted millions of dollars in foundation grants. From 1996 to 2008, the city's tax revenues increased 123%. New businesses became interested in a city with an inspiring vision.

UNITING by design saved Howard, South Dakota. Wise planning transformed Howard from a dying city without hope to a community on the move with the optimistic motto, *Opportunity Lives Here*. Since 2001, Howard has attracted renewable wind energy, organic beef production, and rural community development businesses with 200 new jobs. The high school teacher who encouraged his students to begin the planning for a better future went on to present the story of Howard's return from life support to inspire and guide communities in other states. (2)

In order to unite, a community must begin to align. When a few people align, they can begin to learn together. As they learn, they can develop clarity and communicate their clarity to others. Alignment and planning leads to ongoing dialogue with creative opportunities to assess, realign, act, learn, and course correct. Collaboration becomes effective and wise.

The Elements of Wise Planning

A wise strategic plan has the five elements displayed in the figure below. These elements are interconnected and align the organizational effort that generates enough leverage to achieve positive results. Lesson Five introduced three of these elements that provide the framework for more detailed planning: clear mission; guiding values and principles; and shared vision.

Figure 14

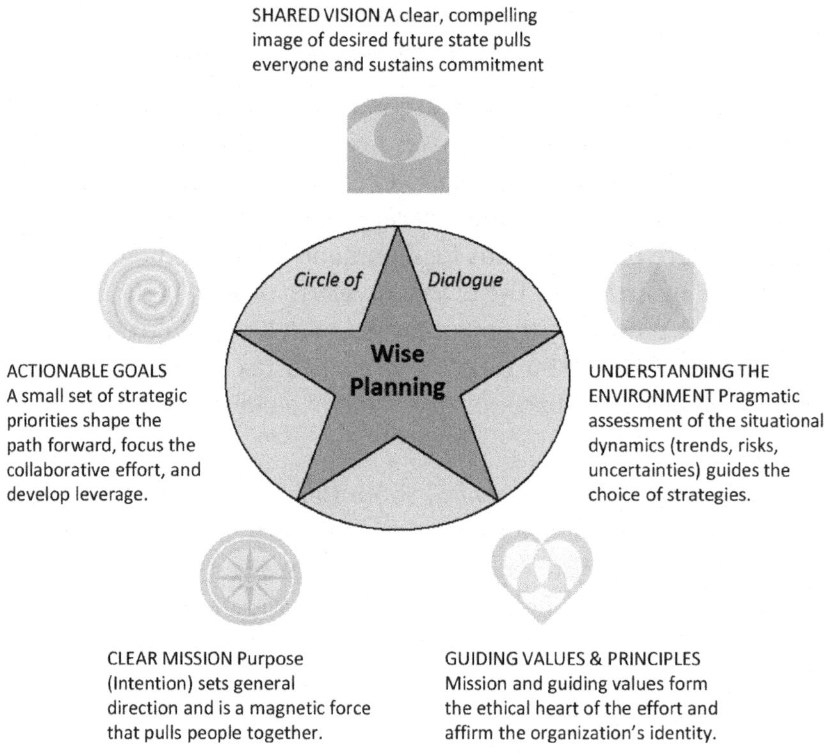

SHARED VISION A clear, compelling image of desired future state pulls everyone and sustains commitment

Circle of *Dialogue*

Wise Planning

ACTIONABLE GOALS
A small set of strategic priorities shape the path forward, focus the collaborative effort, and develop leverage.

UNDERSTANDING THE ENVIRONMENT Pragmatic assessment of the situational dynamics (trends, risks, uncertainties) guides the choice of strategies.

CLEAR MISSION Purpose (Intention) sets general direction and is a magnetic force that pulls people together.

GUIDING VALUES & PRINCIPLES
Mission and guiding values form the ethical heart of the effort and affirm the organization's identity.

An intentional dialogue connects these elements into a learning conversation that turns clarity into intelligent, committed action.

- *Purpose* The WHY of mission, values, and principles that is the foundation of effective strategy.
  (WHY we do what we do) *Is the mission clear and inspiring?*
  (WHY we care about this work together and the way we do it*)*
  Are the core values and guiding principles framed as a strong commitment to the way we will do the work together?

- *Perspective* Understanding the internal organization environment and the external operating environment requires a dialogue that harnesses the power of diverse perspectives.
  (WHAT we must understand in order to engage skillfully) *What is happening in the operating environment now, and likely to happen in the near future?*

- *Performance* Practical progress depends upon a candid discussion of the organization's current strengths and problems.
  (WHAT we can and should improve) *How well is the organization delivering its mission?*

- *Possibilities* In a rapidly changing landscape, a clear idea of the direction the organization wants to go becomes an important source of UNITING. Direction holds the organization together and motivates. A meaningful plan pulls the organization forward to a positive vision of a future state.
  (WHERE we want to arrive at the end of the plan, images of success with our services, partners, results, reputation) *What does success look like in three years?*

- *Priorities* (*Goals/Objectives/Actions*) To act strategically, an organization must wisely choose a few critically important things in order to focus collective effort for superior results. Strategy is about doing the right things. Tactics is about doing things right.
  (How we will commit and act to realize the vision) *How will we be accountable for the actions needed to move forward together?*

Wise Planning Is an Investment

Most leaders are already busy with existing commitments and the urgency of short-term demands. This makes it hard to justify the time investment necessary to step back from these pressures and engage in meaningful wise planning.

It is important for a leadiator to believe the value of the outcome will be worth the investment of time, energy, and money in order to engage and enroll others in a meaningful planning effort. Clarify the necessity for your organization to develop a thoughtful, useful, and flexible plan that will guide your efforts in the near future, however short term. Most groups choose a planning horizon of 2-3 years. These questions will help you focus on the realistic value proposition for Wise Planning in your organization at this time.

Are you credible when approaching funders, donors, and sponsors who provide critical financial support to your organization? Most knowledgeable funders want to be confident that their support will make a difference. A wise strategic plan is credible evidence that the organization knows where it is going, has an intelligent approach to get there, and is prepared to make effective use of the additional support requested. Wise planning demonstrates a commitment to good stewardship of resources and accountability for turning resources into results.

Are your operational efforts carefully coordinated and well-focused to deliver superior outcomes that fulfill your mission? Two common characteristics of successful organizations are coherence and leverage. The work of the organization fits together. Different aspects of the organization complement each other. Wise Planning integrates the talents of the organization's people and its resources to generate mission results.

Do your governing board, leadership, and staff have a unified understanding of the organization's WHY, HOW, and WHAT? Wise Planning enables everyone to stay on the *same page*. Unity is a powerful, tangible quality that can magnify the collective effort to fulfill the mission.

When you recruit and onboard new board members, leaders, managers, and employees how do you effectively orient them to the organization's identity and plans? People are the most valuable resource in your organization. Their talent, commitment, and creativity provide the vital force for all that the organization can and will do. You are more likely to attract the best people to your effort if they want to be part of an organization that is on the move together. When others understand your plan and choose to join you, this increases the likelihood that they will be a good fit, well aligned from the beginning.

How long has it been since you engaged your board, leadership team, and key stakeholders in a strategic conversation about mission effectiveness and vision of success? Organizations can become stale and habitual in their operational patterns. Successful organizations are constructively dissatisfied. An organization remains agile, adaptable, and responsive because it consciously refines its approach to improve results in a dynamic operational environment. Dialogue about strategy is necessary to draw forth the best thinking and creative ideas of others to revitalize the organization's collaborative efforts.

Is your organization facing change and uncertainty with a strategic framework designed for the old normal? The waves of change require fresh thinking about your organization's capacity to adapt. A status quo mindset places the organization at risk as it reacts out of habit instead of responding flexibly to the current and emerging operating conditions.

Leadiators are the stewards of organizational health. A healthy organization is no accident. Like an individual human being, an organization is an organism. It is a social organism that requires care and nourishment to become and remain healthy. Health for an organization begins with the structural elements presented in Lesson Five.

- Clear understanding of why it exists (mission)
- Firm grasp on its commitments (values and principles)
- Line of sight toward its destination (vision)

It is not possible for an organization to align and move forward in a dynamic, effective way without the ability to skillfully coordinate functions, roles, and shared effort. Alignment is not sustainable without focus and communication. *Planning is the ongoing, intentional communication process to come together, learn together, and move forward in unity.*

In *The Advantage: Why Organization Health Trumps Everything*, bestselling business author, Patrick Lenconi, emphasizes that **the fundamental element of organizational health is unified leadership that over-communicates clarity to everyone**. (3) Ongoing Wise Planning is a cornerstone practice that helps a leadiator and leadership team craft a credible, compelling message to employees, partners, and external stakeholders. Everyone understands the current situation, the destination, and the path forward. This message becomes a *steady signal* that keeps the organization on course.

Leadiators help the organization recognize the path of strategic actions and strategic partnerships necessary to achieve its goals. This includes coalitions and alliances of organizations and groups like the young people, elected leaders of a rural community, and citizens in South Dakota who found a creative approach to solve a complex problem by planning together.

Strategic Planning Often Fails to Be Wise

Strategic is an important word that means planned, deliberate, and intentional. Strategic planning is a staple of business life that has become conventional practice for organizations in all sectors including nonprofits and other civil society associations. Strategic planning is a deliberate process to create an approach that helps the organization adapt and succeed.

However, the term strategic planning has been cheapened by overuse and misuse. Too many strategic plans gather dust on shelves. Too many strategic plans were formed without sufficient input from and consideration of stakeholder needs and concerns. Too many strategic plans are clever without being grounded in enduring values and principles. The word *wise* raises the bar above the level implied by the word, *strategic*.

Now, every organization must recognize that the accelerating pace of change assures the irrelevance of traditionally conceived *strategic* plans. To be strategic requires what pilots call, "flying ahead of the plane." It is not enough to look out the window. A pilot must use weather reports and radar to learn about what lies ahead, out of sight. It is wise to intelligently consider the likely and possible conditions that lie months or years ahead. This requires vision. Planning that focuses on matters of fundamental importance to organization survival and success is strategic, even if the plan is short-term.

A typical strategic plan produces a well-drafted document that lays out a carefully prepared set of goals and objectives with detailed actions designed to achieve a vision 3 years from now. However, when accompanied by a mindset that *checks the box* on a fixed product (*We have a 3-year plan.*), it is easy for a plan to become irrelevant as it is executed without enough attention to emerging realities and major uncertainties.

This fixed mindset often begins if the primary motivation to engage in strategic planning is to satisfy the request of a funder, investor, or accrediting body to see the current strategic plan. The focus is on the plan (a noun). Wise planning is a verb and it is motivated by a deep belief in the current and ongoing importance of planning as aligning. Wise Planning doesn't culminate with the creation of a nicely formatted document that inevitably becomes irrelevant. Wise planning is a dynamic process of strategic conversation over time.

In order to be strategic, planning must intelligently anticipate the challenging realities of the organization's environment. Wise planners move beyond conventional, strategic thinking with intentional activities that refine their awareness and analysis.

- Look beyond the study of current and emerging realities in the organization's operating environment to acknowledge uncertainty and consider alternative scenarios that could present a range of challenges and opportunities.

- Continue to exercise the moral imagination to find the most effective ways to fulfill the mission.

- Integrate commitment to guiding values and principles with strategy, goals, and action.

- Respect the needs and concerns of stakeholders.

- Creatively leverage limited resources.

- Build the organization's capacity to adapt to uncertainty and risk.

Wise Planning by Design

Convene with intention and follow a process that implements a good design.

- Establish the need at this time to engage in planning.

- Obtain the full commitment of leadership to support the process.

- Identify the necessary participants and others who need to be consulted.

- Assemble relevant, useful information to enhance perspective.

A sound planning approach begins with honest assessment of the key elements in the organization's current plan and the current performance level of the organization. A new plan may require each element described in Figure 14 on page 166. However, it is important to recognize previous work that continues to provide a solid foundation. Typically, a small core planning team (CPT) will use a checklist like the *Prepare for Wise Planning* worksheet in Appendix 4.

Action Principles

- **Begin with the Right Motivation** Establish the organization's need for planning at this time, beyond the request of others. Determine the necessary scope of the effort and obtain the commitment from leadership.

- **Engage the Right People** Identify necessary participants and others to be consulted

- **Assure Sufficient Support** Provide the resources needed to implement an effective planning process, e.g. time, money, suitable space, planning expertise, and administrative support

- **Prepare for Every Meeting** Prepare for productive planning meetings with clear agendas, useful information, and discussion guidelines that establish a safe, respectful climate for dialogue and creative exploration

---

Include Diverse, Informed Perspectives Wise planning requires thorough consideration of a range of possible issues, confirmation of important values, and review of the current and emerging operating environment. A candid, 360° discussion is fundamentally important. The right people with diverse perspectives need to be in the room (or consulted in a meaningful way) AND feel safe enough to express themselves. Wise planning depends upon precautionary foresight about what could be coming and collective wisdom about how to navigate the operating environment.

Action Principles

- *Study the Territory Together* Begin with an open dialogue to surface the organization's lessons learned, the current and emerging challenges and opportunities, and the possibilities you can imagine together. This learning conversation deepens the analysis and forges better decisions.

- *Think Stakeholders* The clarity, credibility, and durability, of the planning depends upon serious reflection about the needs of the organization's internal and external stakeholders. Fair consideration of stakeholders establishes accountability and demonstrates integrity. Fill in perspective gaps, test assumptions about current plans, and consider alternatives about HOW the organization should move into the future.

- *Include Stakeholder Voices* Generate targeted input from stakeholders that informs the planning team's deliberations through surveys, focus groups, or individual interviews.

Choreograph the Follow Through Planning is an ongoing process. The plan must remain a living document that evolves through periodic review, meaningful assessment of progress, and course correction when needed. Without determined execution, the press of urgent, day-to-day operations can push aside strategic priorities. There must be firm commitment to implement and clear accountability for results. The plan must describe HOW the plan will be reviewed, assessed, and adapted as needed to reorient and keep moving forward toward the desired destination.

Action Principles

- **Align Values and Principles With Action** Your goals, objectives, and actions should be more than strategic responses to the operating environment. Integrate your core values and guiding principles into the plan framework. Align practical realities with your organization's moral compass to navigate inevitable waves of uncertainty and difficulty with the conviction to stay on course toward your vision.

- **Measure What Matters** Establish useful metrics, performance measures, or indicators and determine how you will gather the information needed to assess progress.

- **Be Accountable** Make sure every actionable part of the plan document has the name of a person that has enough authority, resources, and support to be accountable for the execution process. Transparent communication with stakeholders about progress and challenges maintains credibility and earns trust.

- **Refresh the Plan** Schedule periodic review loops to assess, reorient, and course correct as needed. Update the plan document with highlights of progress and difficulties.

Map the Operating Environment

It often improves the dialogue to create a visual representation of the current and near-future landscape. This can be diagrammed on a presentation slide or other digital format. It can be done physically on a white board or with sticky notes on a wall space. The framework shown in figure 15 offers one way to develop this important reference point in the strategic conversation.

Figure 15

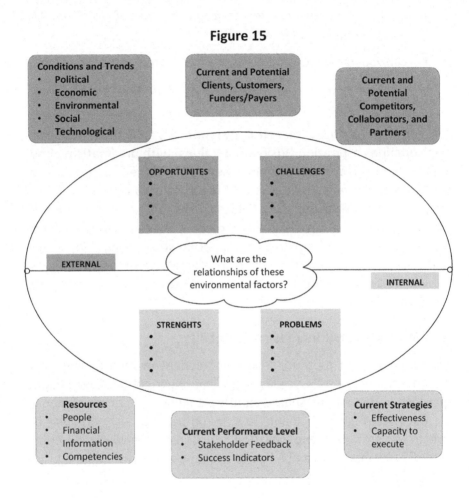

What do you believe to be true? It is essential to have a comprehensive, clear-eyed understanding of the environmental realities within the organization (internal), and outside the organization (external) where it must engage stakeholders and deliver mission performance.

- *What factors are important and should be considered?*

- *Do these factors present as helpful (strengths internally and opportunities externally)?*

- *Do these factors present as difficult (problems internally and challenges externally)?*

- *How do these factors affect the organization's ability to fulfill its mission and realize its vision?*

- *Can you frame these factors as possible strategic issues to address?*

- *Which issues are strategically important enough to be addressed in the planning?*

It is critical to remember that strategy is not only analytical. Wise planning combines aspiration (Vision and Values) with pragmatism about the reality of the operating environment. One of the leading voices of modern strategic planning, Benjamin Tregoe, said, "Strategy is a matter of the heart as well as the head. Values and beliefs exercise a real gravitational pull on the organization's direction; they are going to determine what an organization will or will not do strategically." (4) Deeply held values and core beliefs must be an integral part of the strategy discussion. Make sure there is enough time and space in the planning dialogue to explicitly call forth the heart.

Seek Strategies That Increase Adaptability

A *strategy* is a plan, method, or series of maneuvers for attaining a major aim. At its best, strategic planning is learning together. A well-tested approach to deepen the shared inquiry is to develop a range of scenarios that encourage participants to suspend belief in any particular future. In *The Art of the Long View*, the futurist, Peter Schwartz, describes a set of elements that can be useful to shape alternative planning scenarios. (5)

- Identify **driving macro-forces** in the operating environment. What are the political, economic, environmental, social, and technological trends of importance?

- Identify **predetermined elements**. What are slow-changing phenomena, constrained situations that will continue, things already in the pipeline, and inevitable collisions between forces?

176

- Consider **critical uncertainties** to sensitize participants to plausible, if unlikely futures. Where do our hopes and fears reside about what could happen?

- Sharpen **foresight** by exercising hindsight. Five years ago, what was foreseeable that we missed? What guidance does that give us as we look forward now?

Scenarios help planners frame the future realistically, i.e., the future is uncertain and cannot be predicted. In 2020, we see the reality of an ongoing pandemic, escalating demands for political, social, and economic response to racial injustice, intensifying climate change, accelerating technological development, and global economic gridlock. These powerful forces render the future unpredictable.

All organizations across sectors (private, nonprofit, government) must set wise priorities in order to achieve good results with their limited resources. Remember that results are at the heart of a healthy organization along with an ethical reputation and the adaptive capacity to respond to an uncertain, changing operating environment. (Figure 10, page 157) Wise strategic planning focuses first on the *WHY* rooted in mission, values and principles. With a firm foundation in the heart, move the focus to the *WHAT* before the *HOW*. Strategy is *WHAT* we should do. Tactics and execution are *HOW* we can take action to implement the strategy.

Organizations can improve their capacity to adapt and succeed with strategies that are more likely to perform well amidst uncertainties. There are three important criteria that all organizations in all sectors can use to pre-test proposed strategies. When a proposed strategy meets one or more of these criteria, it is likely to help the organization successfully navigate the inevitable uncertainty and unpredictability in the future operating environment.

Agility When the path forward is unknowable, the ability to maneuver and change course is critically important. Traditional, rigid structures with slow decision timeframes do not respond well to change. *Does the strategy improve the ability to be resourceful and respond, reconfigure, and shift focus or direction ("pivot") within short time frames?*

Unity Resourcefulness is of supreme value. To meet a crisis or overcome a challenge, the organization must be able to marshal all of its resources. *Does the strategy increase the level of integration, coordination, and collaboration within the organization or with external partners?*

Force Multiplication Successful organizations always try to use their human, financial, and material resources to get the most *bang for the buck.* The old name was leverage and the new name is *force multiplication.* Develop and position human and material resources to focus on strategic issues the organization can influence to have the greatest impact on the mission. *Does the strategy strengthen focused effort (talent, creativity, resource sharing, technological capacity, use of collective intelligence) to break through barriers, meet challenges, and capitalize on emerging opportunities?*

> **The intention is not strategic perfection, but a robust framework that can be rapidly implemented, reassessed, and refined.**

In Howard, the breakthrough strategy focused on the ability to influence enough people to make a different choice and spend their money locally. People's pocketbook decision-making was the point of leverage. By influencing a collective shift they multiplied the force of individual decisions, generated a critical mass of new public money to invest in community improvement, and developed a radiating sense of hope that change was possible. **Hope is a powerful force multiplier.**

Figure 16

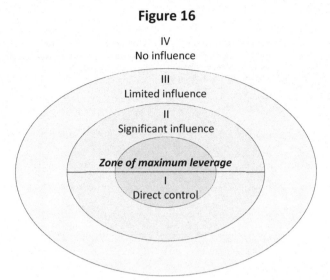

IV
No influence

III
Limited influence

II
Significant influence

Zone of maximum leverage

I
Direct control

Commit to 'Stretch' Goals, 'S.M.A.R.T.' Objectives, and Concrete Action Steps

With clear understanding of the operating environment and the relationship of external and internal realities, the core planning team can identify key issues that must be addressed. Turn an issue into a goal statement by framing an end state with an action verb. For example, consider this issue: *We are likely to face periodic funding uncertainties and lack any predictable income stream.* A large, *stretch* goal might be: *Diversify (verb) funding sources to provide more stability and reduce risk (end state).*

These common verbs frame strong goals, e.g. Build, Increase, Develop, Implement, Improve, Strengthen, Assure. Successful organizations stretch themselves with high expectations. Some stretch goals are enduring without a clear path forward to some point of final resolution. For example, most nonprofit organizations will always have a major goal about securing adequate financial resources. Whether finite or ongoing, a meaningful goal must usually be *chunked down* into key objectives that point the way.

Figure 17

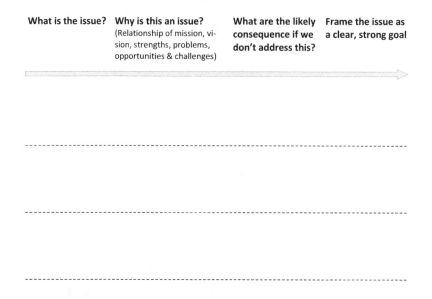

| What is the issue? | Why is this an issue? (Relationship of mission, vision, strengths, problems, opportunities & challenges) | What are the likely consequence if we don't address this? | Frame the issue as a clear, strong goal |

Typically, a good plan is limited to a few major (strategic) goals that direct the organization's resources (leadership and staff time, budget) into a focused, well-coordinated, collective effort on high-consequence issues. There is often an inverse relationship between the number of goals and amount of progress an organization makes. Too many goals will certainly divide the effort and often yield poor or mediocre results. *Stretch goals keep everyone focused on the right priorities that lead to long-term success.*

Now you are ready to identify *S.M.A.R.T.* objectives for each goal with detailed first year action steps for each active objective. These focus engagement and build momentum. Not all goals and objectives need to be active in the same time frame. It is important to be realistic about the priorities for the first year based upon your current capacity.

The right objectives will create a path toward your destination, the GOAL and beyond, to the VISION. Make sure these objectives are practical and designed to produce meaningful outcomes by using the acronym, S.M.A.R.T. (6)

- **S**pecific (*What do I want to accomplish? Who is involved? Where will it take place?*)

- **M**easureable (*How much or many? How will we know we have succeeded?*)

- **A**chievable (*Is it realistic given other responsibilities? Can we address barriers and constraints?*)

- **R**elevant (*Is there high value possible for the level of effort required? Is it practical in the current situation?*)

- **T**ime-bound (*When will it happen? How does it fit in sequence with other objectives?*)

Here are some possible objectives for the goal, *Diversify funding sources to provide more stability and reduce risk.*

- By the end of the second quarter, submit three funding proposals that raise $25,000 to hire a consultant to design a capital campaign.

- Hold four new friend-raising events in 2021 that add at least 200 names to our mailing list.

- By the end of the third quarter, redesign and launch a new web site with a donor portal that attracts 25 new donors.

The ability to respond meaningfully and produce positive results requires a structure of accountability. When people have day-to-day urgencies and full plates of activities, they need to know what has priority. People with responsibility tend to contribute their best effort when the expectations are clear and they are accountable to follow through and deliver.

A historic emphasis on output in planning (level of effort, budget, number of programs, etc.) has shifted to focus on outcomes. There is increased insistence from funders and other stakeholders that organizations be accountable and demonstrate how they use the organization's resources to achieve measurable results. There are many terms used for accountability including: metrics, benchmarks, key performance indicators (KPIs), outcome measures,) objectives and key results (OKRs, and collective impact.

More important than the term used is the organization's commitment to develop, track, and apply *a meaningful set of indicators.* Demonstrate accountability to others, and assess progress over time. Do not track too many things. *Track key indicators that are worth the effort to gather the data, discuss the results, and improve performance over time.*

Another refinement to develop meaningful indicators is to consider the difference between a *lagging* indicator that reflects the ultimate success you want and a *leading* indicator that provides feedback about progress with one or more critical activities. For example, many non-profits have a strategic goal to increase their donations to support their programs. The lagging indicator, is the amount of funds actually raised. Some meaningful leading indicators might be: number of new contacts with potential major donors, size of the fundraising database and mailing list, or number of new grant proposals over $10,000 submitted. Any of these demonstrates progress on the path toward the desired results.

Use a grid like this to develop a tracking document in a table or spreadsheet (often called a "scorecard" or "dashboard") that becomes part of the planning review process. Many excellent templates are available online. (7) Figure 18 provides a logical model to develop meaningful indicators for each goal.

Figure 18

Potential Indicator	Source(s) of Info/Data	Benchmark	Review Loops
What is it and what will it tell you that is useful? (Is it "lagging" or "leading?")	Where will you gather necessary data on the indicator?	What starting level will you use to measure progress?	How often will you review progress & make changes to improve?

GOALS

#1

#2

#3

Many organizations envision change and set goals. The most successful organizations execute their plans with discipline. This requires a structured series of regular conversations to keep everything and everyone on track.

- The key objectives that will be active in year one require a structured action plan that lists major tasks (action steps).

- Each task needs responsible persons assigned to coordinate the work.

- The sequence of the objectives and major tasks must build momentum and lay the groundwork for next steps.

- The necessary resources (staff, equipment, information, budget) must be in place to support successful execution.

- Most organizations use a 6-12 month action plan that is updated monthly or quarterly.

- Place these rows and columns on a spreadsheet, table, or other format so it is easy to update and track.

- Each update of the action plan summarizes the progress made and builds upon it. Another column can be added on the right side of the document for progress comments.

Figure 19

	Objectives	Major Tasks for each objective	Lead Responsibility	Resources Needed	Deadline
Goal #1	1.1				
	1.2				
	1.3				
	1.4				
Goal #2	2.1				
	2.2				
	2.3				
	2.4				
Goal #3	3.1				
	3.2				
	3.3				
	3.4				

Wise Planning is an investment that requires disciplined execution to produce meaningful results. As a cornerstone practice of UNITING by design, it is also a source of cohesion and clear evidence of the organization's integrity as it integrates the mission, core values, and guiding principles with strategy.

These questions for personal reflection and group discussion will guide your organization to consider ways to align through Wise Planning that generates the force of leverage.

Inquiry Into Action

- *What is the value proposition for your organization to invest in Wise Planning? What are the organization's experiences with planning? Are there any positive or negative lessons learned to apply and improve the planning process?*

- *What experience, skills, and resources are available within the organization to design and facilitate a Wise Planning process that includes diverse perspectives and seeks input from stakeholders?*

- *How well does every employee, staff member, manager, and volunteer understand the connection between his or her work and the vision? Does the vision inspire sustained, well-coordinated effort?*

- *How is the vision supported by a clear set of major goals? How is each goal supported by S.M.A.R.T. objectives?*

- *How will the organization's strategic plan become a wise, living plan that is actively used to navigate forward?*

- *What are the meaningful performance indicators that are regularly updated?*

- *What are the regular review loops to assess progress and adapt the plan to changing conditions? How are the results of these reviews transparently communicated to employees and other key stakeholders?*

- *How do the organization's strategies increase agility, build unity, and generate force multiplication?*

Core Ideas From Lesson Six

Planning is the ongoing, intentional communication process to come together, learn together, and move forward in unity.

Wise planning combines aspiration (Vision and Values) with pragmatism about the reality of the operating environment.

The intention is not strategic perfection, but a robust framework that can be rapidly implemented, reassessed, and refined.

Hope is a powerful force multiplier.

Stretch goals keep everyone focused on the right actions that lead to long-term success.

Track key indicators that are worth the effort to gather the data, discuss the results, and improve performance over time.

PART THREE EVOLVING

Adapting to change to fulfill the mission

Organizations have to be able to redefine

themselves at a faster and faster pace.

~ Ray Kurzweil *Futurist*

Lesson Seven Navigating – the Force of Conviction

- Decision Making Shapes an Ethical Organization Culture
- Leadership Integrity Is at the Heart of a Healthy Organization
- Leadiators Use Every Key Decision to Move Forward Together
- A Sound Decision-making Process Is a *Life Preserver*
- Prepare, Prepare, Prepare
- Stick Together with Confident Steps to Form Stronger Decisions
- Leadiators Are Willing and Able to Take Intelligent Risks
- Leadiators Actively Shape Consensus

Lesson Eight Bridging – the Force of Reconciliation

- A Museum Builds a Bridge to Engage Its Stakeholders
- Understanding Conflict and Polarization
- Principled Negotiation Shifts Argument Over Positions to Dialogue About Interests
- Use a Common Language to Increase Understanding (WHAT, WHY, and HOW)
- Generate Possibilities for Agreement
- Remain Centered in Tense Situations to Act Skillfully
- Use a Set of Powerful Principles to Engage Differences

Lesson Nine Adapting – the Force of Agility

- The 21st Century is the Age of Adaption

- An Organization Can Adapt, Pivot, and Show Others the Way

- Integrate Cornerstone Practices and Cultural Characteristics to Increase Agility

- Turn a Flow of Ideas into Innovations

- Shape a Flexible Organization Structure for Agile Response

- Choosing Agile Responses: Wisdom-in-Action

Blueprint for Creative Collaboration

POSITIVE COLLABORATIVE FORCES
Generated by the cornerstone practices, action steps,
and *cultural characteristics* *

Clarity   Perspective   Connection

Understanding   Moral Imagination   Leverage

Conviction   Reconciliation   Agility

SKILLSET

Cornerstone Practices

Values-Based Decision Making
Wise Planning   Principled Negotiation
Dialogue – the Foundational Practice

Designed **N**ecessary **A**ction Steps
that implement the practices

MINDSET
Growth Mindset *

HEARTSET
Integrity *
Psychological Safety *

Lesson Seven NAVIGATING

Integrity is the essence of everything successful.

~ R. Buckminster Fuller *Futurist*

The Force of Conviction

Leadiators demonstrate integrity and accountability by the way they make and communicate key decisions with clarity and confidence.

Key decisions represent important choices about direction, policies, and resources. When they clearly align with core values and guiding principles, stakeholders can better understand and trust the ethics and competence of the leadiator and the organization.

When a key decision involves serious consequences, the decision makers must acknowledge risks and impacts in order to accept responsibility and be accountable.

Key decisions are the means by which an organization navigates through a rapidly changing environment. An organization must be able to shift direction when necessary to fulfill the mission and reach a shared vision. Key decisions make hard choices, set strategic direction, and deploy limited resources. When these decisions align with important values and principles, they radiate a leadiator's conviction that this is the right thing to do.

A leadiator who has the courage of her convictions demonstrates integrity, builds an ethical reputation, earns trust, and strengthens confidence in her leadership among internal and external stakeholders. A leadiator with integrity recognizes *true north* and makes decisions that send a steady signal: people will always be treated in an honest, fair, and principled manner.

Decision-making integrity also hard-wires ethics into the organization's culture by continually reaffirming core values and principles. There are three important connotations of the word Integrity that all have significance for an organization's health.

- **Ethical character** (every leader, manager, and employee understands that ethics goes beyond words to deeds)

- **Structural strength** (commitment to integrity provides the *backbone* needed for an organization to face and tackle difficult problems of every kind)

- **Wholeness** (the ethical fiber of the organization is a cohesive force that pulls people together)

As Lesson Three described, a healthy culture is a psychologically safe environment. When people feel safe and believe that they belong, they contribute fully and creatively to the mission. They also will speak up if they have ethical concerns. Full, creative contributions from everyone give the organization the capacity to adapt, evolve, and thrive.

Each key decision must be credibly communicated to build and maintain a general consensus that the organization is moving in the right direction. *When a key decision aligns with core values and guiding principles, it has an ethical force that can be communicated with conviction.*

In turn, conviction communicates confidence, establishes accountability, and affirms moral authority.

In a time with so much change and uncertainty, leadiators must view every key decision as a valuable opportunity to strengthen the organization. People who must support decisions, implement them, and, at times, bear the consequences of a difficult decision need to recognize the conviction of the decision maker and the *ring of truth* in her message.

Learning Objectives

- Follow seven steps to key decisions with integrity that guide the organization on an ethical course.

- Communicate key decisions to stakeholders that earn trust and gain credibility.

- Build consensus support for key decisions that continue UNITING the organization.

Decision Making Shapes an Ethical Organization Culture

Modern health care organizations must operate in a fiercely competitive operating environment. In 1996, two large, complex nonprofits decided to merge into a new organization with a new name, Centura Health. Each separate organization operated multiple hospitals and other health care facilities and services including physician practices, hospice and home care, memory care facilities, cancer centers, and urgent care. These facilities were located throughout a large region. Each facility had separate leadership on site and often operated with a high degree of independence. The new entity had a workforce of more than 15,000 employees. The vision for the merger was a unified, integrated organization with the capacity to be the leader in the region.

As mentioned in Lesson One, all mergers of large organizations face an uphill battle to successfully integrate separate organizations into a unified whole. The McKinsey and Company study found that more than 80% of business mergers failed to accomplish the stated objectives that justified the merger strategy. One of the common factors identified as a cause of failure was cultural incompatibility. (1)

Centura Health's leadership recognized it faced a particular challenge because its separate organizations had long and different histories, distinct organization cultures, and some values-based philosophical differences. All of these factors posed particular challenges to overcome in order to become one organization.

In addition, key internal stakeholders who were strong champions for the historic nonprofit missions of their respective organizations expressed concerns about the commitment to ethics in the new merged business culture of Centura Health. They were concerned that the size of the new organization and its efforts to maintain a prominent position in a highly competitive marketplace could diminish this commitment.

My partner was Joan Gibson, an expert in health care ethics. She and I were hired to address the concerns throughout the organization with a practical strategy to address the new organization's commitment to ethical practice in its business and operational decisions. In essence, our work was to help them solidify a new, unified culture with a common approach to ethical decision making.

We worked from the *C-Suite* of senior leaders, to the leadership teams of each of their thirteen hospitals. We trained department and division managers throughout the hospitals and in allied organizations that addressed senior care, hospice, and other services.

Within Centura Health, like most large organizations, most key decisions, even when made by one person, usually received input and recommendations from others. This included members of a management team, subject matter experts, or individuals with relevant knowledge to improve the decision maker's perspective and reach a carefully formed decision.

Our first challenge was the attitude of decision makers toward time. Most decision makers experience pressure to meet today's demands and move on to the next challenge. This pressure often shrinks the space for engagement and exploration to a small group of people.

Therefore, the decision-making process needed to be simple to understand, efficient, and effective. There were two design principles at the heart of the process. First, increase the ability of decision makers to respectfully engage different perspectives. Second, use these perspectives to intentionally incorporate Centura Health's core values and guiding principles into key decisions.

The process that emerged through continuous field-testing and revision had a set of sequential steps with each step guided by a central question. *The process was surprisingly simple: ask each question in turn and listen to how others respond. However, a set of check-the-box questions without meaningful engagement and careful listening was not sufficient.*

We learned several important design elements that structure meaningful engagement.

- The steps in the process have to generate an honest dialogue among diverse perspectives to unpack the values dimension of the decision.

- The quality of the dialogue provides the decision maker with greater clarity and conviction to speak directly to the guiding values.

- Address affected stakeholders' concerns with the likely risks and consequences of a difficult decision.

- The decision maker needs to hold back initial comments that send a signal about her preferred outcome. Actively encourage everyone to participate and be candid.

- The final step to a successful decision is remarkably important. Well-made decisions can fail without credible communication that earns the trust of employees and other important stakeholders.

Our work to help decision makers grow Centura Health's unified culture lasted for over a decade. The merger succeeded and Centura has grown to 21,000 employees, 17 hospitals and multiple allied facilities and programs. A key element of its unified strength is its strong values architecture for making hundreds of important decisions. In the many trainings we provided, we learned about the nature of organizational culture, the importance of change over time, and the cornerstone practice of values-based decision making. (2)

The centrality of values in every good decision provided the name for Centura's decision-making process, "Values in Action" or VIA. In Latin, VIA means the way. This process was the way Centura tackled key decisions.

Leadership Integrity Is at the Heart of a Healthy Organization

For the past 15 years, I have asked the same question at the beginning of every decision-making seminar: "Think of a leader you know who has, or had integrity. What does integrity look like in a leader?" I have received remarkably similar answers from participants in many countries who work in government agencies, nonprofits, and corporations. Their responses affirm three universal qualities that demonstrate leadership integrity to others.

- ***Character of the Person*** The foundation of integrity is ethical character. Leaders are honest. They always strive to do the right thing. They align their actions with their principles. They keep their word and their commitments.

- ***Consideration for Others*** Real leaders demonstrate integrity by the quality of their treatment of others. Leaders are not self-centered or arrogant. They do not put themselves above and before others. Rather, they show positive regard for others' dignity by treating them respectfully. They listen carefully to others and sincerely consider their needs and concerns. They care about fairness.

- ***Consistent, Authentic Presence*** Leadership integrity requires a consistent and reliable set of behaviors so others know they can count on the leader. An erratic temperament makes a leader unpredictable and untrustworthy. Lack of trust or mistrust compromises a leader and weakens the organization. Integrity requires the courage to face difficulties directly. Leaders are never *missing in action*. They show up. Employees know a leader has their backs. Also, a leader is not two-faced. Everyone regardless of status, in public and in private, sees the same, authentic face.

Leadership is always about moving the organization forward to fulfill the mission. Leadiators seek to apply the timeless wisdom of Archimedes about the reality of moving large things. "Give me a lever long enough and a fulcrum on which to place it and I will move the world." (3)

Significant forward movement requires effort and leverage. Moral character is the fulcrum where the leader stands on principles in all decisions and actions. When a leader strongly connects with others through considerate, respectful listening and a constant, authentic presence, this lengthens the lever of deep understanding and creativity available to raise up the organization.

Leadership integrity matters from the smallest team to the executive level of a large organization. *There are leaders, and there are those who LEAD.*

Leadiators Use Every Key Decision to Move Forward Together

Decision making is the fundamental means for navigating in our lives. Through key decisions, organizations, groups, families, and individuals imagine the future they want, choose to act, and chart a course.

When a difficult choice presents itself, people need traction. Traction on the road to a good decision comes from deliberate, honest, and respectful talk about what matters. Leaders need to bring the language of values and ethics alive in every key decision-making conversation. Tough choices and good decisions demand nothing less.

- During the pandemic crisis and the resulting economic and social challenges, organizations, communities, and individuals will face more difficult choices.

- In difficult times, key decisions are critically important opportunities to integrate and align the organization.

- A shared decision-making process fosters clear thinking, increases creativity, and builds unity.

An organization's mission and statement of core values are promises to employees and other stakeholders. The faithful use of these important values when making key decisions keeps a promise. Therefore, attention to the conscious, transparent use of declared values in decision making becomes an issue of integrity. A decision is a message to employees and stakeholders that communicates what the organization and the decision maker really value. The message has several parts.

- An explanation of the decision

- The channel of communication used to send the message

- The credibility of the messenger

- Transparency about how the decision was made and who participated

- How the concerns of stakeholders were considered.

The perceptions of employees and stakeholders about decisions shape their beliefs about the organization's real values. Organizational decision making can reaffirm core values and model positive behavior norms. These norms become embedded in the organization's culture.

Decision communication has become more difficult. It is likely that some in the audiences have been deceived in the past by dishonest and hypocritical leaders and organizations whose actions did not align with public statements of their values and principles. They have also been manipulated by ever-present *spin doctors* including public relations advisors, political strategists, advertising executives, and media consultants. Spin is tactical communication designed to accomplish a hidden agenda at the expense of transparency, candor and integrity.

These experiences produce cynicism. *Many hunger for organizations and leaders who will courageously face difficult issues, tell the truth in public, and be accountable to those affected by their decisions.* When your audience does not receive credible, straight talk about an important decision, the reaction can be rumor, negative opinion, and misinformation that circulate through the blogosphere, media channels and by word of mouth with lightning speed. Inaccuracies and misunderstandings quickly spread, affecting reputation and credibility.

Most leaders are motivated to act based on the belief that it is in their best interests to do so. Here are four ways that an intentional approach to values and decisions serves the best interests of leadiators and organizations.

Preserve a Good Reputation WHAT leadiators value defines them in the eyes of others. Values are the motivating WHY in important decisions. When leadiators choose consciously and communicate decisions clearly, their guiding values define them accurately and positively.

Maintain Credibility Now and the Next Time When an organization or a leader declares values publicly in a statement of core values, a credo, or the explanation of a vote, key decision, or position on an issue, this public statement is a commitment. Decisions that clearly honor these public statements keep the commitment, establish accountability, demonstrate integrity, and gain credibility. Credibility in the bank account of trust is a valuable asset that helps a leader communicate future decisions.

Produce a Better Outcome Different perspectives engaged in candid, respectful dialogue (Lesson Four) can shine a bright light on challenging issues and difficult situations with hard choices. The clear light of dialogue about what is truly important produces specific benefits.

- Eliminate blind spots to see choices more clearly.

- Improve understanding of stakeholder perspectives about the issue.

- Increase the probability of a good decision with benefits that outweigh costs.

Save Time Decisions that fall apart or have to go back to the drawing board can be expensive in time, energy and money. Clear, credible communication delivered the first time with ethical conviction provides stakeholders with confidence in the decision. This confidence translates into three elements that generate momentum.

- Support from those who must implement the decision

- Acceptance from those in a position to oppose it

- Decreased need to recall and repair flawed decisions

A Sound Decision-making Process Is a Life Preserver

As your organization looks toward the emerging future, the pandemic and its aftermath along with other waves of change will likely present continuing challenges. Organizations will be faced with difficult decisions to navigate an unpredictable, rapidly changing operating environment. You may be able to anticipate some of these decisions. However, many others may arise quickly and require a prompt response.

Whether or not you have a formal, recognized role as a leader, you can think and act like a leadiator who supports individuals and groups to make decisions with calmness, clarity, and courage. In a crisis, any leader can be driven by a sense of urgency and sink under the weight of uncertainty, information overload, analysis paralysis, and tunnel vision.

However, one person with more calmness can raise a group out of reactivity and panic into clarity and greater capacity. *A clear approach to decision-making can be a life preserver to save an organization and its stakeholders from the consequences of a rushed, poorly considered decision.*

In a difficult time, leaders and groups often make serious mistakes when they rush into critical decisions without the benefit of diverse, informed perspectives. Different ways of seeing and thinking about the situation are essential to inform decision makers and *stress test* their thinking and judgment. A simple, efficient decision-making process can develop collective wisdom, strengthen the current decision, and build capacity to meet the challenging decision around the next corner.

Excessive speed often compromises decision quality. In order to act promptly, leadiators need to master the ability to move with *deliberate speed*.

- Replace jumbled thinking fueled by fear and urgency with an intentional, well-ordered set of steps that move steadily forward with awareness.

- Strive for high quality discussion that rises above low quality argument or win-lose debate.

- At a minimum, have a principled, respectful debate.

- The best practice is a dialogue that generates shared understanding and consensus support.

- A dialogue requires that participants slow down and deepen the communication exchange by listening, reflecting back understanding, asking open questions, and being candid.

- Once a decision has been implemented, it is a good practice to take the time to *audit* the decision and learn to improve process and outcomes in the future. (See Appendix 7)

To find the *gold* in a difficult decision situation, a group has to *mine* the collective intelligence available from multiple perspectives. Dialogue will not develop unless there is enough psychological safety in the group for everyone to candidly contribute questions, concerns, and ideas. Then, there can be shared understanding of the situation, the problem(s) to be solved, and the best available decision option.

There are three stages of decision making.

- *Prepare* to decide. (gather information, develop initial options, identify the right people with perspective and knowledge)

- *Form* the decision. (actively consider relevant information, discuss available knowledge and informed opinion, creatively explore options, discern and choose wisely, prepare to communicate honestly to affected stakeholders)

- **_Implement_** your decision. (enlist support, delegate responsibility, assess progress, modify approach when necessary, learn lessons for the future)

Figure 20 provides a visual *map* of the process. After the decision-making group has convened with all the necessary preparation completed, there are seven steps to deliberately expand the discussion and place values at the heart of the process.

Figure 20

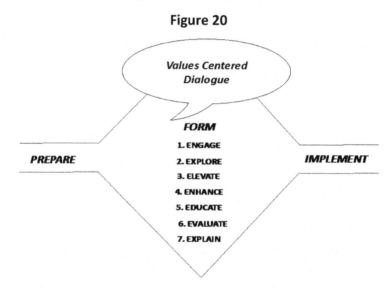

Prepare, Prepare, Prepare

A well informed decision depends upon sufficient preparation. *Scoping* the situation improves perspective to refine the preparation stage. Take a step back and scan the decision situation and the decision process. When a leadiator is conscientious about the elements of preparation many mistakes can be prevented.

Think of a significant decision like a plane that will take off and fly. If you don't want the decision to *crash*, you need to be sure it is ready to *take off*. A pilot begins to prepare by walking around the plane to perform a 360-degree visual inspection and then follows an orderly checklist to get ready to fly.

A group making a decision or advising a leadiator on a decision needs to *walk around* the situation and the problem space thoroughly enough to become familiar with the issue to be decided and then use a checklist to confirm their readiness to decide.

Preparation Checklist

Need and Timing

- Know the drivers and test the level of urgency.
- *Why is a decision necessary now?*
- *Is there a real urgency with a hard deadline for our response?*
- *Is there interim action we can take to buy some time so we can more carefully consider our full response?*

Knowledge

- Facts, informed opinions, and lessons learned provide a firm foundation for a difficult decision.
- What do we know to be true about the situation we are in?
- What do we believe to be true?
- What additional, relevant information are we missing that could help us make this decision?
- How do we access credible sources and curate the information effectively for the decision-making group?
- Have others made decisions like this one so we can learn from their positive and negative experiences?

Key Participants

- Some decisions need group consensus. Some should be delegated to people closer to the frontlines. Others should be made by an individual after meaningful consultation with a group with or without consensus. Be clear who will be accountable for this decision.

- Who has the authority to make this decision?

- Who should make this decision?

- Who else needs to contribute relevant views, experience, and knowledge?

- Who needs to be involved to increase the buy-in and support necessary for successful execution?

Assumptions

- While assumptions may be necessary, they need to be conscious and tested, if possible. (Review the common thinking biases in Lesson One, pages 72-75)

- What is reasonable to assume to be true or likely about the situation we are in?

- How can we acknowledge uncertainty and identify potential risks and opportunities?

- Are we maintaining a healthy degree of humility, openness, and flexibility?

Risks

- It is rare that a key decision is risk free. Do the homework necessary to make sure the decision maker's eyes are open to the risks.

- What risks are there to consider?

- Do we have the information we need to characterize these risks?

- Can we afford to take the time to learn more about the risks?

- Can we afford not to take the time to do so?

- What are the different dimensions of risk? (There is risk in waiting to act and risk in acting without more information. There are large risks and small risks. There are economic risks, market risks, legal risks, health risks, and technological risks.)

Stakeholders

- Integrity, accountability, and credibility are all on the line. Failure to respectfully consider stakeholders' needs and concerns can damage trust in a leader or in the entire organization.

- Which groups and individuals will be benefited or burdened by this decision?

- Will we have participants in the decision-making process who can knowledgeably speak about the needs and concerns of stakeholders?

Options

- A preliminary list of likely options can provide a good springboard for group creativity to expand and refine the list. It can help the decision-making team save time to run these preliminary ideas past a lawyer, accountant, engineer, IT advisor, or other domain expert. Any likely decision options that are not viable can be set aside.

- Are there some possible options that are worth including on an initial list?

- Are there options on the list that should be vetted to cross a threshold of legality, affordability, compliance, or feasibility before convening the decision-making group?

Stick Together with Confident Steps to Form a Good Decision

Values-based Decision Making is a straightforward process with seven steps. Each step focuses on a key question that generates open, productive dialogue about the dimension of values and importance. Participants' diverse, honest views provide the decision maker(s) with improved perspective and clearer understanding to carefully weigh the options and discern the best course of action.

- Listen respectfully to other points of view to better understand stakeholders' values.

- Confirm key statements about importance by *looping* back your understanding. (See Lesson Four, page 120)

- Define the concrete meaning of big values words, e.g. Quality, Fairness, Integrity.

- Weigh risks and consequences.

- Avoid the leap to solutions until you better understand stakeholders and their values.

With a sound process, a leadiator or a leadership group can confidently make key decisions in a way that clearly reflects the organization's mission and values. Decisions develop greater support and acceptance. The process structure develops better decisions because it takes on the realities and challenges of decision making.

- Go beyond argument and debate to develop a meaningful dialogue about what is most important.

- Adapt the structure to limited time periods from thirty minutes to two hours.

- Adapt for individual and group decisions.

- Provide a forum to examine the tension between competing goods.

- Engage participants' best thinking to align key values with available options.

- Build genuine understanding of the downside of a difficult decision.

- Focus on values to develop ethical clarity and conviction about the right course of action.

- Prepare the decision-maker to credibly communicate to stakeholders.

A sound decision-making process builds decision integrity with three characteristics.

- *Accountability* (diligent effort to understand what matters to the organization and its stakeholders)

- *Alignment* (sound connection of key values to the decision)

- *Authenticity* (honest, credible communication to stakeholders)

> *The path through uncertainty and risk has definite steps. You can pause at any time. If you make a misstep you can back up and spend more time at a previous step. If you take a wrong turn, you can get back in step. However, you can't skip a step without weakening your decision.*

Step One – ENGAGE by simply listening to each person's initial perspective to lay the foundation for a learning dialogue.

- Focus Question: *What point of view does each person bring to this decision?*

- Process: Each person takes a few minutes to describe how he or she sees the situation and what seems significant. The decision maker should go last. Allow everyone to speak and be heard without interruption or questions.

Step Two – EXPLORE the range of values and principles involved in this decision

- Focus Question: *Who are the stakeholders affected by the decision AND what is important to them?*

- Process: As a group, work together to develop a comprehensive list of individuals and groups to consider. Then, identify the values and principles that matter to them. This includes the organization itself.

Step Three – ELEVATE your focus to the priority values and principles to guide your choice among the options available

- Focus Question: *Which 2-3 values or principles must be at the heart of our decision?*

- Process: Each person takes a turn to advocate for what is most important and why it matters so much. The decision maker should go last. Make sure that big values words have specific meaning in this decision, e.g. *Fairness, in the sense that everyone should be treated with the same standard.* All the priority values mentioned should be listed and used for reference at Step Six.

Step Four – EXPAND and refine the available options with as much thought and creativity as time permits

- Focus Question: *How can we expand upon the existing alternatives to increase the options to consider?*

- Process: Everyone participates and shares any ideas that add to the alternatives under consideration.

Step Five – EDUCATE each other about the consequences and risks (the downside)

- Focus Question: *What are the probable and possible consequences of each option in addition to the desired outcomes we intend?*

- Process: Everyone participates to make sure that the decision maker is aware of negative consequences and risks associated with each option.

Step Six – EVALUATE and choose the option that most closely aligns with the priority values and principles. Review the risks of the preferred option to develop a plan to mitigate the downside or confirm your willingness to accept the consequences.

- Focus Question: *Which option aligns best with our priority values and principles, and what is its downside?*

- Process: The decision maker receives recommendations about the best option from each advisor. The recommendation should include the downside of the recommended option. The decision maker uses the values priorities from Step Three, weighs the downside, and makes a decision. Advisors can further assist the decision maker to consider ways to mitigate the downside.

Step Seven – EXPLAIN the decision to affected stakeholders (those benefited, burdened, and concerned) in plain, candid language. Include the reasoning that supports the decision and the downside.

- Focus Question: *How can we credibly communicate this decision to those who need to know and understand?*

- Process: The decision maker can use the advisory group to provide feedback on a dry run of the proposed communication.

Additional guidance on the use of all these steps is in Appendix 5. An outline to develop the communication at Step Seven is in Appendix 6.

Leadiators Are Willing and Able to Take Intelligent Risks

In Steps Five and Six of the process, risks are a primary consideration. Acting with Integrity and demonstrating respect for stakeholders requires a reasonable understanding of the risks posed by the decision, from their perspectives. Risk assessment poses two questions:

- *What is the probability that something will happen?*

- *If it happens, how large is the likely impact?*

Be deliberate. Figure 21 can be drawn on a whiteboard or flip chart to clearly display possible risks. Risks must be considered on a spectrum of likelihood and size. After assessing the risks, use the three broad categories to acknowledge the level of risk. Then, consider your risk tolerance. Can you accept the level of risk? If you believe you should accept the level of risk, do you have any ability to take action that reduces or mitigates the level of risk? If you do have the ability to act, are you willing to make the investment of time and resources (human and financial) to manage or mitigate the risk?

Figure 21

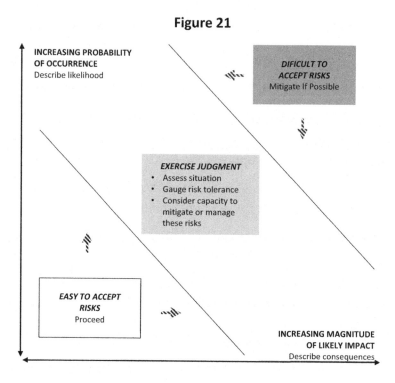

Hastiness, sloppy analysis, wishful thinking, and rationalization are common human behaviors. Each of them can lead to a failure to recognize and adequately assess the risks and costs of a decision. *A decision maker with integrity needs to acknowledge the risks and explain how they were weighed in the decision.*

Once a decision maker recognizes the possible or likely negative consequences of a decision, there is additional inquiry. In some circumstances, it may be wise to act to reduce the impact of the consequences or manage the risk. Risk mitigation presents an opportunity and a challenge. With a painful decision, sincere effort to deal with the impact can build trust. However, when a decision maker's efforts to mitigate are half-hearted or insincere, this can destroy trust and place future credibility at risk.

Use these guidelines to ensure that any mitigation efforts are effective.

Steps to Take

- Be specific and describe what will be done, who will do it, and when it will happen.

- Affirm your personal level of commitment to follow through.

- Clarify how you will communicate with others about the follow up on your words of commitment

Mistakes to Avoid

- Vague, or general statements about what you intend to do

- Over-promising and under-delivering

- *Feel-good* statements or insincere empathy without real commitment and action

- Minimizing the risks or downplaying the burdens that others may experience

Monitor Implementation and Learning

As discussed in Lesson Four, successful organizations adapt. Adapting requires continuous learning. Key decisions provide rich opportunities to review the decision-making process, examine the process of implementation, evaluate, and learn. (See Appendix 7 for a Decision Audit worksheet)

Leadiators Actively Shape Consensus

No organization is immune from the waves of change. The organizations that survive in a transformed landscape of new risks, challenges, and opportunities will be those with leadiators who know how to keep people together. Some organizations will learn to thrive.

At the heart of the capacity to thrive is an organization's coordinated ability to shift direction when necessary. This ability to shift direction and move together requires the organization to have a center. This center is a general consensus that the organization's leadership is ethical and competent. Consensus means there is shared understanding of the answers to four essential organizational questions.

- WHO are we? (the WHY of our common purpose, our core values, and principles and the principles that guide our work and the way we treat people – Lesson Five)

- WHERE are we going? (the vision – Lesson Five)

- HOW are we going to get there? (a small set of major goals that unify the effort and the practical strategies that will achieve the goals – Lesson Six)

- HOW do our key decisions align with our values, vision, and goals?

Leadiators must understand how to mold and sustain a working consensus among the leadership team, managers, employees, and strategic partners. (4)

Think Clearly About Consensus

A dictionary definition of consensus focuses on unanimity, agreement, and harmony. However, these words are too general to guide a leadiator to mold a meaningful consensus in these extraordinary times.

- ***Consensus Does Not Require Unanimity*** Everyone does not need to approve or like a decision. Emphasis on the importance of unanimity before the organization can move forward presents real risks. It could place disproportionate power in the hands of a small minority to withhold support and control the outcome. It could freeze the organization when action is imperative. It could lead to a watered-down compromise that offends no one and assures mediocre results.

- **Beware of False Consensus** Too often, unanimous agreement is only the illusion of agreement. This illusion is called *group think*. People withhold their true views to act in apparent agreement with the majority. Group-think happens because there are pressures to conform, to be seen as a loyal *team player*, or to get in line with the leader or the majority.

- **Don't Take Silence For Agreement** An organization needs a psychologically safe environment that makes it possible for everyone to express candid, diverse perspectives and build meaningful consensus.

- **Recognize the Weakness of Simple Majority Votes** Even when the organization or group has formal rules that permit a majority to vote and pass a measure, it is important for an organization to patiently seek to build the degree of support that is desirable or necessary in this particular situation. A 4-3 vote by a team or Board may be valid. It may also be wholly insufficient. Without broad backing, there may be active or passive opposition, half-hearted implementation, and poor results.

Real Consensus is Wise

The root meaning of consensus is from the Latin word *consentire, to think and feel together.* Organizations, communities, and collaborative partnerships must learn together. Leadiators must actively guide the process to mold a wise consensus.

- **Value and engage diverse perspectives** to think, feel, and learn together. Diverse perspectives are essential to build robust outcomes with sufficient support. Like the pieces in a mosaic, they can be shaped into an understanding of what is essential, true, and right to do.

- **Honest dialogue activates learning**, increases shared understanding, and applies ethical intelligence to difficult issues.

- When a leadiator has the authority and responsibility to decide, it is wise to *learn whether there are significant concerns* and a lack of support before the final decision has been made.

- If voting will be used, ***don't move quickly to majority voting***. Patiently take the time necessary to build broad support for important issues. Typically, a wise consensus requires a super-majority (3/4ths or more) of the participants whose support is more than lukewarm.

- ***Respectfully acknowledge sincere disagreement*** and accept different degrees of enthusiasm. Take time to carefully consider concerns and opposition. This builds psychological safety.

- At the heart of wise consensus is ***alignment of purpose***, general acceptance of the plan or idea, and real willingness to move forward together.

- Think beyond the resolution of the current issue. **Recognize that wise consensus is an investment in the organization's future**. Strengthen working relationships to respond to the next critical decision.

Test Consensus Openly with a "Fist to Five"

This simple poll with a show of hands may not always fit inside a particular organizational culture or a particular decision-making context. However, I have used it often enough in diverse organizations to recommend that you try it. After substantial discussion, it is often useful to *test the waters*. A visual support spectrum helps everyone see the current level of support. Each participant simultaneously raises a hand with a number of fingers reflecting the degree of support for the proposed action.

5 – Full Support "Yes!!!"

4 – Strong Support "I'm on board."

3 – Acceptable "OK by me"

2 – Can live with it "Let's move on"

1 – Serious reservations "Count me out"

0 (Fist) – Strong opposition "NO!!!"

A leadiator can use this approach in a meeting of staff or with a leadership team to find out where people stand at any point in the discussion. If a formal vote is necessary like the vote of a board of directors, a consensus approach might include a *straw* vote taken by hand with each person simultaneously holding up a hand showing their current degree of support.

If any are strongly opposed or have serious reservations (zero or one), a healthy process provides at least one more opportunity for those with concerns to fully express themselves to make sure others listen carefully and sincerely try to comprehend. When concerns are well understood, this may lead to an improved proposal or a new idea to consider. Even if nothing changes, a transparent process demonstrates respect for those with a minority position. When people with objections have been heard and can respectfully agree to disagree, it is not uncommon for a minority who continue to disagree to step aside and gracefully accept the decision. The organization can remain united in the importance of moving forward with the mission. (5)

Inquiry Into Action - Here are some questions for personal reflection and group discussion. They will guide your organization to consider ways to strengthen the organization's culture of integrity.

- *Even when leaders have the authority to act and make a decision, do they consult with others and learn from different perspectives?*

- *What process does your organization have for making key decisions? What would it take to assure the consistent use of a clear, effective process?*

- *How does your organization integrate its core values and guiding principles into key decisions?*

- *How well defined and meaningful are your organization's core values and guiding principles?*

- *How does your leadership make sure that all leaders and managers are held accountable to consistently act in alignment with the core values and guiding principles? What would it take to make sure that leaders hold themselves and others accountable?*

- *How clearly do leaders and managers communicate key decisions to those affected? What would it take to increase clarity of communication?*

- *How do these key decisions explain the values driving the decision and acknowledge the downside (negative consequences, likely risks)?*

- *How important is consensus in your organization? Where, when, and how do leaders and managers use consensus?*

Core Ideas From Lesson Seven

Leadiators demonstrate integrity and accountability by the way they make and communicate key decisions.

When a key decision aligns with core values and guiding principles, it has an ethical force that can be communicated with conviction.

The perceptions of employees and stakeholders about decisions shape their beliefs about the organization's real values

A clear approach to decision-making can be a life preserver to save an organization and its stakeholders from the consequences of a rushed, poorly considered decision.

The decision-making path amidst uncertainty and risk has definite steps. A decision maker with integrity needs to acknowledge the risks and explain how they were weighed in the decision.

At the heart of the capacity to thrive is an organization's coordinated ability to shift direction when necessary. This ability to shift direction and move together requires the organization to have a center. This center is a general consensus that the organization's leadership is ethical and competent.

Blueprint for Creative Collaboration

POSITIVE COLLABORATIVE FORCES
Generated by the cornerstone practices, action steps,
and *cultural characteristics**

Clarity   Perspective   Connection

Understanding   Moral Imagination   Leverage

Conviction   **Reconciliation**   Agility

SKILLSET

Cornerstone Practices

Values-Based Decision Making
Wise Planning   **Principled Negotiation**
Dialogue – the Foundational Practice

Designed **N**ecessary **A**ction Steps
that implement the practices

MINDSET
Growth Mindset*

HEARTSET
Integrity*
Psychological Safety*

Lesson Eight BRIDGING

As we build bridges and even become bridges,
we will be doing a service to the world.

~ **John A. Powell** *Racing to Justice*

The Force of Reconciliation

Differences, conflict, and polarization
are common challenges in organizations.

Leadiators need the courage and skills to face these challenges.

Diversity can become an organizational strength.

The cornerstone practice of Principled Negotiation can bridge
differences by turning: barriers into understanding; understanding
into acceptance and creativity; creativity into just agreement; and
just agreement into reconciliation and peace.

A peaceful organization is more inclusive,
equitable, creative, and productive.

A peaceful organization is better
able to navigate the waves of change.

The fourth cornerstone practice of Principled Negotiation integrates Mindset, Heartset, and Skillset to navigate difficulties, bridge differences, reach agreements, and generate healthy working relationships today and tomorrow.

Many organizations declare a commitment to "Diversity," "Equity," and "Inclusion." Follow through is less common. The challenges to live into these three words are often bigger than the organization's capacity. There is a large, but manageable first step that a collaborative organization must take to build enough healthy capacity for the important work to assure respect, inclusion, and equity for diverse people from different backgrounds.

The organization must first be able to *negotiate* differences. Organizational differences come in many forms (race, gender, age, generation, ability, disability, culture, language, sexual orientation, education level, socio-economic status, professional status, perspective, values, learning style, work style, experience level, expertise, religion, politics etc.). Any of these differences alone or in combination can become a barrier that divides individuals and groups inside the organization, limiting the capacity to work well together.

To negotiate a situation is to navigate difficulty or challenge. This often requires the capacity to recognize, bridge, and accept differences. A bridge must be built from both sides. It does not eliminate differences. It connects and provides a way to meet and engage.

Leadiators need the Mindset, Heartset, and Skillset to transform differences into a valuable asset. Mindset provides the intelligence, heartset provides the will, and skillset provides the ability. Leadiators must set an example so that others can learn and engage in this important work. Commitment to be in positive relationship with people who are different generates the will to treat others with basic respect, listen well, and patiently work through challenging issues. Diverse perspectives must be accepted and then embraced so differences can be bridged. Then, it becomes possible to openly address conflict and seek reconciliation with equitable agreements.

The authority to impose a leader's will on an individual, a team, or an organization must be sparingly used as this use of power usually includes risk. To be effective, leadiators don't just announce and impose their authority. Even when a leadiator is right and has full authority to act, the use of power to decide and impose may backfire. Others may comply and do so with resentment. Grudging compliance can lead to low morale, chronic complaining, gossip, speculation, or downright sabotage, also known as "malicious compliance."

Negotiation is not limited to making agreements. There are issues that need to be resolved by agreements that people will carry out in good faith. Then, there are issues and situations that need to be navigated with awareness because the *negotiation* seeks other important outcomes from different stakeholders.

Leadiators need to balance the use of power and authority over others with principled behavior to negotiate these constructive outcomes.

- Gain acceptance and support for key decisions.
- Generate understanding, cooperation, and patience.
- Build consensus and trust.
- Increase willingness to creatively engage.
- Reach agreement to disagree with respect and move forward together.

Learning Objectives

- Understand conflict and the signs of polarization.
- Practice Principled Negotiation to bridge differences with respect, creativity, and practical agreements.
- Equip leaders and managers as first responders who can constructively engage and resolve conflict.
- Create a climate of positive engagement where differences can be bridged and honorably reconciled.

A Museum Builds a Bridge to Engage Its Stakeholders

The Museum of Indian Arts and Culture (MIAC) is operated by the State of New Mexico and it is filled with art work, objects, and stories about the Native peoples of New Mexico. Once before, I had been asked by a director of the museum to guide the staff through a strategic planning process to envision and plan for the future success of the museum. In June 2013, a new director had just arrived and asked me again to help with this work.

The new director asked me to propose a way to respectfully seek out the perspectives of representatives from *Indian Country* in New Mexico. She wanted this to happen early in the planning process so these diverse perspectives could help shape the MIAC staff's plans and influence the direction of the museum.

This was a straightforward request, but it needed a careful response. Planning always takes place within a context shaped by history. In New Mexico, there are 23 recognized tribes and pueblos. It is a common mistake to group them into a single category with a unified set of concerns and views. However, each tribe is a sovereign nation with a particular history and unique cultural dimensions. Respect requires inclusion and acknowledgement of the diversity of culture, concerns, and ideas about "Indian Arts and Culture."

Also, any consultation by a government institution with Native people happens as part of a chain of consultation within the complex history of Native people in the state. This history has been very difficult for Native peoples. In New Mexico, there is also a complex history of the relationship between museums and Native people. There are examples of museums that have displayed Native objects and images, portrayed Native people, and interpreted Native history and culture in ways that lacked sensitivity and respect. Finally, meeting formats and discussion behaviors have embedded dominant culture norms that may not encourage respectful intercultural exchanges and honest sharing of diverse points of view.

Ultimately, the director determined to convene MIAC's large Native American advisory committee along with other invited representatives totaling about 50 people. I recommended a process for large group dialogue called the *World Café* as the best way to offer respect, maximize participation, engage and bridge diverse perspectives, and learn together.

The *World Café* process is a remarkable social *technology* that can be used to convene groups of 12-1200+ for well-structured, important conversations. It has an extraordinary track record, actively field-tested for the past 25 years. The process works for a large group to come together and imagine a positive future for an organization, a neighborhood, or a community. It has been used effectively all over the world in many different countries and cultural settings. (1)

- In large cities and remote rural communities

- With major corporations and small nonprofits

- With scientific elites and with young people who are still in their early education experiences

These conversations can be about specific issues to understand, differences to bridge, or problems to solve. They can also be used more broadly to shape an organization's future.

The process consistently works well in different settings because its design principles are elegantly simple and deeply respectful. It uses the structure of an informal conversation at small café tables with 5-6 people for a set of simultaneous conversations. The structure helps limit the influence of vertical hierarchy and status with a horizontal exploration to understand and learn together. Everyone has an opportunity to speak, to listen, and be listened to. The conversation is structured around a few "questions that matter" and people spend 20-30 minutes at a table before moving to a different table and speaking with others. In large meetings, where many will not be able to give voice to their ideas, the World Café encourages full participation by many within a modest timeframe.

There are only a few guidelines.

- Focus on what matters.

- Listen deeply.

- Contribute by speaking your mind and heart.

- Link and connect ideas.

- Make room for others to speak.

Although I had confidence in the process based on other experiences, I had not seen it used before in this kind of a setting. The spirit in the conversation in the room that day and the quality of the input offered by the participants was remarkable. The consultation with Native stakeholders identified key themes that directly influenced the subsequent meetings of the MIAC staff to envision the museum's future with programs and partnerships that are respectful of and relevant to Native stakeholders. Within a long history filled with so much separation and misunderstanding, the process built a small bridge of mutual understanding.

The day confirmed my belief in the practical power of diverse perspectives when voices come together, engage with respect, think together, and bridge differences. The wisdom of the *World Café* process is a generous gift available to everyone as *open source* social software. The guidelines are available online to any organization, team, or group that wants to convene diverse perspectives to have "conversations that matter." (2)

Understanding Conflict and Polarization

Sometimes, the dynamics of differences escalate into conflict. In an organization, conflict usually results from an unwillingness to be in good relations with others. Conflict is a state of disagreement, opposition, contention, competition or tension between individuals or groups of people. These are predictable patterns encountered at every level in every culture, in workplaces, communities, neighborhoods, faith-based organizations, and families. Although conflict can be destructive, there is also latent constructive potential in conflict. It should not be feared, but respected, understood, and, when possible, resolved. (3)

However, in many organizations the high level of collaboration necessary to fulfill the mission is often compromised. Common causes interfere with respectful, constructive engagement. These include poor communication, unprofessional behavior, lack of trust, unmanaged conflict that festers without resolution, unresolved disagreements, power plays, and ongoing feuds. The inability to collaborate can impose costly consequences on the organization: wasted time; low morale; staff turnover; and lost opportunities to excel in delivering the mission.

When an organization develops healthy norms to engage conflict, the organization gains opportunities to transform differences into agreement that can shift negative dynamics and generate a positive change of direction. These positive norms counter and redirect reactions shaped by three negative mindsets.

- Conflict is a CONTEST that requires a winner and a loser and will be measured by how much each person gains or must give up.

- Conflict is a WAR, a struggle from which only one person or group will emerge (survive) intact and this struggle justifies the use of any means necessary.

- Conflict is a MESS, an unpleasant, negative situation without any constructive possibilities.

Like professional mediators, leaders and managers need a framework of principles and skills that they adapt to day-to-day conflicts and differences that arise inside most organizations. A leadiator does not have to be officially neutral or viewed as impartial to act with purpose and skill to create a positive climate for constructive discussion of issues and concerns.

Effective engagement with conflict requires an appropriate place and enough time. When a constructive forum is available, capacity to change and grow becomes more possible.

- Address challenging situations.

- Reestablish respectful working relationships.

- Increase the ability to communicate effectively.

- Collaborate consistently.

- Bridge differences.

- Solve problems.

Leadiators understand the costly consequences of conflict and develop norms of behavior that address conflict in healthy, proactive ways. These norms can be communicated from the first day a new person joins the organization. When new employees or volunteers join an organization, the onboarding process is an opportunity to introduce the organization's norms about communication and working with differences.

Every challenging situation provides an opportunity for existing leaders, managers, and staff to learn and to reinforce what is expected and what is not acceptable. Managers are the organization's *first responders* and can have a disproportionate impact (positive or negative) on organization conflict norms because they are closer to the day-to-day action. Therefore, they are often able to be the first to respond. Response that is confident and skillful reinforces the desired norms for those directly affected by the conflict and bystanders. Like first responders in our communities, organization *first responders* need training, orientation, and experience to fulfill this critical organization role.

Respect the Danger of Polarization

Let's begin with an example. Three Black men won a lawsuit against an organization that had never hired a non-White employee. The organization was forced to hire them and pay them damages for lost pay since the date they had been rejected as job applicants. They started their new jobs. So far so good.

Although now employed with a fair salary, the collective hostility of many existing employees toward the three men resulted in orchestrated, silent treatment to ostracize them, discourage them, and drive them out of the organization. Except for minimal communication necessary to do their jobs, no one would speak to them, help them, or acknowledge their presence. No one would sit within ten feet of them in the company cafeteria.

No formal leader of the organization--President, Department Director, Team Leader, Union President, or Union Shop Steward said or did anything to address the issue.

After about a week of this treatment, John, a middle-aged White man without any formal title or authority, respected by everyone, became a leadiator. With his cafeteria tray in hand, he simply paused at the table where the three men sat, separated from everyone. He asked if he could join them. They accepted. The next day he returned and joined them again. On the third day, he invited a friend to "come meet the new guys, you'll like them." On the fourth day, he asked two other friends to "come meet the new guys, you'll like them."

These simple acts sent a powerful message about how the organization's culture needed to change and how people should be treated. More employees began to follow John's example. Over a period of weeks, the large majority of the workforce stopped the silent treatment and either warmly welcomed or respectfully accepted the three men.

While all the formal leaders were *missing in action*, John quietly stepped forward to become a leadiator, guiding his organization with a quiet example, opening communication channels, developing relationships, bridging the division, and making a small, but powerful move away from racial discrimination toward a more inclusive workplace. ***There are leaders who carry formal authority and titles, and there are those who LEAD.***

In four decades as a professional mediator, I have seen polarization dynamics that damage and, at times, tear apart work teams, family businesses, university academic departments, nonprofit organizations, companies, and communities.

I have encountered more than a few organizations where the people with the titles were unable, or unwilling to lead. Particularly in situations of crisis and division, a failure of leadership can produce serious harm to an organization's health. However, I have also observed people just like John in the middle or lower ranks of organizations who care deeply about the organization's mission and guiding values. With the mindset, heartset, and skillset of a leadiator, they quietly lead by example every day as they do their work and interact with others. They show the way to work in creative collaboration. Visible examples of leadership integrity at all levels are crucial to build and sustain a healthy organization.

How Polarization Works

Polarization is a state of hostility, antagonism, antipathy, conflict, and repugnance with powerful emotions. Polarization has the capacity to fester and infect every member of an entire social structure. As each side takes action to promote or defend its interests, territory, and priorities against the other, the consequences of their actions can hurt non-aligned stakeholders, alienate or pull others into the conflict, and weaken the whole organization.

Polarized social conflict generates a *fog of war* that confuses and blinds much like the escalation of military conflicts. In a polarized climate, perception is often distorted by the weight of powerful emotions (anger and fear), moral righteousness, arrogance, lack of humility, and diminished capacity for reflection and deliberation.

In this perceptual *fog*, each side tends to strongly identify with the sense of being wronged or mistreated by the other. Individuals and groups on opposite sides tend to develop a story about their own rightness and being victimized by the other. This self-serving narrative releases them from accountability. It dismisses the value of the other side's concerns. The struggle continues to devalue others. It is fueled by moral justification without any willingness to listen, learn, or understand.

Recognize the negative power of polarization. A common cold is not a problem. A pandemic is dangerous. ***The three primary behavioral characteristics of polarization are dangerous because they have a disease-like capacity to multiply and spread unless addressed.***

- *Volatility* Everyday interactions can turn into a clash that can rapidly deteriorate into hostility and aggression. Anyone involved may intensely react to a real or perceived provocation as "disrespect" or "a personal attack."

- *Suspicion* When people see others as adversaries, they tend to perceive actions, words, and events in a way that fits into an existing story about "who they are and how they treat us." For example, an honest inquiry can be misinterpreted as "a trick to manipulate us to their advantage." Adversaries often choose to

228

segregate and avoid direct communication. This increases mistrust and intensifies the polarization dynamic.

- **Oversimplification** Complex issues become binary choices: us vs. them; either you are with us or against us; right or wrong; and win or lose. Human beings are reduced to stereotypes with labels, e.g. jerk, bully, slacker, and other negative characterizations.

As in the example above, a leadiator like John can model proactive strategies to counter these powerful patterns. These strategies require courage and integrity to implement. They have the power to shift the dynamics, improve communication channels, and **create a bridge for dialogue**.

- Use guidelines for acceptable behavior and *neutral* facilitation to **establish and sustain respectful interactions**.

- Seize small opportunities to **build a working level of trust** by demonstrating empathy and being willing to learn the other's deeper story. One researcher who has studied political and social polarization refers to this as "climbing the empathy wall." (4)

- **Strengthen the non-polarized middle (the "third side"). Enlist others to act as bridge builders, voices of moderation, and advocates for the common good. As the third side grows, the power of those with extreme positions diminishes.** (5)

There are no quick fixes for polarization. It is a journey that requires patience, a strong will, and some skill. A leadiator focuses skillful effort to bridge differences with the last of the four cornerstone practices, Principled Negotiation.

Principled Negotiation Shifts Argument Over Positions to Dialogue About Interests

Principled Negotiation within a current or prospective collaborative relationship recognizes that two things are in play to reach agreement on an issue: the issue and the working relationship. This includes the current and future relationship. A person with enough authority to impose his preferred outcome could also affect the morale, motivation, and willingness to cooperate, now and in the future. This may be for an individual or members of a group.

Traditional give-and-take bargaining over positions is a hit-or-miss approach to reaching agreement. Each party to the negotiation competitively exercises his or her power in order to achieve a desirable outcome. Competitive tension may incentivize people to use bluffing, posturing, threats and deception to improve the result. Typically, this power contest produces a low to moderate satisfaction compromise that everyone can *live with*. The competitive focus on each side's preferred outcome often forecloses creative exploration of alternatives. This approach also risks impasse and escalation of the conflict.

Traditional bargaining is not the preferred means to address differences in ongoing work relationships. Instead of power over or power against, Principled Negotiation becomes more skillful with power dynamics by understanding the forms of power that people bring to working relationships. For example, the Executive Director who is "negotiating" the acceptance and whole-hearted support among a group of employees for a challenging reorganization is dealing with others who lack formal authority but have information about work flows, control over procedures, the capacity to cooperate at higher or lower levels, and the ability to accelerate or moderate the progress of the transition.

Principled Negotiation provides an effective way to use power <u>with</u> others to reach higher satisfaction outcomes. The negotiation becomes a way to work with each other. It is this practice that strengthens the collaborative relationship over time. Recognize the many forms of power to build this skill.

> *Authority*... comes from a formal structural position that delivers power and influence to the holder of the position, e.g. judges, executives, managers, parents
>
> *Sanction*... comes from the perceived or actual ability to inflict harm or to prevent another from achieving their goals
>
> *Information*... comes from expertise, possession of key information, or control over access to information

Nuisance... often available, even to those who seem to be without power, and comes from the ability to delay, discomfort, or inconvenience others to some degree

Association... an indirect form of power that comes from proximity to, alliance with, or relationship with others possessing power

Personal Characteristics... includes determination, communication ability, confidence, and the ethical character to invoke moral principles and appeal to values held by others

Resources... stems from the ability to deliver or deny desirable resources such as money, land, labor, and materials to others

Status Quo... rests with the person/group who benefits from or is satisfied with the existing situation because it usually requires more effort to change a situation than to continue as things are

Reward... comes from providing incentives and things people desire such as money, recognition, promotion, or social approval

Procedure... comes from managing or controlling the processes that must be used to accomplish a task

A principled approach to negotiation has four major elements.

- Take care of your own needs and concerns. *That won't work for me because _____. Now that I have put my idea on the table for you to consider, I want to explain my reasoning about this approach as fair to you and to me.*

- Be willing to understand and consider the other's needs and concerns. *Could you give me an example of how your idea could be implemented? What is important to you that needs to be addressed right away?*

- Actively listen and educate to build the level of understanding. *So I hear three things that you said are important, A.B.C. Did I miss anything? I want to be clear with you about what I am struggling with in your proposal. Am I being clear?*

- Creatively explore possible solutions that satisfy everyone's needs at some level. *What if _____? Is there another way we can look at this?*

What makes negotiation principled is more openness and honesty, more disclosure of one's sincere interests (needs, concerns, and values), AND more willingness to understand and consider the other side's sincere interests.

A principled negotiator can skillfully guide other people in the shift from arguing over positions to exploring interests. With better understanding, the negotiators can seek to find a collaborative outcome that is balanced and mutually satisfactory. Figure 22 shows this movement from "Half Way" compromise to "Our Way" mutuality.

Figure 22

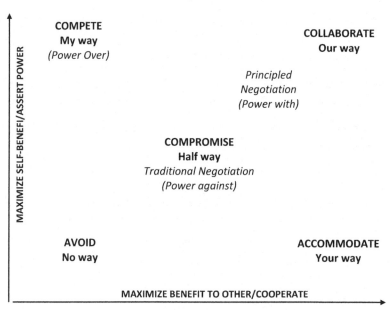

Use a Common Language to Increase Understanding (WHAT, WHY, and HOW)

The practice of Principled Negotiation requires an honest dialogue about importance. The road to a positive outcome (some meaningful improvement over the status quo) begins at a *table* where the issues that must be addressed can be identified and explored.

Use this simple framework with a clear sequence to guide the conversation forward and avoid detours into defensiveness and aggressive debate. Begin to identify the issues that need to be addressed. Think of the issues as **WHAT** we have to discuss and negotiate about, i.e. the topics.

The Issues Define the Problem

Effective problem solving requires that the problem be clearly understood. There are different ways to state issues. Some people rely on a topical checklist. I recommend that you frame them as one or more questions that need to be answered.

For example, two co-workers may have difficulty getting along, are unable to communicate effectively, or cooperate. In one sense, the overall issue to talk about is the topic of *our working relationship*.

- *State as a basic question: How can we improve our working relationship?*

- *State as part of a higher goal: How can we improve our working relationship so it better serves the customers and is mutually satisfactory to us?*

- *Frame as a Set of Questions: How can we improve our working relationship?; What should our communication look like? (frequency, channels); What are the clear, shared expectations for each of our roles and responsibilities?; How will we manage the upcoming field research project?; If we have disagreements in the future, how will we address them?*

It is important to state issues so they do not presuppose a particular solution that may favor one side, e.g. *How much money does A need to reimburse B?* This narrow focus on money may leave out other parts of the problem. It also suggests that some amount of reimbursement is necessary. A more neutral statement leaves open the possibility of shared responsibility to solve the problem. *What steps do we need to take to fully resolve this issue?* In particularly challenging situations, great care may be required to frame issues clearly. Then, sequence them to enable small steps forward that can build momentum and confidence to keep talking.

Once **WHAT** has been identified and there is basic understanding of the situation, go deeper.

WHY Is the Reason the Issue Matters. The key to resolving issues collaboratively is an understanding of the **WHY** that underlies the WHAT. **WHY** does the issue matter to me and to you? **WHY** are you or they interested in this WHAT? The word *interest* embraces two underlying sources of **WHY** something matters to an individual or a group: their needs to be met or the values they believe are affected.

Figure 23 provides a logical structure to refine your thinking of **WHY** with three major categories of underlying interests. Consider an example of a conflict in an organization with a small group of employees in a large team who are unhappy with their treatment in terms of pay, job assignments, and recognition.

Substantive interests underlie tangible things like money, work roles, equipment, and benefits. For an employee, economic security is a powerful **WHY** that underlies the desire to receive a pay raise. Someone may also care about a raise because of an interest in the family's RESPECT for his capacity to support them.

Procedural interests underlie the ways things are done. Beyond what I am expected to do, who do I have to report to and how do I have to document my work? If I find the reporting and supervision burdensome and unnecessary, fairness and respect may be **WHY** someone wants a change. Someone may also have a need for AUTONOMY to do the job in her own way.

Psychological interests represent the way you feel about yourself and your image in the eyes of others who you care about. If your family has money troubles and you are under pressure to *stand up for yourself* and demand a raise, your sense of self-worth or the respect of your spouse may also be WHY you want a raise or recognition. Is what you are being asked to do in line with your position in the organization? Or, is it a de facto promotion or demotion? (6)

Figure 23

1. Remember that people have different types of interests. Interests are needs and values, i.e., the REASONS WHY you want something or place a value on having something. They underlie the something. Money is not an interest. The reason you want the money is the interest.

> **Substantive interests** underlie tangible things people want such as property, money, resources, position, or authority

> **Procedural interests** underlie the way people want things to be done, time frames, and methods used for input or decision making

> **Psychological/Relational interests** underlie how people want to be treated or seen and regarded by others

2. Uncover the the interests. Identify the key stakeholders in this negotiation (individual, group, organization) and what matters to them (the interests they have).

3. Consider how the participants' interests interrelate. Look for the connection between these interests. Are they common, different without being in conflict, or actively in conflict?

> **Shared** - Common ground where there is mutual gain when this is satisfied.   *(Strategy: **Build Upon**)*

> **Complementary** - Differing but not in conflict. If one benefits, this takes little or nothing away from the other.
> *(Strategy: **Dovetail/Fit Together**)*

> **Conflicting** - Zero sum because satisfaction for one always comes with direct cost or loss to other.
> *(Strategy: **Compromise, Tradeoff or Package** positive and negative outcomes into an overall acceptable agreement)*

4. Search for options that address underlying interests. Durable agreements and positive working relationships are based on some acceptable level of satisfaction. Satisfied interests are the key to a positive outcome.

Generate Possibilities for Agreement

HOW is the place in the conversation to creatively explore possibilities. After you have some clarity about *WHAT* and *WHY*, you can work together to surface ideas of **HOW** to address the *WHAT* and satisfy (to some degree) the *WHY*.

Dialogue (Lesson 4) continues to be a crucial practice. It is the way you explore, learn, and create.

- Discover people's underlying interests.

- Differences in perspective become clearer.

- Assumptions can be tested.

- Misunderstandings can be corrected.

Even when the solution itself may not be very satisfying, there can be a negotiation of acceptance, understanding, respect, and face-saving. These outcomes protect the ability to work well together in the future.

The value of a constructive working relationship in the future calls for creative exploration to find the best possible option. With the climate of dialogue and respect, you gain the capacity to conduct a resourceful search for possibilities. Pay particular attention to ideas that build on shared interests or address complementary (differing) interests of those directly involved and for other key stakeholders. ***Creativity takes effort to uncover possibilities. Ask questions that force you to think more deeply about the interests of stakeholders.***

Then, take the options list and put them side-by-side with the shared, complementary, and conflicting interests. It is often more effective to make this side-by-side assessment in a visual form to *step back* and look for patterns of possibility. Consider a white board or a large piece of flip chart paper. See Figure 24.

Questions Can Open Doors

- *What if.....?*

- *Where else can we look for ideas?*

- *What unwritten rules can we break?*

- *What would (name the wisest person you know) do if he or she were here?*

- *How can we combine skills and resources to satisfy key interests on both sides?*

- *What assumptions are we making?*

- *What different assumptions might we make?*

- *How can we expand the list of options with variations on existing ideas? (use the acronym, SCAMPER: What can we.... S ubstitute, C ombine, A dapt, M agnify, M inify*, P ut to other uses, E liminate, R everse?) * to change by reducing in scope or size (7)*

- *BRAINSTORMING. Can we take five minutes, without criticism, and come up with as many ideas as possible?*

Figure 24

A's Interest	Possible Options	B's Interest
Shared		Shared
Complementary		Complementary
Conflicting		Conflicting

Remain Centered in Tense Situations to Act Skillfully

Difficult situations in groups and between individuals emerge from time to time that challenge the capacity to collaborate. When we react to conflict and difficulty, we often move automatically into one of three modes: Fight; Flee; or Freeze. Leadiators can best serve the organization and the people who look to them for guidance and wisdom by overcoming anger, fear, or anxiety-based reactions. They need to move into *Flow*. This word implies engagement, movement with the situation, flexibility, and responsiveness.

Even in a large group situation, one person can make a difference by responding instead of reacting. One person who remains non-reactive can behave and act in a way that changes an entire group. Earlier in this Lesson, you met such a person. While his coworkers remained in a state of negative reaction, John responded in a calm, centered way. In Lesson One, Jasminka *flowed* with the many difficulties while others around her were in fight, flee, or freeze mode.

Here are four concrete moves any person can make to break a cycle of reaction and RESPOND and flow forward with more awareness and skill.

Focus on Short Term Goals - *How am I going to get through the next five minutes/hour/day with this situation/person?*

Narrow your focus to what is in front of you right now that you might be able to control or directly influence. Clarify what you want to happen next. This avoids the overwhelming scope of the problem and applies your full capacity to perform at a higher level on a specific task. This dynamic works in all pressure situations: athletic performance, public speaking, a difficult conversation with a neighbor, or a messy interpersonal conflict at work. An immediate goal might be to control your temper, find the firmness to speak an uncomfortable truth in a calm voice, or listen to a difficult person without reacting and arguing.

Use Mental Rehearsal - *What does a successful outcome LOOK LIKE?*

Most of us don't take the time to prepare before going into a difficult meeting. Take a few minutes to clearly and vividly imagine a good resolution to a situation that is causing difficulty and anxiety. SEE what it will look like when you do this difficult thing well. Notice how you FEEL in your body, what you HEAR, and even what you SMELL. When you do this and repeat it, you are giving your brain the experience of success and strengthening your will to act and persevere. This practice has been extensively developed to help athletes increase their capacity to respond skillfully under pressure. (8)

Replace Negative Thoughts With Positive Self-Talk - *What is the inner dialogue that is influencing me?*

Most of us are susceptible to an inner chatter that can have a profound influence on our feelings and behavior. Pay attention to this self-talk and promptly intervene to stop negative, unhelpful messages that pull you away from a good result. Just say NO, STOP, CANCEL, or REWIND. Replace the negative message with a short, clear reminder that prompts you to move forward positively. For example, *I can do this__ Keep my eyes on the prize__ Just take the next step__ Remember, they are doing the best they can__ Don't take it personally because it's not about you.*

Control Your Physical/Emotional Arousal Level - *How can I stay calm and centered in my body?*

A sinking feeling in the pit of the stomach, a shaking, angry voice, or mounting panic, if uncontrolled, limit your behavioral options. Even if your safety is truly threatened, calm dynamic response is usually better than hasty or panicked reaction that could make the situation worse. Excuse yourself to take a break, get a glass of water, or use the bathroom. INHALE deeply, count to six, hold for a count of two, exhale for a count of six. Repeat 3X. In less than one minute, this simple technique lowers your blood pressure, calms the nervous system, fills the brain with oxygen and immediately increases your capacity to think and RESPOND consciously.

Clear the Air to Move Forward Together

When it isn't possible to let an issue or a situation go, there is an art to addressing a troubling issue that comes up between individuals or within a group. Many people have a common pattern to avoid conflict, confrontation, or an unpleasant conversation. This is different than making a deliberate choice to let something go and move on.

> *The consequences of remaining silent and ignoring an issue can be significant. Without clear understanding, firm words and, in some cases, correction of problematic behavior, unacceptable behavior and conditions may continue or worsen. If the situation remains unaddressed, this may damage or limit the capacity to collaborate.*

The structure of a positive setting for a difficult conversation has some basic elements.

- *Place* There is an appropriate location with sufficient privacy so people will speak candidly

- *Space* There is enough time for key people involved to speak and listen

- *Pace* A conversation level of exchange allows for effective exploration of WHAT, WHY, and HOW with the ability to check out perceptions and develop understanding

- *Face* There is enough self-control with enough structure to maintain civility and assure mutual respect so no one's dignity is at risk

A leadiator has an important role to cultivate forums where these conversations can happen. The cohesion and functioning of the group or organization will be shaped by how problematic behavior or violated expectations are addressed. A leadiator must show others the way.

Action Steps for challenging conversations about collaboration:

- *Avoid surprises* Let the person(s) know what you want to talk about and schedule an appropriate time and place. Seek their agreement about the way to have the discussion. Consider whether you need ground rules and/or a third party.

- *Deepen the Listening* Summarize the issue at the start of the meeting and ask for their perspective before you spend too much time laying out everything that you want to say. Try to *chunk down* the discussion so there is a balanced exchange back and forth with each participant talking, listening, and looping back (see Lesson Four page 120).

- *Use Precise Words* When you speak, make clear distinctions between facts (*II observed that...,*) emotions (*When you said _____, I felt angry/ sad/worried*), needs or values (It *is important to me that I receive because _____*)*., beliefs/assumptions/judgments I assume that the most workable approach is _____ because_____, and requests (What I am asking you do to address this is _____).*

- *Maintain Climate Control* Do not allow their words or emotions to provoke a reaction from you. Remain under self-control. Exchanging heated words is only a non-listening argument. Keep the pace moderate and the tone calm.

- *One Step at a Time* It may not be possible to reach agreement or resolve the issue. Acknowledge the differences in perspective, goals, and expectations. Discuss possible next steps. Keep the line of communication open between you.

Use a Set of Powerful Principles to Engage Differences

Leadiators in every organization, at every level, can apply universal principles that harness powerful forces able to generate the force of reconciliation. Here are some examples of this practical wisdom developed by leadiators with experience in harsh conditions. Use them to help individuals and groups bridge seemingly irreconcilable differences and sustain practical collaboration within the organization, between groups and organizations, and in the community. (9)

The Power of Dignity - Always give and insist upon no frills respect. Treat people like they already are who they could be to help them become what they could be.

> *Genuine dialogue is the only path forward to meaningful collaboration and this cannot happen in a climate of disrespect.* It is often the case that individuals or groups with the greatest need to collaborate hit an immediate dead end because they veer into competitive debate and argument, accusation and blame-fixing, and the endless recycling of historic grievances.

> There is a distinction between having *RESPECT* for someone (which must be earned) and treating another with no frills respect (a universal, human right). You can insist that others treat you with this basic level of respect. You can find the willingness, courage, and self-control to retain dignified dominion over your emotions while talking to others with whom you disagree or are in conflict. No frills respect is a necessary investment to bring everyone to the table where open conversations and Principled Negotiation can surface and explore hidden possibilities.

The Power of Forgiveness (Letting Go) - Release yourself from the prison of the past. Resentment in your heart toward others hurts you more than them.

> Many collaborative efforts never progress due to an unwillingness to leave past grievances and focus on the present and future. It is a mistake to think that forgiveness is about the other. It is about you.

The growing science of the neurology of the heart shows that holding anger or resentment in the heart is physiologically unhealthy and it is a likely non-success strategy because it continually focuses in the rearview mirror.

In order to leave the past, it is fundamental to recognize what is in your best interest, and in the interest of the organization. Focus on the present and the future, not the past. Forgiveness does not forget the past. It is a shift in focus from the past to look forward, and move on. (10)

The Power of Perspective - Speak a common language to reach the head and the heart. *What someone needs and values lies at the center of the issue.*

When perspective, motivation, or world-view is quite different, it is even more important to be able to speak to those on the other side in a way that increases understanding. The willingness to listen, learn, and see through the eyes of the other is frequently lacking in situations with a history of competition, mistrust, or conflict, just when it is most needed.

When people with differences approach communication as debate or argument, they do not yet have a common language that can reach the other's heart and go to the essence of the issue. Contentious debate easily degrades into blaming or attacking the other side, defending oneself, and avoiding any share of responsibility for the issue. These actions cut off opportunities to learn something from the other, shift perspective, and find common ground that can be built upon.

When you find a common language of interests (needs and values), you increase the capacity to see the world through the eyes of those on the other side of the gap. With this capacity you have new ability to build a bridge for a peaceful transition to a better relationship.

We are interested in and care about what we believe that we need and what we value as important. These needs and values motivate us to take action to promote, protect, and defend what matters.

This is the language that may be able to reach the other, shift perspective, build a small degree of trust, and begin the journey toward possibility. **Straight talk about needs and values balanced with a strong helping of mutual respect is the common language of the heart.** See Figure 23

> This journey toward peace in a working relationship, a team, or an organization requires will to begin. *It is essential to find the courage and the will to reach out instead of turning away, to respond and open up, instead of reacting against or closing down.*

The Power of a Clear Vision – Focus on the desired outcome and take patient steps. All journeys begin with steps.

For most of us, the circumstances in organizations that challenge us to seek and build collaboration can be improved or transformed. Consider these examples of challenging circumstances.

- Working to improve practices and outcomes inside a bureaucratic organization that resists change and fails to honor and support its employees

- Healing unresolved family issues inside a family-owned business that contribute to chaos, low morale, or mediocre performance in the organization

- Addressing unresolved conflict between members of a governing board, business partners, or professional colleagues who do not work well together

- Sustaining an organization's efforts to develop a workplace that is diverse, equitable, and inclusive

From my experience inside a wide variety of organizations, I observe how discouraged people can become. It is common that many allow the weight of negative history and their perception of the degree of difficulty to convince them that nothing can be done. *To inspire collaboration for positive change in an organization requires the time to forge a powerful, compelling vision of what the working relationship could be.*

Leadiators need a positive vision that focuses committed action and sustains motivation over time to effect the desired change. Leaders and potential change agents give up hope that things can change and resign themselves to the status quo. Leaders without hope may simply leave. Or they *retire in place*, remaining discouraged and cynical, unwilling to try to do anything beyond the basic requirements of their jobs until they can retire or move on to something better. A jaded belief that nothing can be done becomes a self-fulfilling prophecy.

We live in a society that values increasing speed and quick fixes. However, many barriers to collaboration in organizational systems, between organizations and individuals, and in communities require patient effort to overcome. To be an agent for UNITING, you need hope. This is not naïve or wishful. It is muscular and hard-headed about WHAT IS. This form of hope requires determination to take action and remain firmly committed to WHAT COULD BE. A strong vision of what you want the collaboration to create and deliver can sustain whole-hearted effort over time.

Inquiry Into Action

- *How do members of your team address strong differences and disagreements when they arise with each other?*

- *How do members of your team address strong differences and disagreements with the organization's clients/ customers and community stakeholders?*

- *How does the team leader address strong differences and disagreements within the team?*

- *How does the leader of the organization confidently and creatively address strong differences and disagreements within the organization?*

- *If you have a conflict with someone else on the team or elsewhere in the organization, what skills do you and others have to work it out respectfully and directly?*

- *What could it mean to the organization if team members, managers, and leaders had the capacity to confidently and creatively address strong differences and disagreements?*

- *When a conflict situation is too difficult for you to resolve on your own, where do go to get help in the organization? (your team leader, a mentor, HR, a mediator)*

- *If any team member has a serious disagreement with the team leader or a senior leader, can she approach the person directly to talk about the issue with confidence that he will be treated fairly and respectfully?*

- *How much gossip and backbiting is there in the organization? (backbiting is complaining and speaking negatively about others when they are not present)*

- *In your organization how do departments, divisions, and teams work together cooperatively to avoid office politics, power plays, and feuds?*

- *If your organization speaks about the importance of diversity, equity, and inclusion, what are the visible signs that its leaders want to address these issues?*

Core Ideas From Lesson Eight

Differences, conflict, and polarization
are common challenges in organizations.

A bridge must be built from both sides.
The bridge does not eliminate differences. It connects
and provides a way to meet and engage.

When an organization develops healthy norms to engage conflict,
the organization gains opportunities to transform differences into
agreement that can shift negative dynamics and generate a positive
change of direction.

What makes negotiation principled is more openness and honesty,
more disclosure of one's sincere interests (needs, concerns, and
values), AND willingness to understand and consider the other side's
sincere interests.

When perspective, motivation, or world-view is quite different, it is
even more important to be able to speak to those on the other side in
a way that increases understanding.

It is essential to find the courage and the will to reach out instead of
turning away, to respond and open up, instead of reacting against or
closing down.

Straight talk about needs and values balanced with a strong helping
of mutual respect is the common language of the heart.

Blueprint for Creative Collaboration

POSITIVE COLLABORATIVE FORCES
Generated by the cornerstone practices, action steps,
and *cultural characteristics**

Clarity   Perspective   Connection

Understanding   Moral Imagination   Leverage

Conviction   Reconciliation   *Agility*

SKILLSET

Cornerstone Practices

Values-Based Decision Making
Wise Planning   Principled Negotiation
Dialogue – the Foundational Practice

Designed **N**ecessary **A**ction Steps
that implement the practices

MINDSET
*Growth Mindset**

HEARTSET
*Integrity**
*Psychological Safety**

Lesson Nine ADAPTING

The greatest force is adaptation and inventiveness,
if we can operate well together.

~ **Ray Dalio** *Legendary financial investor*

The Force of Agility

Adapting requires the ability to move with agility. With increased agility an organization can respond skillfully to uncertainty and change instead of reacting.

Skillful response draws upon collective intelligence from diverse perspectives to act wisely.

Leadiators cannot predict the future. They can enable it by integrating the cornerstone practices of Creative Collaboration into a unified, flexible organization.
Then people can move agilely as one.

Agile organizations generate a flow of creative ideas and adapt to change by turning the best ideas into small and large innovations.

Ideas and learning can flow rapidly in all directions when organizational structures have open, flexible channels of communication.

In a rapidly changing, risky environment, the organizational capacity to adapt, shift course, and move in a different direction becomes critical. This ability to turn and alter course is often referred to as a *pivot*. In order to pivot and remain balanced when in motion, a human being needs a center of gravity and coordination. Like a human being, an organization can stumble and fall by losing its *balance* when changing direction.

An organization's center of gravity comes from shared core values and guiding principles that clearly link with a powerful mission. Leadiators help the organization remain united and centered on its values and principles, ready to agilely pivot together.

The operating environment will continue to present challenges. Instead of panicked reaction or habitual response, adaptive organizations must respond in a principled, deliberate, and wise way. A leadiator has the duty to prepare the organization to respond.

A well-coordinated organization has a flexible structure and shared skills practices, strongly rooted in its values and principles. The four cornerstone practices of Dialogue, Values-based Decision Making, Wise Planning, and Principled Negotiation tap collective intelligence, generate creativity, and lead to wiser responses.

An agile organization also has the capacity to turn creative ideas into practical innovations that improve what customers, clients, and stakeholders receive. An innovation doesn't need to be a grand breakthrough like a stunning technological invention to be important. Many organizations achieve excellence with small, *bread-and-butter* innovations in processes and procedures that aggregate into big gains in capacity.

Learning Objectives

- Develop agility by integrating the cornerstone practices as organization habits that guide response.

- Recognize that innovation is the end of a process that begins with an environment safe enough to generate a steady flow of creative ideas from people at all levels of the organization.

- Design the organization structure to maintain open channels of engagement and communication.

- Cultivate practical wisdom to make better decisions, plan more effectively, and solve problems more resourcefully.

The 21ˢᵗ Century is the Age of Adaptation

In 2005, after ten years of experience guiding strategic planning, I had an encounter that changed the way I understood this work and how I guided my clients to engage the emerging future. I sat in a conference room with fifteen members of a division leadership team in a large science and engineering laboratory. This group had a unique opportunity to prepare for their planning together with a master class on effective strategy and the uncertain future. One member of the team had a college friend who had become one of the leading futurists in the world. As a favor to an old friend, he agreed to fly in and kick off their planning effort. He presented a way to think pragmatically and strategically about the next twenty years called Seven Revolutions. He described the year 2025 and the powerful trends that would transform our 21ˢᵗ century lives as organizations and individuals. (1)

I filled a pad with notes on his key points that I continue to refer to fifteen years later. In my work with organizations and leadiators, I often reflect upon the accuracy of his vision of the future. Here were a few of his key predictions with examples of some current developments.

- Pressures from *1.5 billion more people in the world seeking safety and security* will overwhelm borders and social service systems and challenge stable democracies to respond. e.g. the ongoing refugee crisis in Europe and worldwide.

- *Accelerating, tsunamis of change* (social, political, technological, and environmental) will cascade around the world, taxing the capacity of leaders and organizations to make decisions and adapt. Information overload and increasing issue complexity will decrease time to respond effectively. Many leaders and organizations will remain confused and unable to respond effec-

251

tively. e.g. the interlocking crises of COVID-19, the global economic slowdown, extreme weather events, and racial justice movements.

- *If unchecked by effective leadership and governance structures, fear and polarization will generate divisions* in communities and societies that promote unskillful reaction instead of wise response. e.g. the political polarization in the U.S. (national, state, and local) and elsewhere since 2016, and the rise of extremism globally, magnified by social media.

- Organizations in all sectors (corporate, government, and nonprofit) will only remain relevant if their leaders guide them to evolve, partner across sectors, and *develop new methods of work that increase the collective capacity to respond and adapt*. e.g. the worldwide partnerships of Project ECHO described in this lesson.

Adaptive capacity is now centrally important for every organization. The futurist highlighted the need for a new generation of leaders with the vision, understanding, and skills to build more adaptable organizations with more flexible structures and approaches. This includes the necessity to form new types of strategic coalitions, partnerships, alliances, and networks within and across all sectors: government, international, corporate, and civil society. I believe this new generation must become leadiators who know how to build bridges.

His take-away message had three essential points:

- Adaptability will become ever more critical to organization survival and success, so leaders need to deliberately cultivate this capacity in organizations. *(In my words, adaptive capacity must be a leadiator's true north to cultivate the force of agility.)*

- Difficult problems cannot be solved at the same level of consciousness that created them, so leaders need to be catalysts for new levels of resourceful thinking. *(In my words, leadiators must facilitate the flow of dialogue, collective intelligence, and creative ideas that lead to innovation.)*

- A leader's task is not to predict the future, but enable it. *(In my words, a leadiator must harness the forces of moral imagination and leverage to direct the collaborative energies of the organization to deliver positive results.)*

These three keys can be integrated into a single leadership imperative across sectors. **Leadiators have the duty to develop the organizational adaptive capacity to respond resourcefully to the inevitable, unpredictable changes ahead.** This becomes one question, *How adaptable are you and your organization?*

During the first decade of the Age of Adaptation an acronym (VUCA) emerged from business theory and military experience that is often used to characterize the revolutionary world forecast by the futurist. ,(2)

- **V**olatility - the dynamics and velocity of change in the operating environment

- **U**ncertainty - the inability to predict and the probability of being surprised without awareness or knowledge

- **C**omplexity - the overload of factors to consider that can produce confusion and paralysis

- **A**mbiguity – lack of clarity to discern the operating environment along with risks of misunderstanding and mischaracterizing opportunities, challenges, problems, and threats

These elements are the reality that makes the *new normal* an illusion. Coordinated navigation of a VUCA world requires agility and adaptation that can only be developed through shared understanding and Creative Collaboration throughout the organization.

An Organization Can Adapt, Pivot, and Show Others the Way

In the introduction, you learned about Project ECHO and its founder, Dr. Sanjeev Arora. ECHO continues to evolve and adapt in health care with its mission to serve the underserved by moving knowledge, not people. In March, 2020, in the midst of a global pandemic, ECHO made a major pivot and redirected its worldwide partnership network to focus on the crisis and rapidly disseminate knowledge of best practices to build expertise in isolated and underserved communities to prevent and treat COVID-19.

In early August, 2020, in another pivot, ECHO is rapidly expanding its capacity to deliver a program many times larger than its other offerings. ECHO was asked to adapt and scale its model for delivery to nursing home staff and administrators to improve their ability to prevent and treat COVID-19 where the most vulnerable people reside. This is a critical issue as data indicate that the deaths of elderly in nursing homes are approximately 39% of all US deaths due to COVID-19. (3)

Recently, Dr. Arora stated that he believes the biggest health impact from the ECHO model will not be from its direct mission work to impact a billion lives through improved health care. He envisions that the ECHO model will be adapted and used widely to improve public education, reaching even more people. His conviction is based upon substantial public health research that confirms education level as one of the most powerful social determinants of health, i.e. improve education for people and you improve their health. (4)

ECHO's virtual network operating model and community of practice principles are extraordinarily adaptable and are now spreading and scaling worldwide in the field of public education. The 2019 Public Broadcasting System documentary on ECHO features a leading educator in India sharing the best practices from her innovative school with isolated rural teachers and administrators. This movement demonstrates that creative collaboration is an abundant resource. Innovation in one field can be borrowed, repurposed, and rapidly circulated around the world. (5)

Beyond public education, change agents in other domains have also begun to borrow and repurpose the ECHO model. Advocates for better access to the court system for low-income people, specialized police training to work skillfully with mentally ill suspects, and others, are adapting ECHO's network design principles to tackle difficult issues by bringing expertise and best practices from where they are abundant to where they are most needed. The principle to "Move Knowledge, Not People" has universal value.

ECHO is committed to scientific rigor and carefully tracks outcomes from the use of the model. They continue to demonstrate that the quality of care provided with this approach is equal to the quality of care provided directly in the traditional way when patients travel to be treated by experts. As ECHO grows, its continuing commitment to the quality and impact of its services generates recognition and financial support that spurs improvement and innovation. Here are some of the verifiable outcomes.

- Better access for rural and underserved communities
- Reduced disparities in treatment received
- Improved quality and safety of treatment
- Rapid dissemination of best practices
- Increased consistency in care and practice
- Greater efficiency in the delivery of care

ECHO's motto is simple and powerful: RIGHT KNOWLEDGE, RIGHT PLACE, RIGHT TIME. The *secret sauce* in its operating model is its capacity to *increase learning velocity.* Collective wisdom spreads worldwide via readily available technology through a respectful, creative community of practice. Health care practitioners connect with experts and with peer practitioners to learn, share, and grow together. Its expandable design is deeply collaborative. ECHO openly shares its intellectual property, makes training available for free, and aggressively seeks partnerships to join this "hub and spoke," knowledge-sharing network. All of these design features reduce *friction*. With increased flow of ideas and knowledge, the network learns together and adapts rapidly.

Integrate Cornerstone Practices and Cultural Characteristics to Increase Agility

Agility requires Mindset, Heartset, and Skillset. An agile organization has high levels of these attributes.

- Being alert and on the lookout to notice and assess the need to shift direction.

- Maintaining a psychologically safe, respectful, and inclusive work environment so everyone remains connected and engaged to make creative contributions.

- Being nimble, coordinated, and able to shift direction.

Previous lessons have laid out the steps leadiators and organizations can take to integrate the organization and become more agile. The four cornerstone practices and three cultural characteristics are inter related and synergistic. Each one supports and augments the others to increase your organization's agility.

Psychological Safety (Lesson Three BELONGING – the Force of Connection) A sense of belonging grows when people feel safe enough to connect and a willingness to speak up and contribute. Adapting usually requires people to leave their comfort zones and leadiators have a critical role to keep the safety level high enough to encourage them. Everyone needs to be fully engaged with their jobs AND they need to be ready to contribute creative ideas and honest feedback. Adapting can be hard work and everyone needs to share the load.

Dialogue (Lesson Four LEARNING – the Force of Understanding) The foundation practice of dialogue engages the right people in critical conversations to learn from each other and harness the power of diverse perspectives. Open, honest questions and respectful listening invite participation and full, creative contributions. Learning conversations are essential to all the other cornerstone practices. Only dialogue grows a large, reliable conversational learning zone to fully tap the organization's collective intelligence. Successful adaptation requires a clear-eyed, hard-headed view of reality, probability, and possibility.

Growth Mindset (Lesson Four LEARNING – the Force of Understanding) A constructive way of framing all issues and challenges begins with the attitude that you can learn from every challenge and every mistake to improve skills, and build capacity. Change requires an organization to try new things. Trying new things usually involves making mistakes. In order to adapt, these mistakes need to be rapidly transformed into learning that guides the process of adaptation. An adaptive organization maintains a high rate of learning velocity.

Integrity (Lesson Five ENVISIONING – the Force of Moral Imagination and Lesson Seven NAVIGATING – the Force of Conviction) Strength and balance at the core of an organization come from its purpose and ethical character. Ethical character comes from a clear set of values and principles that are fully alive in the organization's practices and processes. Integrity is also structural. Like a well-engineered building, the leadership team, management teams, and operating teams must be well integrated internally and well connected with other teams. Roles, responsibilities, rules, and expectations must be clear, consistently implemented, and accepted so everyone is willing to be accountable as part of a healthy, integrated organization. All of these elements of integrity require leadership that acts in ways that send a consistent message of respect.

Wise Planning (Lesson Six ALIGNING – the Force of Leverage) Aligned with core values and guiding principles, the organization's wise plan is a guide and a lever. The plan's goals and objectives show the organization's leadership team, managers, and employees where to focus (the fulcrum) and how to coordinate their collective efforts (the lever) to move the mission forward amidst change. As previously cited in Lesson Seven, Wise Planning applies the timeless wisdom of Archimedes. "Give me a lever long enough and a fulcrum on which to place it, and I will move the world." (6)

Leadership uses planning to remind everyone of the destination. When facing resource limitations and other difficult realities of change, leadiators must help everyone SEE where the organization is going and WHY it is worth the effort. The tension in the gap between where the organization is and where it wants to go frames the importance of adaptation and change. An organization needs alignment (unity) and well-coordinated effort to leverage available resources into mission results. The leadership team must consistently and clearly communicate with everyone to assure this unified effort.

Values-Based Decision Making (Lesson Seven NAVIGATING - the Force of Conviction) Key decisions always set the course or change the course. They are the adaptation power tools. When an organization can make high consequence decisions that align with core values and principles, this demonstrates integrity and accountability. The leadiator and the organization remain credible in the eyes of employees, investors, funders, community stakeholders, and partners. The resulting trust enables the organization to move with agility and unity at what Stephen M.R. Covey, calls "the speed of trust." (7)

With a clear, disciplined process for making decisions, the organization can hard-wire the process in its divisions and management teams. This builds an ethical culture that can scale through internal growth or by merger with another organization.

Principled Negotiation (Lesson Eight BRIDGING - the Force of Reconciliation) When everyone is already united and already wants to work well together, there is no extra friction to slow down the process of adapting. Every team at every level can orient and respond. However, unresolved conflicts, historic grievances and resentments, relationship tension, and lack of trust produce friction that inhibits collaboration and slows response.

Leadiators and managers need a Mindset, Heartset, and Skillset that faces and engages differences and conflict. When issues arise amidst the stress of changing ways of working, differences can be bridged and reconciled effectively. A peaceful organization can respond and adapt.

Figure 25

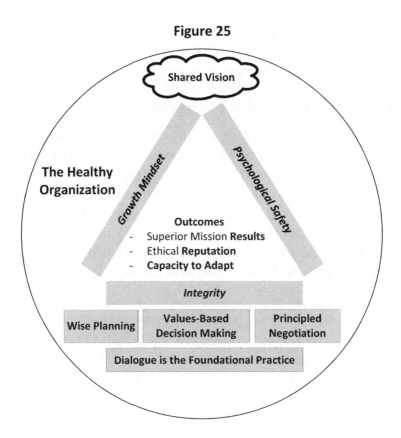

Integration The four cornerstone practices and three cultural characteristics fit together to form a structurally strong, healthy organization. This structure acts as a force multiplier that generates creativity, collaboration, and agility.

A leadiator can guide the organization's examination of its current level of capacity with the assessment tool in the Appendix 8,9, and 10. The tool incorporates the list of cornerstone practices and cultural characteristics, providing seven indicators of organization health.

There are separate versions for a leadership team and a work team. When all work teams across a larger organization, department, or division complete this assessment, the compilation of responses can be useful to assess the larger organization. The assessments can be used as a group discussion checklist for a team, private reflection by a leadiator to consider opportunities to strengthen collaboration, or a survey to get input from others that provides a composite picture of the organization's strengths and weaknesses.

Turn a Flow of Creative Ideas into Innovation

Many of the organizations I have advised must work with significant resource limitations. They are not huge corporations with big research and development budgets. They are not well-funded tech startups trying to disrupt with innovation *home runs* or *moon shots*. They are businesses, nonprofits, and government agencies with 5-5,000 employees. For them, innovation is not some sort of exotic activity. Instead, innovation is a practical discipline that comes in the form of continuous improvement to adapt and thrive. They have the necessity to serve and do more or do better with less.

There are shelves of books on creativity techniques. In Lesson 8, Page 237, there is a checklist of ten questions and actions that can generate ideas. However, the most powerful way for leadiators to generate a flow of ideas in an organization is to create a safe enough environment, regularly invite people to share their ideas, and then always treat what they share with respect by carefully listening and sincerely considering what they hear.

The story of the USS Benfold in Lesson Three is an eloquent example. The needed ideas were literally hiding in plain sight in the hearts and minds of the ship's alienated crew, waiting for a leadiator who had the wisdom to ask. For example, Captain Abrashoff found out that the crew really disliked the regular scraping and painting of the ship to remove rust stains from the superstructure. So he arranged to replace the rust-producing fasteners with rust-resistant, stainless steel fasteners. The net result: decreased menial labor, increased morale, and time saved to devote to performance enhancing training and activities. A simple, practical idea delivered a cornucopia of benefits.

One of the first principles of creativity is to look for ways to adapt existing materials and resources by rethinking an existing approach. Another is to search for others who have solved a similar problem and adapt their solution to your situation. There is an entire society that specializes in this approach, to do more with less. India has been doing this for a long time with a huge population and many people that live on the economic margins of society. For millions of people, the proverb, "Necessity is the mother of invention" is not a quaint saying. It is a day-to-day reality.

The Indians have a word, *Jugaad*, which means frugal innovation. Because it is frugal, it usually involves tremendous practicality, using limited resources to creatively work around or *hack* a problem or situation with an improvised fix born of adversity. Observers of this approach, distill three replicable principles that your organization can apply.

- Keep it simple.
- Do not reinvent the wheel.
- Think and act horizontally. Scale out, not up. (8)

In other words, ***innovation to adapt as an organization is not complicated. Common sense combines with open minds to tap the power of collective intelligence.***

Therefore, innovativeness is a resource in every organization waiting to be tapped. Consider again, the example of the navy ship and the power of simplicity. The ship's captain simply took the time to ask three hundred sailors the same question, *What is one idea you have to make the ship better?* He sorted the answers for the best ideas that were within the ship's operating budget and were not prohibited by naval policies. Then he started trying them. Some worked well. Some worked OK. And some didn't work. He gave credit to the sailors for their ideas. He asked for more ideas, continued to try out the best ideas, and gave credit.

A leadiator doesn't need to know how to innovate. A leadiator needs to know how to generate a healthy supply of creative ideas. People need to believe that they belong and have a contribution to make. A leadiator's example and consistent messaging are critical to *prime the pump* and keep the ideas flowing.

The flow of ideas will not turn into innovation unless the leadiator, leadership team, and managers continue to partner with employees and external partners to turn the most promising ideas into prototypes. There must be a willingness to experiment and see what works and what doesn't. Many organizations have not developed this risk muscle that treats unsuccessful attempts as learning (positive) instead of mistakes (negative). Innovation is a learnable discipline. (9)

Monte del Sol (Lesson 2) did not reinvent the wheel. Mentoring is a well-understood and effective process for human development with centuries of history. In Homer's *the Odyssey,* Odysseus entrusts his son to his good friend, Mentor, to guide his growth and development. MdS took this ancient *wheel* and adapted its design to create a comprehensive program in a community charter school in Santa Fe, New Mexico in 2000.

This *innovation* turbocharged the learning experience of hundreds of students and even changed some students lives. Earlier in this lesson, you learned that Project ECHO is taking its well-designed model (wheel) of working with chronic disease conditions for individual patients and adapting it to a global pandemic at a much larger scale.

The MdS program also followed the principle of thinking and acting horizontally. As they began the program in one grade of the school, learned, improved and then scaled it horizontally to another grade until all the high school students were covered by the program. The ECHO model of "hubs" is a beautiful example of rapid horizontal scaling. The home organization in New Mexico does not keep growing vertically and owning or controlling new programmatic sub parts. Instead, ECHO partners with other organizations horizontally as hubs by fertilizing them with its intellectual property and experience. There is also a higher level of partnership called a "superhub" that receives the authority to provide their own training and the capacity to start additional "hubs." This is a higher form of horizontal scaling.

Every organization has the opportunity to open the faucet of creativity and establish a flow of ideas. This requires leadiators who are willing to be vulnerable, admit they don't know, ask for help, acknowledge mistakes, and be grateful for the ideas they receive from others. In order to find the most promising ideas, an organization needs a steady supply of ideas to consider. The most reliable supply of ideas comes when organizations unleash the powerful life force of collective intelligence.

In the natural world, there is an expression of life force called the *edge effect.* In the edge areas where ecological zones overlap, biodiversity increases with more types of plants, animals, birds, and insects. Organizations can increase the diversity of ideas by structuring overlap between the operating zones of the organization. In this fertile learning zone, the engagement of diverse perspectives generates creative thinking. The Museum of Indian Arts and Culture (Lesson Eight) used the *World Café* to create a learning zone of participants from different tribes and pueblos with diverse perspectives to open the *faucet* of ideas about the museum's future.

**The winning formula for creativity is
DIVERSE PERSPECTIVES + ENGAGED DIALOGUE =
COLLECTIVE, CREATIVE INTELLIGENCE**

Innovation requires the courage to turn a creative idea into a prototype to test and see how it works. Some organization environments are so risk averse that they are unable to innovate. These organizations fail to innovate and adapt because they fear the word FAILURE too much. No organization wants to fail. But failure and mistakes are powerful sources of learning and growth. This is why a Growth Mindset, introduced in Lesson Four, is a critical cultural characteristic to establish the virtuous cycle of CREATIVE IDEA-PROTOTYPE-LEARN-GROW-ADAPT-SUCCEED. *Adaptive organizations love learning more than they fear failure.*

Shape a Flexible Organization Structure for Agile Response

Organizations are malleable, living structures. They can be shaped to reflect lessons learned and respond to changes in the operating environment. These organization development moves may help your organization build a structure that can turn crises and challenges into opportunities to adapt and navigate cascading change.

Confirm Your UNITING Narrative It is easy to become complacent in a calm operational environment when the waves of change are small. If you are blessed with calm seas, use this opportunity to bring your leadership team together. Stress-test your UNITING narrative. *Is each member of your leadership team aligned?* Confirm each element of your steady signal message that will continue to clarify the path forward and help the organization remain aligned to navigate any challenges that lie ahead. MISSION, VALUES, VISION, FOCUS. Make sure each leadiator knows how to show others the way.

There are many examples of organizations with well-crafted statements of mission, beliefs, and values with operations that fall short of their professed identity and ideals. The identity of mission and values must be lived and integrated through consistent actions. When the organization's leadership is consciously aligned, credibility is strong and norms of behavior (HOW we work together and with others) remain clear. A positive culture only takes shape through predictable, constructive behavior over time. *Does your organization clarify what the big core values words mean? Do you have a set of action principles that are intentionally practiced by people at all levels of the organization?*

Now more than ever, amidst the waves of change and uncertainty, every organization needs a compass, UNITING and guiding the organization toward the vision. If your organization is already in lean times or a crisis and hard choices must be made, there is an opportunity to have a transformative dialogue about what matters most. ***An organization that understands its core values can exit a crisis with increased adaptive capacity because its values have been stress-tested, clarified, and affirmed.*** A strong set of core values and guiding principles provide a directional positioning system for key decisions to keep everyone *swimming* together in the right direction.

Choose Employees, Managers, and Partners Who Align It is not so easy to discipline non-conforming employees. It is never easy to fire them. Make sure your hiring, orientation, and evaluation processes are designed to identify people who share your core values and demonstrate the capacity to fit in with your organization culture. This is why the core values need more specific guiding principles and supporting behaviors that orient and explain the expectations. Psychological Safety (Lesson Three) requires trust and trust requires "predictable, constructive behaviors." (Figure 5) When problem behaviors arise, managers must have the confidence and skills to address the issues. Most messy terminations should have been addressed earlier. This is a most common mistake. If orientation to the behavioral expectations needed does not result in correction and alignment, a respectful termination that carefully complies with the law and the organization's procedures is necessary to protect the trust level for everyone else. However, many people with the responsibility to lead and manage are, in my experience, *conflict averse.*

Turn Every Supervisor into a First Responder Change increases pressure and stress in organizations. One of the common symptoms is increased workplace conflict expressed in victim thinking, resentment about increased or decreased workloads, blame-fixing, and other maladaptive reactions to change. Supervisors must be the organization's *first responders* to promptly address conflict situations. They can be trained to confidently triage and address conflict early before it escalates. First responders prevent unhealthy conflict habits from forming. They model positive, proactive engagement. Healthy conflict habits make the organization more adaptable. Supervisors also have day-to-day opportunities to encourage ideas, reinforce lessons learned, and cultivate psychological safety.

Commit to Cross Training Organizations that cross train employees to fill in, shift roles, and combine duties when necessary are better able to flex and adapt to changed circumstances. Making painful cutbacks and operating with less may also provide opportunities to cover responsibilities in more flexible ways or innovate to a different way to fulfill the mission.

Utilize Cross Functional Teams Separated *stovepipes* or *silos* that reflect functional parts of the organization's mission work may be outdated habits rather than wise responses to emerging realities. It is easy for an organization to continue to operate inflexibly and unimaginatively in the absence of rich, creative communication between other parts of the organization. Flexibility is strength. Operational rigidity is not. Interdisciplinary networks of people with different backgrounds and experiences can become a creative resource to *crack the code* on difficult problems.

Create Processes That Tap Collective Intelligence Leadiators need to normalize and broaden the change conversation to remain agile. This requires open forums with healthy, group dialogue that engages the hearts and minds of everyone. There may be a need to address difficult financial or operational constraints, tap the best thinking of your people to solve a novel problem with creativity and wisdom, or review and evaluate important projects and decisions. Leadiators convene diverse perspectives to candidly explore what happened, acknowledge what went well, identify mistakes, harvest lessons learned, and improve in the future.

Excellent organizations in widely disparate fields from military operations, movie production, restaurants, schools, and hospitals have different names for this common practice, e.g. "After-Action Review," "Brain Trust," "Key Decision Audit," "Knowledge Marketplace," "Brain Bank," and "Focused Event Analysis." Likely design elements include presence of multiple perspectives from across the organization, flattening rank and hierarchy to encourage full participation, commitment to candor, and some simple guidelines that support truth-speaking without blame-fixing. Dialogue affirms the reality that "we are in this together; everyone has something to contribute; and we need to stick together." (10)

Your organization needs to know how to make the space for and design participatory meetings that engage everyone. When everyone is feeling overwhelmed with work or circumstances, having a meeting can feel like a waste of time. Time together needs to be an organizational value like it was at Monte del Sol. If you don't know where to begin, the *World Café* (Lesson 8) is a great model. In addition, there is a superb guide on general meeting design. A *Facilitator's Guide to Participatory Decision Making* has specific, well-explained techniques and wise recommendations. It belongs on every leadiator's bookshelf. (11)

Turn Onboarding into an Integration Springboard Adaptation amidst change and uncertainty requires everyone to be fully engaged. Onboarding should not be a check-the-box activity. It is an investment in readiness to fully contribute. How the organization's managers and employees welcome, orient, engage, and integrate new arrivals sends a set of belonging cues (Lesson 3) that prepare them to be full contributors. The onboarding process sets behavioral expectations, sends a message of accountability, and reinforces cultural patterns. The organization's values can come alive on day one. The culture of the organization becomes real.

Distribute Decision-Making Authority and Skills When every request and idea has to go to the top for approval and action, an organization cannot be agile and efficient. Organizations of any size can distribute authority to operating divisions and work teams to make important decisions and authoritative recommendations. People closer to operational action and the customer or client often make more informed decisions. In my experience, when leadiators extend trust and responsibility, they increase engagement and develop employees with greater job satisfaction and higher motivation. In order to build this decision-making capacity, leadiators must model an effective decision-making process that honors the organizations core values and the values of its stakeholders. (Lesson Seven)

Prepare Your Teams to Adapt to Virtual Operating Conditions For most organizations, their operations must embrace a distributed workforce that communicates virtually as the exclusive, or primary means of functioning through late 2021. Some organizations will permanently integrate work-from-home as an important part of their operations. Therefore, leadiators must assure that teams and organizations can function effectively in virtual operations. The three primary challenges that leadiators must overcome to enable virtual collaboration are misunderstandings, miscommunication, and difficulties with coordination. (12)

This is new territory for many organizations. However, large corporations with national and international operations, global non-governmental organizations, and government agencies have been learning how to do this for decades. Every one of the cornerstone practices and cultural characteristics presented in this book becomes even more valuable when an organization must function virtually. These skills and attributes support collaboration by strengthening communication and coordination. When the typical opportunities for physical face-to-face meetings and informal communication are limited or non-existent, leadiators cannot take these building blocks of organizational health for granted.

- *Dialogue* is the gold standard for misunderstanding-free communication that builds positive working relationships. Organizations can offer training to virtual teams and make sure managers know how to facilitate online dialogue in team meetings. Organizations can use large group, virtual formats to gather people for conversations that matter, e.g. The World Café.

- *Psychological Safety* has been shown to help meet the challenge of dispersed operations and virtual communication. (13) In a high anxiety environment, the perception of safety encourages everyone to speak up and contribute. Organizations must select managers to lead virtual teams who understand how to apply the action steps in Lesson Three to earn the trust and confidence of team members.

- When an organization must change and adapt its operations, *Wise Planning* is critical to build understanding. The mission, vision, values, and major goals must be clear. Then distributed operations can stay aligned and coordinate, roles, responsibilities, processes, and tasks to better fulfill the mission.

- *Values-Based Decision Making* enables leadiators and other decision makers to communicate well and ensure understanding by distributed employees and stakeholders. The organization demonstrates accountability, establishes *Integrity*, earns credibility, and builds trust. The organization remains unified and on course.

- Virtual communications have inherent limitations. Therefore, leadiators must do everything in their power to help managers and virtual team members develop the skill of **Principled Negotiation**. Without this skill, unmanaged conflict and disagreement can quickly erode virtual communication, diminish effective coordination, and damage team functioning.

- When an organization culture promotes a **Growth Mindset**, this open, honest approach to mistakes and learning generates knowledge sharing throughout the distributed organization. Creative ideas flow and multiple perspectives can be engaged to search for innovation opportunities.

Use the worksheet in Appendix 8, 9, and 10 to evaluate your current virtual practices and assess additional steps your organization can take to improve its capacity to collaborate virtually.

Choosing Agile Responses: Wisdom-in-Action

The choices and challenges ahead are not likely to be easy. As a leadiator, you can seek wisdom from ancient and modern sources to deepen the capacity to guide and encourage an organization. The work of Schwartz and Sharpe and other neuroscientists clearly connects traditional wisdom teachings from indigenous, western, and eastern sources to leading edge research on the functioning of the brain. *Perennial wisdom about collaboration provides practical principles that integrate with emerging knowledge about the brain and decision making.* (14)

One of the most widely recognized experts on the nature of leadership, John Maxwell, said, "Leaders KNOW the way, SHOW the way, and GO the way." This maxim elegantly integrates perennial elements of wisdom for modern leadiators. (15)

Purpose (Know the Way) Wisdom is rooted in deliberate, calm, purposeful awareness. Leadiators can guide others through a practical process to align principles and actions. Do the right thing (WHAT), for the right reasons (WHY), and in the right way (HOW).

Presence (Show the Way) Leadiators always lead with the example of integrity in their behavior and their decisions. They consistently show up with wise, virtuous qualities that build trust and inspire others to join, work, learn, and stick together.

- *Be values-based and principles driven* Risk and uncertainty abound amidst accelerating change. Firm connection to core values and guiding principles is *North* when you are navigating. Leadiators and organizations make decisions and plans by consciously choosing to align with their moral compass.

- *Be humble* Avoid arrogance and fill in blind spots by listening carefully to different perspectives. A leadiator recognizes the limits of her knowledge and understanding. Admit uncertainties and ask for help. Make "I don't know" a natural part of your approach along with "Let's find out" and "What do you think?"

- *Be centered* Remain calm and patient. Remain aware of emotions while avoiding reactivity or being flooded with feeling. Emotions are a source of information about what matters and what may be at risk. Emotions may be indicators that point toward something important, but they are not, in their inherent nature, wisdom.

- *Be open hearted* Empathy and compassion will strongly connect a leadiator with what the organization, colleagues, and stakeholders value and need. Difficult choices can be painful. Acknowledge the discomfort of necessary tradeoffs in right vs. right decisions.

- *Be courageous* Turn toward what is difficult to face. Leave the comfort zone to embrace diversity and engage with those who see things differently. A leadiator always lets others know that he stands together with them.

Practice (Go the Way) Leadiators are diligent practitioners and teachers of **D**esigned **N**ecessary **A**ctions. These skilled behaviors build and sustain collaboration over time. Leadiators earn trust with their competence in day-to-day actions that consistently align well with principles.

270

- **_Seek perspective_** Improve your view of the situation, issue, and choices to better understand who is affected, what is important to them, and what is important to you.

- **_Promote dialogue_** Willingly engage others with open questions and deep listening to learn together how to move forward constructively. Move beyond *either-or* to explore *both-and* possibilities

- **_Access intuition_** Find a silent space and become centered. Listen for the still, small *voice* of your moral compass that may point toward a bigger perspective beyond personal priorities toward fundamental fairness or a practical balance between extreme positions.

- **_Tap the moral imagination_** Apply lessons learned and the positive examples of people you admire to find an effective, ethical way to navigate challenges. (*What would* _____ *do?*) Consciously seek to reconcile or balance differing interests. Integrate action with priority values and principles.

- **_Develop precautionary foresight_** Acknowledge uncertainties. Weigh the probability and magnitude of risks and consequences before acting. Accept the burden of leadership to go beyond the expedient, short-term option. Be a steward of the future for others.

Wisdom comes down to the ability to make the best choice possible with the available information when you make a decision or offer wise counsel to others. Two interconnected processes are at the heart of the essential life practice of decision making, as a decision maker or as an advisor to others. First, you need to clearly perceive and comprehend the reality of the situation. Second, you must be able to reflect upon this comprehension and then discern what is most important in order to choose wisely.

Clarity of perception and discernment of importance go beyond raw intellectual capacity. Intuition, common sense, life experience, and emotional intelligence all contribute to being wise.

When a leadiator remains in the humble position of a life-long learner, no matter how educated or experienced, she gains more capacity to think clearly and understand what matters, moving towards wisdom. When he fails to do so, he moves away from wisdom. Lesson Seven provides a disciplined decision-making process that encourages fair consideration of different perspectives and wise reflection.

Wisdom in action has three elements.

- **Common sense** to pragmatically grasp the situation and the possibilities

- **Humility** to admit mistakes, listen to others, and learn from them

- **Ethical intelligence** to align right purpose and guiding values with action

---

To thrive in the Age of Adaptation, leadership teams need to stretch and move beyond their current level of capacity. They must move out of denial and transform limiting patterns of interaction. They must become proactive and responsive instead of reactive.

Leadiators must guide the organization to embrace, adapt, and move with the waves of change. The leadiators needed in this emerging era are women and men at all organization levels who are always uniting others, facilitating learning, and strengthening the capacity to adapt and work together in collaboration.

Like it or not, organizations are a form of community where many of us spend a significant percentage of our lives. Leadiators must accept the responsibility to be guardians of the organizational community's culture and health. Therefore, amidst accelerating change, it is up to leadiators to be practitioners and teachers of a change mindset and a common language that unifies the organization internally and with its external partners.

If you are ready to engage others in a serious dialogue about your organization's future, you can begin here.

Action Steps

- **Confirm the vision** Leadiators must help others see what success looks like and link the desired destination with the initiatives and changes needed.

- **Connect everyone to the leading edge of change** Leadiators must be evangelical to spread the word and engage many in the necessary collective effort to adapt and grow.

- **Find a way through** Leadiators must resolutely identify what is in the way and focus the effort to navigate past the barriers (structure, attitude, skills, resources) that keep the organization in status quo mode.

- **Change behaviors to change minds. Belief in a possible future will not precede practical action. People need to deliberately practice their way into believing that it is possible to thrive amidst change.** Leadership must keep the focus on key behaviors that can be changed to support a mental and emotional framework that will sustain the movement toward the vision.

- **Examine your example** Review the assessment in Appendix 8 for yourself as a sole leader, or for your leadership team and consider your strengths and weaknesses.

- **Begin with small steps** Sustainable change requires a structure. Take action to integrate the cornerstone practices and the cultural characteristics with a set of intentional steps.

Inquiry into Action

- *How can I set the example as a leadiator?*

- *As a leadership team, how can we set the example?*

- *What are my/our strengths to build on?*

- *What are the weaknesses/gaps we need to address in order to build a more agile, adaptive organization?*

- *How can we establish and maintain an open and engaging organizational structure?*

- *How can we use proven approaches like cross-training, cross-functional teams, and large group review of important decisions, events, and challenges to tap diverse perspectives and collective intelligence?*

- *How can we begin to use or improve our use of these approaches?*

- *How can our leaders and managers develop the willingness and skills to engage employees and stakeholders and elicit their ideas, contributions, and concerns?*

- *How can our managers become first responders with the training and coaching needed to address conflict, concerns, and problems when they arise?*

Core Ideas From Lesson Nine

Adapting requires the ability to move with agility. With increased agility an organization can respond skillfully to uncertainty and change instead of reacting.

Leadiators cannot predict the future. They can enable it by integrating the cornerstone practices of Creative Collaboration into a unified, flexible organization that can move agilely as one.

Innovation to adapt as an organization is not complicated.

Common sense combines with open minds to tap the power of collective intelligence.

Every organization has the opportunity to open the faucet of creativity and establish a flow of ideas. This requires leadiators who are willing to be vulnerable, admit they don't know, ask for help, and be grateful for the ideas they receive from others.

The winning formula for creativity is DIVERSE PERSPECTIVES + ENGAGED DIALOGUE = COLLECTIVE, CREATIVE INTELLIGENCE

An organization that understands its core values can exit a crisis with increased adaptive capacity because its values have been stress-tested, clarified, and affirmed.

Perennial wisdom about collaboration provides practical principles that integrate with emerging knowledge about the brain and decision making.

Conclusion

Common Sense for Uncommon Times

Wisdom meaning judgment acting on experience, common sense, available knowledge, and a decent appreciation of probability.

~ Barbara Tuchman *Historian*

Swimming Together

I arrived in Europe in 2017 to support the World Health Organization with an initiative called "The Respectful Workplace." My job was to introduce a respectful process for making ethical decisions using dialogue about values.

Europe was in the midst of a migrant refugee crisis like the trend forecast by the futurist in 2005 (Lesson Nine). The situation overwhelmed the capacity of the European Union countries to respond and adapt.

At a video training center in Budapest, Hungary, I stood in front of a camera and a large video screen delivering an interactive presentation to participants in Egypt, Iran, Iraq, Pakistan, Tunisia, Afghanistan, and Jordan. I was in a place I had never been before, speaking with people I did not know who were located in countries I had never visited. I was in unknown waters for a 21st century swimming lesson.

We were linked together by state-of-the-art technology in a collaborative, learning conversation. The question we discussed was, "How can your worldwide organization grow its unified capacity to adapt and address the current decision-making challenges?" As each participant spoke, the software's voice activation seamlessly shifted the primary video window, placed the current speaker in the center of the high definition screen, and returned the previous speaker to a small window frame at the bottom. There were no glitches or noticeable delays in the conversation.

I didn't know it then, but this novel experience (for me) would soon become commonplace for millions of us. In early 2020, every organization began to function through this technology to navigate the waves of a virus pandemic that almost overnight, stopped every organization on the planet from functioning in all the ways leaders take for granted.

I left Hungary with growing conviction that every organization needs to become a healthy, learning community. Only by UNITING can an organization generate and sustain the capacity for an intelligent, coordinated, and innovative response to the challenges ahead. Technology will continue to play a central role to connect us, but it is not nearly enough. Organizations need a shared blueprint so they can coordinate and move together as one.

I have integrated the futurist's 2005-2025 forecast about the critical nature of adaptive capacity with the past 15 years of experience to propose three assumptions that organizations must embrace in their planning and operations.

- Organizations need everyone to engage and contribute their full creative capacity in order to respond and adapt to the waves of change and uncertainty.

- Organizations need a practical, resourceful framework (Mindset, Heartset, Skillset) to build and sustain adaptive capacity.

- Organizations can only become fully resourceful through disciplined practices that consistently generate learning velocity and a flow of creative ideas that produce innovations. (1)

> *The only way for human beings to learn fast enough and adapt effectively in this strange landscape is to implement a 21st century version of what humans have done since the Upper Paleolithic era about 40,000 years ago. Form communities of mutual support, coordinated action, and innovation.*

In other words, we need to *swim* together. Think of an organizational community as a school of fish and Creative Collaboration as a form of organized swimming amidst the growing waves of change. Join together, learn together, and stick together. Project ECHO (Introduction and Lesson Nine) is a successful model of a technologically enabled, globally networked community that can adapt and scale to the size of the waves.

For many of us, the community outside of our immediate families where we *swim* the most is the workplace. Then, there are organizations where we affiliate: faith-based organizations, nonprofits, and neighborhood associations. These are the *communities* where each of us can engage, participate, and have influence. These communities can become centers of hope amidst the larger forces of change. In these centers, we have the opportunity to recognize our interdependence and *swim* together by learning, adapting, and responding.

Listen to the Common Sense Wisdom of the Heart

Organizations need leadiators who are catalysts, bringing people together to creatively collaborate. Therefore, I want to speak directly to your wise heart. Discern what is essential and what is possible by intentionally using the resources in this guide for UNITING BY DESIGN. Imagine that you are a leadiator who can bring wisdom to your community. Wisdom is not so common, but it is within everyone's reach. The writer Samuel Taylor Coleridge helps us demystify this powerful word. "Common sense in an uncommon degree is what the world calls wisdom." (2)

Recognize That This Time Is Different We live on a beautiful planet. Earth's ecosystems with their diverse species of life are threatened. An estimated 2.0 billion more people will arrive in the next thirty years. Increased pressure to meet the needs and desires of all these people will intensify these threats. (3) Financial and health issues that arise on the other side of the world will continue to rapidly cascade through our globally integrated systems to affect people far away. Common sense understanding of the size of these challenges points to the importance of joining together to marshal strong, creative responses. Adaptive responses are needed at all levels: international; national; regional; and local.

Have Conviction that We Are Better Together Common sense points to the urgent need for UNITING and resourceful action. The phrase I use for this higher level of resourcefulness is Creative Collaboration. When people fully engage, they unleash forces of learning, understanding, and possibility. People become capable of action from "the better angels of our nature." They bring out the best in each other. (4)

Act Locally Within Your Sphere of Influence You are a member of multiple communities. With resourceful leadiatorship, each one of these communities can grow in health, UNITING by design. Experience and common sense confirm that anyone can become a leadiator, take action with others on a small scale, and make a difference. Helen Keller, the visionary social activist, said, "Alone we can do so little, together we can do so much." (5) It is unwise to ignore opportunities to act locally while waiting for national and international leaders to step up and take dramatic, large scale actions.

Tap the Renewable Power of the Heart The size of the challenges can become emotionally and rationally overwhelming. People can be left without clarity about what to do or the heart to act. "Heart" means spirit ("stout-hearted"), character ("faithful heart"), and willingness ("whole-hearted" effort). In the past two decades, developments in neuroscience and imaging provide us with greater knowledge about the extraordinary design of the operating system of the whole human being. The sophisticated communication network of brain and heart is not yet fully understood. However, this network seems to be deeply implicated in the social bonds of empathy and belonging that grow our capacity to work together, build trust, and sustain healthy relationships with emotional intelligence. In our hearts, we can recognize and know, e.g. "In my heart, I knew she was right," "my heart went out to him," and "I want to know whether you have the heart for this." (6)

21st century knowledge about mind-body connection aligns with perennial messages of wisdom traditions, indigenous elders, spiritual teachers, and poets around the world who universally affirm the heart as a source of wisdom, deeply connected to the design of the intelligence system of consciousness in each human being. However, this remarkable power source requires each of us to make a journey of conscious recognition. *What is essential? Is now the time to act? What is my particular way to step forward, connect with others, and contribute?* Agnes Baker Pilgrim, a member of a circle of wise elders called the Council of Indigenous Grandmothers, reminds us that this journey is long. "The greatest distance in the world is the 14 inches from our minds to our hearts." (7)

Practice, Practice, Practice Sustainable Creative Collaboration is not possible without a continuous flow of predictable actions directly connected to the heart. A leadiator guides an organization with shared meaning and purpose deeply rooted in acts of respect, caring, and generosity. With this guidance, an organization can continuously regenerate enough trust and collective will to sustain focused, resourceful effort over time.

Without heart-felt commitment, the inevitable challenges that arise between individuals and within organizational structures will interfere with the connective, relationship tissue necessary to stick together. The civil rights movement of the 1960's reminded everyone to "keep your eyes on the prize." We need moral imagination to lift our eyes toward a brighter horizon with the possibility of better days. Remember the long vision of Tomorrow's Women (Lesson Five) that rests in the belief in future generations of women leading their peoples to peace. Remember Jasminka (Lesson One) as she stood in the ruins of a Bosnian city and imagined a youth center where peace was possible. Remember how Project ECHO (Lesson Nine) sees a world with a billion people receiving better health care. Remember Monte del Sol (Lesson Four) helping every student find her place in the world. Organizations need vision in order to keep moving forward together. However, vision must be deeply connected with practice. Organizations need to use the Mindset and Heartset of Creative Collaboration to practice the Skillset.

Share the Load Now is the time for leadiators to support good people to stand together and share responsibility. You can learn from courageous leaders who faced great challenges and persevered. They didn't do it alone. They engaged and enrolled others to join them. The civil rights leader, Lena Horne, said, "It's not the size of the load that breaks you down. It's the way you carry it." (8) We can show each other how to carry the load and, at times we can help another carry it together.

When you think of the big picture of all that is happening now and the uncertainty about what will happen, confusion, fear, or despair could arise. A sense of isolation and powerlessness promotes that kind of mental/emotional state. However, our reality is interdependence. When you come out of isolation and seek diverse perspectives, you begin to see more clearly amidst complexity. Partners and trusted advisors help you maintain a Growth Mindset so you and others ALWAYS learn from every mistake and setback, grow stronger together, and overcome difficulties with the victory of learning. As Nelson Mandela said, "I never lose. I either win or I learn." (9)

> *Leadiators can step up with the Mindset, Heartset, and Skillset to serve others and bring them together to share the load.*

Say NO! to Cynicism The journey of UNITING is not sustainable without leadiators who demonstrate courage and hope. These embodied virtues radiate a positive force that builds organizational health, unity, and adaptive capacity. You can help others engage by spreading hope in an environment where anxiety and fear can isolate, alienate, and paralyze. We need each other to act courageously in the face of difficulty.

Cynicism prevents courage and hope from developing in the heart and generating the will to act. Healthy skepticism about the practicality of the Mindset-Heartset-Skillset resource model presented in this book is natural and welcome. However, beware of the cynical voice that disempowers so many in this world. Relentless waves of negative media and social media messages shape individual and collective perceptions of what is possible. Some of these messages are designed to manipulate.

People are subject to form a belief that the situation is too big, too complicated, and nothing can be done. A belief that it is too complex or too hard leads to a self-fulfilling prophecy that nothing will make any difference. If so, why bother making the effort?

CALL TO ACTION – Be a Leadiator and Force Multiplier for the Common Good

Our civil society can be strengthened by thousands of small, positive forces UNITING in workplaces, faith-based organizations, neighborhoods, nonprofits, coalitions, alliances, and communities. We need the adaptive capacity to come together, learn together, innovate together, and stick together.

We need wise leadiators who want to be a force for UNITING with the Mindset, Heartset, and Skillset to guide others. Traditional leaders can grow into leadiators (a ship captain in Lesson Three and a head learner in Lessons Two and Four). People without a title and formal authority can step forward with good will and strong hearts to become leadiators (a school teacher in Lesson One and an employee with a lunch tray in Lesson Eight).

The blueprint in this book has been actively field-tested to guide the building of Creative Collaboration. The organization architecture is sound. The resources of Mindset, Heartset, and Skillset provide you and other emerging leadiators with clarity about what to do, why it matters, and how to engage with others to take action. However, this approach is not an algorithm or a rigid checklist. A true leadiator helps others use an uncommon degree of common sense to adapt these design principles to an organization's unique history, setting, and challenges.

> *The essence of Creative Collaboration is adapting.*

Collaboration only becomes robust and creative when it goes beyond basic cooperation. Creative Collaboration is cooperation PLUS+++.

Leadiators facilitate the meaningful alignment of positive purpose and positive principles with positive action.

A leadiator with resources becomes a force multiplier. A force multiplier makes other people better together. A force multiplier's words and deeds have ripple effects that touch others she has never met. A force multiplier generously gives away his lessons learned and good ideas. A force multiplier taps the renewable energy of the heart by inspiring and encouraging others to have real hope. This is not just a wish for better days. Real hope is an alchemical mixture of wisdom, moral imagination, and common sense action. When hope develops from disciplined practices and daily action steps, it becomes a radiating, positive force.

Hope can grow in the heart because working together in creative alignment makes sense, no matter how things turn out. Each leadiator who rises above fear with **COURAGE**, above despair with **HOPE**, and above cynicism with **WISDOM**, assumes a small, important place in a large movement of UNITING to respond to the challenges of our times, right now.

Frame your situation carefully. Reflect on your life through the lens of your multiple roles: parent, colleague, professional, employee, manager, neighbor, faith-based community member, nonprofit board member, and community volunteer.

- *Where are you connected to organizations?*

- *Do you already have formal decision-making authority as a leader or manager?*

- *If you do not have formal authority to lead, do you have influence with a formal leader as a trusted advisor or a participant in important decisions?*

- *What is the need for people to come together by UNITING in your organization or community?*

- *How might you take the first step to show up with the capacity of a leadiator?*

You frame a situation accurately when you keep the stakeholders who are affected in the center of your field of vision. As you reflect on what can be done, you need cognitive intelligence for practicality and emotional intelligence for connection to others. These ways of knowing through the mind and the heart operate like a set of binocular lenses that can be focused together with intention. This combination allows you to practically assess the situation, develop empathy for others who are engaged, and reflect upon what is important to them.

The Mindset and Heartset of a leadiator can become a positive catalyst that initiates and helps cultivate the nine collaborative forces needed for people to adapt and navigate change together: Clarity; Perspective; Connection; Understanding; Moral Imagination; Leverage; Conviction; Reconciliation; and Agility.

With empathy for the people (including yourself) who may be affected, you can exercise moral imagination. This uniquely human ability can generate a picture of how various options may unfold and mobilize the will to act. This ability is directly connected to wisdom. With moral imagination you can begin to use the Skillset of a leadiator and guide others.

Now it is time to act.

- You have a blueprint to guide the process of building Creative Collaboration.

- You have a set of honest, respectful questions to begin a dialogue that engages others in important conversations about your organization's health and its future.

- You are a part of one or more organizations: a business, government, or nonprofit workplace, a nonprofit board or volunteer, a member of a faith-based community, or a member of a neighborhood association. Your organization may be a part of a coalition, partnership, or alliance of organizations working together.

- You have four cornerstone practices and **D**esigned **N**ecessary **A**ctions to form a healthy organizational culture.

- You have core values and guiding principles as a compass to keep you on course as Creative Collaboration emerges.

Listen to your wise heart.

- *Do you have conviction that your organization or your community needs UNITING to become more healthy, resilient, and adaptable in these times?*

- *Are you willing to become a leadiator who serves others as a force multiplier?*

- *Do you want to be a leadiator UNITING others by design?*

- *Are you ready?*

Hope is always accompanied by the imagination,
the will to see what our physical environment
seems to deem impossible.

Only the creative mind can make use of hope.

Only a creative people can wield it.

~ Jericho Brown *Poet (10)*

The Force of Positivity

I AM a hopeful leadiator expecting positive results

from UNITING others, no matter what I see around us.

We will continue to organize and collaborate creatively.

We will face all challenges together.

We will celebrate our victories.

We will turn any every mistake or setback into learning.

We will navigate forward with moral imagination.

Endnotes

Introduction

1. Peter Diamandis and Steven Kotler, *The Future is Faster Than You Think: How Converging Technologies Are Transforming Business, Industries, and Our Lives*, Simon and Schuster, (2020)

2. https://www.youtube.com/watch?v=QqvUz0HrNKY Accessed November 9, 2020

3. Paul Wilson, *Disturbing the Peace, Chapter 5: The Politics of Hope*,

4. https://en.wikiquote.org/wiki/V%C3%A1clav_Havel quote Accessed October 30, 2020

5. *Project ECHO: A Democracy of Knowledge* https://www.pbs.org/video/project-echo-a-democracy-of-knowledge-d2nejv/ Aired November 21, 2019 Accessed October 30, 2020 https://en.wikiquote.org/wiki/Present#L Accessed October 30, 2020

6. Annual Message to Congress (December 1, 1862) https://www.goodreads.com/quotes/72422-the-dogmas-of-the-quiet-past-are-inadequate-to-the Accessed November 10, 2020

7. Michael McMaster, *The Intelligence Advantage: Organizing for Complexity*, Butterworth-Heineman, 1996, 9-14

Lesson One

1. Author interview with Jasminka Drino Krilic

2. Corrie Ten Boom, *Clippings From My Notebook*, T. Nelson (1982)

3. Lou Gerstner, *Summary: Who Says Elephants Can't Dance*, BusinessNews Publishing (2014), 20

4. IBM 2010 Global CEO Study: Creativity Selected as Most Crucial Factor for Future Success https://www-03.ibm.com/press/us/en/pressrelease/31670.wss Accessed November 1, 2020 This interview of over 1500 CEOs, senior managers, and senior public sector leaders represent all sizes of organizations in 60 countries and 33 industries.

5. Dan Lovallo and Olivier Sibony, *"The Case of Behavioral Strategy,"* McKinsey Quarterly 2:30-45 (2010)

6. Stephen M.R. Covey, *The Speed of Trust: The One Thing That Changes Everything 26*, Free Press (2006)

7. Steve Jobs, https://www.quotespedia.org/authors/s/steve-jobs/if-you-are-working-on-something-that-you-really-care-about-you-dont-have-to-be-pushed-the-vision-pulls-you-steve-jobs/ Accessed November 11, 2020

8. Stanley McChrystal, et al. *Team of Teams: New Rules of Engagement for a Complex World* Penguin/Portfolio (2015) The team of teams framework was developed and field-tested on the complex 21st century battlefield and has migrated to non-military organizations that must adapt to complexity, uncertainty, and change.

9. W. Felps, T. Mitchell, and E. Byington, *"How, When, and Why Bad Apples Spoil the Barrel: Negative Group Member and Dysfunctional Groups," Research in Organizational Behavior* 27 (2006). For a highly readable explanation, see Daniel Coyle, *The Culture Code: The Secrets of Highly Successful Groups*, Bantam Books (2018), 3-6

10. Eric Berne, *A Layman's Guide to Psychiatry and Psychoanalysis* (Penguin 1976) 295, see generally, https://en.wikipedia.org/wiki/Identified_patient Accessed November 1, 2020

11. Satya Nadella, 9-18-17 *Fast Company* https://www.fastcompany.com/40457458/satya-nadella-rewrites-microsofts-code Accessed November 11, 2020

Lesson Two

1. Muriel Rukeyser, https://www.goodreads.com/author/quotes/30010.Muriel_Rukeyser Accessed November 5, 2020

2. Alan Kay, https://quoteinvestigator.com/2018/05/29/pov/ Accessed November 5, 2020

3. Daniel Kahneman, *Thinking Fast and Slow*, Farrar, Straus and Giroux (2011) 85-88

4. Ibid. See also, Edward Russo and Paul Schoemaker, *Winning Decisions,* Currency/Doubleday (2002) and, by the same authors, *Decision Traps* Doubleday (1989). The various biases are covered in detail throughout the work of these authors.

5. John Dewey https://www.quotenova.net/authors/john-dewey/q5w76w Accessed November 5, 2020

6. Kahneman, *Thinking Fast and Slow* 408-418. These universal principles are distilled from my decades of experience to align with the author's closing observations about speed and perspective in decision making.

7. Ibid.

Lesson Three

1. Michael Abrashoff, *It's Your Ship: Management Lessons From the Best Damned Ship in the US Navy,* Warner Books (2002)

2. David Foster Wallace, quoted in https://www.newyorker.com/books/page-turner/this-is-water Accessed November 7, 2020

3. There are many examples. An excellent resource on this topic is Daniel Coyle, *The Culture Code: The Secrets of Highly Successful Groups*, Bantam Books (2018) 3-6. The author identifies best in class organizations and reverse engineers the common elements of their healthy cultures to crack the code on universal principles to apply. See also, James Collins and Jerry Porras, *Built to Last: Successful Habits of Visionary Companies*, HarperBusiness (1994).

4. Stephen R. Covey and Rebecca Merrill, *Summary: First Things First* 11, Business News Publishing (2013)

5. Charles Duhigg, *What Google Learned From Its Research to Build the Perfect* Team, New York Times Magazine (February 25, 2016) https://www.nytimes.com/2016/02/28/magazine/what-google-learned-from-its-quest-to-build-the-perfect-team.html Accessed November 20, 2020

6. Amy Edmondson, *Teaming: How Organizations Learn, Innovate, and Compete in the Knowledge Economy*, John Wiley and Sons (2012) and *The Fearless Organization: Creating Psychological Safety in the Workplace for Learning, Innovation, and Growth*, Wiley (2019)

7. Edmondson, *The Fearless* xiv-xxi. The author's extensive research findings that support this declaration are spread throughout the book. However, her summary of the range of research findings is covered in Chapter 2, *The Paper Trail*.

8. Edmondson, The Fearless Organization 4-5

9. Edmondson, The Fearless Organization 103-123

10. Eric Schmidt, From University of Pennsylvania Commencement Address, 2009 http://www.quotationspage.com/quote/40991.html Accessed November 1, 2020

11. Tom Peters, *Thriving on Chaos: Handbook for a Management Revolution*, HarperCollins (1987)

Lesson Four

1. Alfred Mehrabian, *Silent Messages,* Wadsworth (1971) https://en.wikipedia.org/wiki/Body_language Accessed November 14, 2020

2. C. Otto Scharmer, *Essentials of Theory U*, Berrett-Koehler (2018) 43-47. See also, Adam Kahane, *Solving Tough Problems: An Open Way of Talking, Listening, and Creating New Realities,* Berrett-Koehler (2007)

3. John Dewey, https://www.goodreads.com/quotes/7702317-a-problem-well-defined-is-a-problem-half-solved Accessed November 14, 2020

4. Edmondson, *The Fearless Organization* 154

5. Attributed to many. https://quoteinvestigator.com/2015/02/03/you-can/

6. Peter Senge, *The Fifth Discipline: The Art and Practice of the Learning Organization Second Edition*, Deckle-Edge (2006) (original edition published in 1990) and Peter Senge, et al., *The Fifth Discipline Fieldbook,* Currency/Doubleday (1994)

7. Rick Hanson, *Hardwiring Happiness: The New Brain Science of Contentment, Calm, and Confidence,* Harmony Books (2013). For an excellent summary of the principles, see the author's short article, https://greatergood.berkeley.edu/article/item/how_to_grow_the_good_in_your_brain Accessed November 16, 2020

8. Donald Hebb, Canadian neuropsychologist, https://en.wikipedia.org/wiki/Hebbian_theory Accessed December 10, 2020

9. Carol Dweck, *Mindset: The New Psychology of Success,* Ballantine Books (2006, 2016) 108-146

10. Satya Nadella, *Fast Company* September 18, 2017

11. https://www.fastcompany.com/40457458/satya-nadella-rewrites-microsofts-code Accessed November 11, 2020

12. Ibid.

13. Satya Nadella, *Hit Refresh: The Quest to Rediscover Microsoft's Soul and Imagine a Better Future for Everyone,* HarperCollins (2017)

14. Attributed to many. https://quoteinvestigator.com/2017/05/23/culture-eats/ Accessed November 15, 2020

15. Dweck, *Mindset* 263. Examples of the behaviors of fixed and growth mindsets are discussed at length throughout this excellent resource. A diagram on this page provides a visual summary of the differences.

16. Ibid.

Lesson Five

1. Margaret Mead,
    https://quoteinvestigator.com/2017/11/12/change-world/
    Accessed November 22, 2020

2. Paul Hawken, From a 2009 commencement address at the
    University of Portland, referenced in Anne and Jeffrey Rowthorn,
    God's Good Earth: Praise and Prayer for Creation, 326, Liturgical
    Press (2018)

3. Tomorrow's Women website,
    https://tomorrowswomen.org/about/ Accessed November 22,
    2020

4. Nelson Mandela, *Long Walk to Freedom: The Autobiography of
    Nelson Mandela* Nolwazi (1994)

5. Simon Sinek, *Start with Why: How Great Leaders Inspire Everyone
    to Take Action* Portfolio/Penguin (2009). The author's much
    watched TED talk can be viewed at
    https://www.ted.com/talks/simon_sinek_how_great_leaders_insp
    ire_action?language=en Accessed November 22, 2020

6. Mark D. Bennett and Joan McIver Gibson *A Field Guide to Good
    Decisions: Values in Action*, Praeger (2006) xvi

7. Ibid, 3-9.

8. https://www.centura.org/about-centura/mission-and-values
    Accessed December 12, 2020

9. John Paul Lederach, *The Moral Imagination: The Art and Soul of
    Building Peace,* Oxford University Press (2005)

10. See epigraph from Rosabeth Moss Kanter at beginning of this
    lesson.

11. Robert F. Kennedy, campaign slogan paraphrasing the words of
    George Bernard Shaw.
    https://politicaldog101.com/2018/03/robert-kennedy-did-george-
    bernand-shaw/ Accessed November 22, 2020

12. Steve Jobs, https://www.reddit.com/r/quotes/comments/ gn9oja/if_you_are_working_on_something_that_you_really/ Accessed November 22, 2020

13. Interview with CIL Executive Director, Tony Delisle. For more information about CIL, see their website http://www.cilncf.org/about-us/ Accessed November 22, 2020

Lesson Six

1. Website of the city of Howard, South Dakota https://www.cityofhoward.com/about Accessed November 24, 2020 website

2. Detailed account in the excellent book on change in organizations and communities, Chip and Dan Heath, *Switch: How to Change Things When Change is Hard*, Broadway Books (2010) 67-71

3. Patrick Lenconi, *The Advantage: Why Organizational Health Trumps Everything* 141-151, Jossey-Bass (2012)

4. Benjamin Tregoe, cited in George Dixon, *What Works At Work: Lessons From the Masters*, Lakewood (1988) 256

5. Peter Schwartz, *The Art of the Long View,* Doubleday/Currency (1991)

6. *Original credit to George Doran, There's a S.M.A.R.T. Way to Write Management's Goals and Objectives, Management Review, Vol. 70, Issue 11, pp. 35-36 (1981). This concept is widely used in planning work.*

7. Robert S. Kaplan and D.P. Norton, The Strategy-Focused Organization: How Balanced Scorecard Companies Thrive in the New Business Environment. *Harvard Business School Press (2000). For examples, see* https://www.google.com/search?sa=X&sxsrf=ALeKk03_yH1H13Cf3J Rs2ljaRfinalQLhQ:1606330289997&source=univ&tbm=isch&q=bala nced+scorecard+examples+of+companies+pdf&client=firefox-b-1-d&ved=2ahUKEwjlys7Srp7tAhUEwVkKHY6zAgsQjJkEegQICBAB&biw =1685&bih=1020 Accessed November 25, 2020

Lesson Seven

1. Dan Lovallo and Olivier Sibony, *"The Case of Behavioral Strategy,"* McKinsey Quarterly 2:30-45 (2010)

2. Centura Health website https://www.centura.org/about-centura Accessed December 21, 2020

3. Archimedes, https://www.goodreads.com/quotes/207927-give-me-a-lever-long-enough-and-a-fulcrum-on Accessed November 25, 2020

4. Sam Kaner et al., *Facilitator's Guide to Participatory Decision-Making , 2nd ed.*, Jossey-Bass, (2007) 275-287

5. Ibid. See also, David Straus, How to Make Collaboration Work: Powerful Ways to Build Consensus, Solve Problems, and Make Decisions 58-66 Berrett-Koehler (2002)

Lesson Eight

1. Juanita Brown and David Issacs, The World Cafe: Shaping Our Futures Through Conversations That Matter, Berret-Koehler (2005)

2. http://www.theworldcafe.com/ The website generously offers guidance and recommendations for using the process.

3. William Ury, Getting to Peace: Transforming Conflict at Home, at Work, and in the World, Viking (1999) 41-56

4. Arlie Hochschild, Interview, https://onbeing.org/programs/arlie-hochschild-the-deep-stories-of-our-time/ Accessed March 3, 2021. See Arlie Hochschild, Strangers in Their Own Land: Anger and Mourning on the American Right, The New Press (2016)

5. Ury, Getting to Peace, 3-26

6. There is a well-developed set of resources that describe the field of Principled Negotiation. It is also called "Interest-based Negotiation," "Mutual Gains Negotiation," and "Win-Win Negotiation." Two excellent references are Roger Fisher and William Ury, Getting to Yes: Negotiating Agreement Without Giving In Second edition, Penguin, (1991) and William Ury, Getting Past No: Negotiating in Difficult Situations, Bantam (1991)

7. Proposed by Alex Osborn, leading expert on creativity in 1953. It was further developed by Bob Eberle in 1971 in his book, SCAMPER: Creative Games and Activities for Imagination Development. Prufrock Press (2008)

8. Luke Behncke, Mental Skills Training for Sports: A Brief Review in Athletic Insight, The Online Journal of Sports Psychology http://peterliljedahl.com/wp-content/uploads/SkillsPDF.pdf Accessed December 20, 2020

9. Although there are many examples, Nelson Mandela stands out as a master of bridge building and reconciliation amidst extreme challenges. See many examples in this fine book that summarizes his philosophy and strategy. Richard Stengel, Mandela's Way: Lessons on Life, Love, and Courage, Crown (2010) 135

10. Ibid. See also Desmond Tutu and Mpho Tutu, The Book of Forgiving: The Fourfold Path for Healing Ourselves and Our World, HarperOne (2014)

Lesson Nine

1. https://csis-website-prod.s3.amazonaws.com/s3fs-public/legacy_files/files/publication/7r-key-developments.pdf Accessed December 21, 2020

2. Nathan Bennett and G. James Lemoine, *What VUCA Really Means to You* Harvard Business Review, January-February 2014 https://hbr.org/2014/01/what-vuca-really-means-for-you Accessed December 21, 2020

3. https://www.nbcnews.com/know-your-value/feature/39-covid-19-deaths-have-occurred-nursing-homes-many-could-ncna1250374 Accessed December 21, 2020

4. https://www.thelancet.com/journals/lanpub/article/PIIS2468-2667(20)30144-4/fulltext Accessed December 21, 2020

5. *Project ECHO: A Democracy of Knowledge* https://www.pbs.org/video/project-echo-a-democracy-of-knowledge-d2nejv/ Aired November 21, 2019 Accessed October 30, 2020

6. https://www.goodreads.com/author/quotes/661188.Archimedes Accessed December 21, 2020

7. Stephen M.R. Covey, *The Speed of Trust: The One Thing That Changes Everything*, Free Press (2006)

8. Navi Radjou and Jaideep Prabhu, *Frugal Innovation: How to Do More With Less,* Economist (2015). See also, Ted talk by Navi Radjou, https://www.ted.com/talks/navi_radjou_creative_problem_solving_in_the_face_of_extreme_limits?language=en Accessed December 21, 2020

9. See generally, Tom Kelley, *The Ten Faces of Innovation*, Tom Kelley, Currency/Doubleday (2005). IDEO is well-recognized as an leader in the understanding of the method, mystery, and magic of innovation in organizations. For a detailed account that demystifies IDEO's magic, see Coyle, *Culture Code* 49-154, 160-161.

10. Coyle, *Culture Code 98-99*. Edmondson, *Fearless Organization* 157-158

11. Kaner et al., *Facilitator's Guide*

12. Edmondson, *Teaming* 201-205

13. Edmondson, *The Fearless Organization 43*

14. Barry Schwartz and Kenneth Sharpe, *Practical Wisdom: The Right Way to Do the Right Thing*, Riverhead Books (2010). See also Stephen Hall, *Wisdom: From Philosophy to Neuroscience* Vintage Books (2010) for the author's distillation of the eight neural pillars of wisdom.

15. John Maxwell, The Right to Lead, Simple Truths LLC (2009) https://www.inc.com/peter-economy/44-inspiring-john-c-maxwell-quotes-that-will-take-you-to-leadership-success.html Accessed December 21, 2020

Conclusion

1. See generally, Kelley, *Ten Faces of Innovation*.

2. Samuel Taylor Coleridge, The Complete Works of Samuel Taylor Coleridge, Volume 5, 2012, Ulan Press.

3. https://www.un.org/development/desa/en/news/population/world-population-prospects-2019.html Accessed October 30, 2020.

4. This comes from the closing paragraph of Abraham Lincoln's 1st Inaugural Address, delivered on March 4, 1861: "I am loath to close. We are not enemies, but friends. We must not be enemies. Though passion may have strained it must not break our bonds of affection. The mystic chords of memory, stretching from every battlefield and patriot grave to every living heart and hearthstone all over this broad land, will yet swell the chorus of the Union, when again touched, as surely they will be, by *the better angels of our nature*."

5. Helen Keller, *The Story of My Life* General Press (2018)

6. For a general overview of this topic, see https://en.wikipedia.org/wiki/Emotional_intelligence. See Daniel Goleman, *Working With Emotional Intelligence* Chapter 4 The Inner Rudder, Bantam (1998). Goleman is a pioneer in this field.

7. https://www.idlehearts.com/authors/agnes-baker-pilgrim-quotes Accessed October 30, 2020.

8. https://www.goodreads.com/quotes/314889 Accessed October 30, 2020.

9. Nelson Mandela, *Nelson Mandela by Himself: The Authorised Book of Quotations*, Pan Macmillan South Africa, 2011.

10. https://kenyonreview.org/conversation/jericho-brown/ Accessed October 30, 2020.

Bibliography and Resources

In the knowledge economy of the 21st century, the futurist, John Naisbet observed, "We are drowning in information, but starved for knowledge." I have only included in this list a curated selection from a much longer list of worthy resources about the themes I developed in this book.

I have included the resources that most directly influenced my thinking in order to respectfully acknowledge the authors' works.

The list is organized under primary themes. Many of these books cover multiple themes in this book, so I have placed it under the theme that relates most directly to its influence on my thinking. As most of us have insufficient time to read as much as we would like, I place my top recommendation first in each category with an *asterisk.

DIALOGUE

Facilitator's Guide to Participatory Decision-Making, 2nd ed., Sam Kaner et al., Jossey-Bass, 2007. Many collaborative groups need help to generate respectful, powerful dialogue that keeps the decision-making process focused and moving forward. A skilled facilitator can play an essential role in challenging situations. This book is a superb resource providing the tools and methods that groups need to stick together, dialogue, and make decisions.

The World Cafe: Shaping Our Futures Through Conversations That Matter, Juanita Brown and David Issacs, Berrett Koehler, 2005. This open-source social technology describes a valuable, flexible, easy-to-use process for fostering collaborative dialogue, sharing mutual knowledge, and discovering new opportunities for action. It has been "field-tested" all over the world for two decades bringing together groups of 12-1200 in all sectors. The website provides excellent guidance to get you started. www.theworldcafe.org

Solving Tough Problems: An Open Way of Talking, Listening, and Creating New Realities, Adam Kahane, Barrett-Koehler 2004, 2007. This is an inspiring guide by someone who has worked on some of the toughest problems in the world. It all comes down to the ways to bring people together to truly talk and listen to one another. Simple to state, not so easy to practice successfully.

Dialogue and the Art of Thinking Together, William Issacs, Doubleday/ Currency, 1999. When decisions have impacts beyond the individual, it is often necessary to 'think together' in order to come up with a superior decision that anticipates concerns and is based on the values that matter most. Thinking together requires dialogue, and this book by an experienced practitioner deepens our understanding of the way to do it.

DECISION MAKING

* Thinking Fast and Slow, Daniel Kahneman Farrar, Straus and Giroux, 2012. One of the most important thinkers in neuroscience and decision making, a psychologist and winner of the Nobel Prize in economics, explains the two thinking systems that drive the way we think and how they work together to shape our judgments and decisions.

A Field Guide to Good Decisions: Values in Action, Mark D. Bennett and Joan McIver Gibson, Praeger, 2006. A practical guide to using values to make difficult decisions with clear illustrations for use by organizations, leaders, and groups. The book provides a five-step process to harness the power of diverse perspectives to make and communicate decisions that demonstrate integrity and accountability, earning trust and credibility.

Decisive: How to Make Better Choices in Life and Work, Chip Heath and Dan Heath, Crown, 2013. Provides a clear blueprint to the principles and road map for better decisions. The authors clearly illustrate each principle with evocative stories from corporations, NGOs, and communities.

How Good People Make Tough Choices: Resolving the Dilemma of Ethical Living, Rushworth Kidder, William Morrow Publishers, 1995. This is a good overview of the subject of ethics and making difficult decisions with integrity. The author uses true case study examples drawn from government, corporate and personal experience to illustrate his approach. He provides a specific three-part model for examining ethical dilemmas.

COLLABORATION

*Mindset: The New Psychology of Success__How We Can Learn to Fulfill Our Potential, Carol S. Dweck, Ph.D., Ballantine Books, 2006, 2016 (updated version). A leading researcher on how to turn around public schools that serve students living in poverty, has exported her findings to organizations. It is "mindset" that holds the key and she demonstrates the power of a "growth mindset" that encourages continued learning and development. Learning together is at the heart of Creative Collaboration.

How to Make Collaboration Work, David Straus, Berrett-Koehler, 2002. Provides a clear model of the architecture of collaboration with examples. The description of the use of a "process map" to create a path forward is particularly helpful.

The Power of Collective Wisdom and the trap of collective folly, Alan Briskin et al. Berrett-Koehler 2009. Skilled guidance on how to navigate beyond groupthink and polarization to reach the promised land of the extraordinary potential of united minds and hearts working together to do extraordinary things.

Teaming: How Organizations Learn, Innovate, and Compete in the Knowledge Economy, Amy Edmondson, Jossey-Bass, 2012. The author is a researcher and thought leader who has broadened our understanding of creative collaboration as the essential capacity for a fast-moving, successful 21st century organization.

The Art of Gathering: How We Meet and Why It Matters, Priya Parker, Riverhead, 2018. The author is a master facilitator and conflict resolution specialist who provides a useful framework to increase intentionality and construct more effective containers for group interaction.

WISDOM AND PLANNING

* Wisdom: From Philosophy to Neuroscience, Stephen S. Hall, Vintage, 2011. A comprehensive, interdisciplinary journey that blends modern science, history, and philosophy. The author is an experienced science journalist who mines the current research for nuggets of wisdom.

Practical Wisdom: the Right Way to Do the Right Thing, Barry Schwartz and Kenneth Sharpe, Riverhead Books, 2010. Integrates current neuroscience with ancient philosophy to examine ways to cultivate wisdom within organizational systems. The proliferation of rules and incentives in modern life erodes the capacity to develop judgment and wisdom.

Wiser: Getting Beyond Groupthink to Make Groups Smarter, Cass R. Sunstein and Reid Hastie, Harvard Business Review Press, 2015. The authors draw on wide organization experience to update the classic work on the perils of "Groupthink" where honest, diverse contributions are distorted or thwarted by a variety of group dynamics. The second half of the book presents eight strategies that improve group dynamics and increase collective intelligence.

The Dance of Change: The Challenges to Sustaining Momentum in Learning Organizations, Peter Senge et al. Doubleday/Currency, 1999. Written by leaders in the organization learning movement. This book provides a theory and a large toolbox for the practice of possibility and wise action. You don't need to read the whole book. Just open it, look around, and find something to inspire and help you.

Manifesto for a Moral Revolution: Practices to Build a Better World, Jacqueline Novogratz. Henry Holt and Company, 2020. The author is a philanthropist with deep experience building collaborative relationships. Her creative work with social entrepreneurs worldwide is informed by a deep commitment to core values and guiding principles. The book is filled with inspiring stories of moral imagination and Creative Collaboration that succeeded against large odds.

The Future is Faster Than You Think: How Converging Technologies Are Transforming Business, Industries, and Our Lives, Peter Diamandis and Steven Kotler. Simon and Schuster, 2020. The level of acceleration in technology in the next ten years will represent as much change in the world as the previous one hundred years. The authors describe the specific innovations in the pipeline that will transform every sector of our lives. They assert that the technology solutions to our largest problems are coming. The unanswered question is whether human beings are capable of the collaboration necessary to implement the solutions.

The Art of the Long View: Planning for the Future in an Uncertain World, Peter Schwartz. Doubleday/Currency, 1991. The author is a leading futurist who helped pioneer the use of alternative scenarios as a way to plan for and engage the inherent uncertainty of the future. Though written almost thirty years ago, the author's predictions about the increase in uncertainty and volatility are even more relevant today.

LEADERSHIP AND ORGANIZATIONS

* The Culture Code: the Secrets of Highly Successful Groups, Daniel Coyle, Bantam, 2018. The author is a skilled storyteller who has reverse-engineered breathtakingly diverse, ultra-successful organizations to identify a *code* that is common. The code has three parts: Build Safety; Share Vulnerability; and Establish Purpose. Each section ends with practical recommendations for leaders to put the code into practice.

The Fearless Organization: Creating Psychological Safety in the Workplace for Learning, Innovation, and Growth, Amy Edmondson, John Wiley and Sons, 2019. A leading academic researcher with deep consulting experience inside organizations makes the case that psychological safety is the foundation for full engagement by employees that leads to superior performance. If you want to examine the evidence, the author provides extensive references to research studies.

The Intelligence Advantage: Organizing for Complexity, Michael McMaster, Butterworth-Heinemann, 1996. A very useful view of organizations as organisms that can be shaped for intelligence and adaptability. The book offers clear design principles, effective management ideas, and constructive work practices.

Primal Leadership: Realizing the Power of Emotional Intelligence, Daniel Goleman, Harvard Business School Press, 2002. A leading authority on emotional intelligence builds on his earlier work and focuses on the qualities of effective leaders who are transparent and able to speak directly and courageously about what matters to them.

Switch: How to Change Things When Change is Hard, Chip and Dan Heath, Broadway, 2010. The authors present an elegant, simple formula to respond to complexity and change. The book is very readable and filled with stories from all organization sectors. It has been translated into over 20 languages. It is an excellent backgrounder for a team that needs to come together and respond to change.

The Advantage: Why Organizational Health Trumps Everything Else in Business, Patrick Lenconi, Jossey-Bass, 2012. Every organization that wants to accomplish its mission at the highest level must invest in the development and maintenance of a healthy organizational environment. This consultant and writer of several best-selling books on teams and organizational performance underscores the critical nature of an aligned leadership team that "over communicates their clarity" about mission, values, vision, and strategy to everyone else.

PEACE AND BRIDGING DIFFERENCES

* Getting to Peace: Transforming Conflict at Home, at Work, and in the World, William Ury, Viking, 1999. This book provides a taxonomy of ten roles for leadiators. Only peaceful organizations have the opportunity to fully carry out the mission. Of particular value to a leadiator is clear framing of the work to prevent conflict and bridge differences using the roles of provider, teacher, and bridge-builder.

Mandela's Way: Lessons on Life, Love, and Courage, Richard Stengel, Crown, 2010. Do not dismiss the relevance of the leadership of Nelson Mandela to your situation because he was a great man. Mandela's example offers superb guidance and inspiration to leadiators everywhere. His principles and strategies to build bridges and generate the force of reconciliation have been tested in extreme circumstances.

The Power of a Positive No: How to Say NO and Still Get to YES, William Ury, Bantam, 2007. There is great power in simplicity. This elegant book looks at the core of critical communications about boundaries, forks in the road, and vital choices. Leadiators need to guide with positivity, firmness, principles, and love. The guidelines in this book are practical and powerful to bring candor, principles, and compassion to key conversations.

The Moral Imagination: The Art and Soul of Building Peace, John Paul Lederach, Oxford University Press, 2005. In the quest for wisdom that can guide collaborative action, this author draws on deep experience as a peace builder in difficult situations around the world to underscore the power of imagination aligned with principle.

Appendices

1. Psychological Safety - Assess Your Leadership As an Individual and a Team

2. Assess Your Team's Dialogue Skills

3. Improve Dialogue With Open Questions

4. Prepare for Wise Planning

5. Summary of the Decision-Making Steps

6. Decision Communication Worksheet for Step 7

7. Decision Audit Worksheet: Reflect on the Process and the Results to Learn

8. Health Assessment #1 Creative Collaboration - Leadership Team

9. Leadership Assessment Worksheet

10. Health Assessment #2 Creative Collaboration - Work Team

11. Leading Virtual Collaboration – a Checklist

1. Psychological Safety - Assess Your Leadership As an Individual and a Team

Prepare for a leadership discussion about Psychological Safety. Rank your current level of performance for the activities described in each bullet: 5 Excellent; 4 Good; 3 Fair; 2 Poor; 1 Not at All . Rank your own level and the level of your leadership team as a group. In your discussion, explain the reasoning for your rankings.

Providing Context

- Frame the nature of the work. (Have I been clear enough about the interdependencies of our work that require openness and everyone's voice? What does everyone need to understand about the current and emerging challenges? Have I made it clear that we can acknowledge and learn from failure as a necessary part of our work?) Ranking: _____

- Affirm mission and purpose. (Is our WHY vibrantly clear to everyone? Why do we make a difference? Who do we serve? Does everyone understand where we are going together?) Ranking: _____

- Breathe life into core values and action principles. (Does everyone understand the standards for our work and the way we treat each other? Does everyone understand how we turn our values into practical action?) Ranking: _____

My Observations and Ideas to Discuss:

Facilitating Engagement and Speaking Up

- Be open and humble. (*Help me think this through… I am not sure how to proceed. What do you think?... I blew it. Let's discuss how I can do a better job with issues like this in the future… There's always more to learn and we need everyone's perspective to fill in the gaps.*) Ranking: _____

- Establish dialogue/learning conversation as the norm for important conversations. (Do I ask open and honest questions because I want to know the answer? *How do you see this issue? Walk me through your reasoning so I can better understand your concerns?* Do I balance how much I talk with how much I listen and seek to clarify my understanding? Do I patiently grow wider, deeper conversations?) Ranking: _____

- Build an organizational container that encourages psychological safety. (Have I thought about ways that our structure and channels of communication can consistently draw forth questions, concerns, and ideas at all levels of the organization? Can I observe the signs of full engagement? Am I vigilant for the warning signs of a lack of psychological safety?) Ranking: _____

My Observations and Ideas:

Responding Constructively

- Lead with respect and gratitude. (Do I generously listen? Do I regularly let others know that I value their contributions? Do I sincerely thank people who come to me with problems, concerns, and questions?) Ranking: _____

- Turn mistakes into learning. (When there is a mistake, failure, or bad news, do I take a positive approach that emphasizes learning, offers help, and moves things forward?) Ranking: _____

- Maintain healthy boundaries. (Do I clarify where the behavioral guardrails are? Do I even-handedly enforce consequences when conduct is serious enough to merit action? Do I provide coaching and orientation to influence future positive behaviors by the individual, and by other members of the team?) Ranking: _____

My Observations and Ideas:

2. Assess Your Team's Dialogue Skills

Key Behaviors	Current Level
	5= We do this well
	1= We do this poorly

Don't Beat Around the Bush Speak directly and clarify what has meaning and importance for you.

R.E.S.P.E.C.T. Speak respectfully and honestly at all times.

Air Traffic Control Only one person talks at a time. Do not cut others off and avoid 'cross-talk.'

Candor Without Aggression Express disagreement directly and honestly without making any personal attack or negatively characterizing the motives, beliefs, or ideas of others.

Question to Understand Ask open and honest questions that invite others to clarify their views and increase your understanding of their goals, needs, and concerns.

Share the Back Story When you have a strong position, share it AND describe the reasoning that led you to this opinion, recommendation, or conclusion.

Adopt a Learning Mindset Listen with the intent to learn rather than confirm what you already believe or find a weakness in their position.

Leave Some Oxygen for Others Be brief and share the air time so others have a full opportunity to speak.

Connect the Dots Link ideas and highlight common threads or areas of possible agreement.

3. Improve Dialogue With Open Questions

Uncovering Values	Considering Stakeholders (Individuals or groups who have a stake in the issue)
Why is this important to you?	
What's important here to examine?	What are our duties and obligations here? To whom?
What do you think lies at the heart of the matter?	Who should we consider as we make this decision? Why?
What matters to you most in this situation?	Who will bear the burden of this decision?
What can you tell me that will help me understand the importance of this issue to you?	What seems to be important to them?
What is significant about this question for you?	What standards do you think they (name a stakeholder group) will use to judge the fairness/rightness/goodness of our decision?
What is at risk in this issue?	
What worries you about this issue?	What do you think the effects/consequences (intended and unintended) of our decision will be for _____?
How are our core values and other important values in tension here?	What impact will this have on the value perceived by those we serve?

Ethics and Principles	Outcomes
How do you know that this is (not) the right thing to do?	*What would you like to see come out of this? Why?*
What makes this an inappropriate way to proceed?	*What do you hope for?*
What standards should we use to make this decision?	*When we look at the balance of costs and benefits for this option, what does that tell us?*
Why do you think this a good decision?	*When we look back on this decision one year from now, how will we know we did the right/best thing?*
What is the fairest course of action for our community stakeholders? Why?	*If your teenager asked why you made this decision, what would you say to her?*
If _____ (a person you respect for her wisdom and integrity) were here and we asked for her perspective, what do you think she would she say to us?	*How would you explain the basis for this decision if the daily newspaper ran a front page story on this issue, and quoted you about the decision you propose to make?*

4. Prepare for Wise Planning

Prudence - Avoid Common Mistakes ❖ Insufficient Commitment (lack of motivation) ❖ Wrong Group Composition (lack of key perspectives) ❖ Inattention to Important Values & Principles (lack of integrity) ❖ Inadequate Opportunities for Dialogue About Concerns and Ideas (lack of candor) ❖ Need for Practical Foresight by Planning Team (lack of awareness of risk and uncertainty) ❖ Failure to Track and Use Success Indicators (lack of accountability) ❖ Flawed Execution (lack of will and discipline)

Make a Commitment - Set Clear Intention

1. Is there a leadership consensus about the need for the planning effort and the desired outcomes?

2. Is there shared commitment by senior leadership and management to invest the time, energy, and money that will be necessary to plan effectively and fully execute the plan?

Confirm the Scope - Identify Necessary Plan Elements to be Developed

3. Do we already have a clear, compelling Mission statement? Do we already have a clear statement of our core values and guiding principles? If so, do we need to review them as part of the planning process?

4. Is there a current assessment of the operating environment? If not, how should we prepare one?

5. What is our planning horizon? (Usually 1-3 years amidst so much change) Do we already have an inspiring, shared Vision of where we want to be at the end of the plan in ___years?

6. Do we already have a solid plan that needs to be updated or do we need a full set of new goals, objectives, action plans, and success indicators/performance measures?

Tap Collective Intelligence - Engage the Right People With Key Perspectives

7. Who needs to be directly involved in a core planning team that will shape the plan?

8. Who needs to be interviewed directly to provide influential input to the core planning team? Who needs to provide perspective through surveys, focus groups, or other indirect channels?

9. Do we need a facilitator/consultant to help us design the process, guide us, and support our ability to work together effectively?

10. What roles/responsibilities need to be assigned during the planning process? E.g. Do we need a few people to coordinate the effort? Who will update employees, staff, and other stakeholders?

Become Ready - Provide the Necessary Information, Resources and Logistics Support

11. Do we have a full assessment of our most recent strategic plan to inform our current effort? (a. progress made; b. list of unachieved goals and objectives; and c. lessons learned)

12. What relevant information exists about our current organizational performance? (a. financial results; b. satisfaction levels of customers, stakeholders, employees; c. budget forecasts)

13. In our operational mission space, what relevant information could be useful to the planning participants? (trends, best practices of partners and competitors, opportunities and challenges)

14. What is a suitable location? (Size, convenience, seating/tables, wall space for posting notes)

15. What is the timeline and schedule? What additional resources are necessary? (AV, food, materials)

Execution and Credibility - Coordinate Follow Through and Build Accountability for Results

16. Who needs to be informed about the final plan?

17. How will we maintain accountability for execution and results? (a. track progress with goals, objectives, and actions; b. document results; and c. inform stakeholders)

18. Who will be responsible for overseeing each part of the plan during the execution phase?

19. How will we regularly review the plan, assess progress, and course-correct when necessary?

20. What communication channels will we use to share key information with stakeholders about the execution phase and the results? When?

5. Summary of the Decision-Making Steps

Plan the Steps to a Strong Decision

Step	Focus Questions and *Activity*
1. ENGAGE by simply listening to each person's initial perspective to lay the foundation for a learning dialogue.	**What point of view do I bring to this decision?** *(Each person takes a few minutes to describe how they see the situation and highlights what seems important.)*
2. EXPLORE the range of values and principles involved in this decision.	**Who are the affected stakeholders AND what is important to them?** *(the group works together to develop a comprehensive list of individuals and groups to consider. Then, identify what matters to them.)*
3. ELEVATE your focus to the priority values to guide your choice among the options available.	**Which 2-3 values must be at the heart of our decision?** *(Each person takes a turn to advocate for what is most important with their supporting reasons. The decision maker(s) should go last.)*
4. EXPAND and refine the available options with as much thought and creativity as time permits.	**How can we expand upon the obvious alternatives to increase our options?** *(Group discussion)*
5. EDUCATE each other about the consequences and risks. (the downside)	**What are the probable and possible negative consequences of each option in addition to the desired outcomes that we intend?** *(Group discussion)*
6. EVALUATE and choose the option that most closely aligns with priority values. Review the risks of your preferred option to develop a plan to mitigate the downside or confirm your willingness to accept the consequences. each other about the consequences and risks. (the downside)	**Which option aligns best with the priority values?** *(Each person makes a recommendation to the decision maker(s) about the best option. This includes his or her reasoning AND the downside of the option. After hearing from everyone, the decision maker(s) presents the decision with reasons and risks. If anyone thinks the decision maker(s) don't fully appreciate the risks, they have a final opportunity to advise.)*
7. EXPLAIN the decision to affected stakeholders (those benefited, burdened, and concerned) in plain, candid language. Include the reasoning that supports the decision and the downside.	**How can we credibly communicate this decision to those who need to understand what was done, why it was done, and why it is a good decision?** *(The decision maker(s) consults with the group to receive their advice and ideas.)*

6. Decision Communication Worksheet for Step 7

Step 7: Explain the Decision So Stakeholders Understand

Step/Question(s)	Notes
Essential Background to 'Tell the Story' *Why did we need to make this decision now?* *What process did we use to make the decision?* *What alternatives were considered?* Set context to help audience understand. Demonstrate your seriousness and diligence. If appropriate to audience, begin the communication with this background	
Decision: What is decision/recommendation? Make a clear, direct statement **Responsibility**: Who made the decision/recommendation and is accountable? Be accountable. Own decision. If a group, provide names and titles.	
Guiding Values and Benefits: *WHY is the right decision... a good decision?* Clarify the values reasoning that supports the conclusion to take this action. Confirm any measures to assess the outcome and demonstrate accountability.	
Downside: *What difficulties and burdens do you recognize will or could be experienced?* Level with stakeholders about negative consequences and risks. Consider what, if anything, you are willing to do mitigate these negatives (P.14). Be concrete and accountable about any plant to mitigate the downside.	

7. Decision Audit Worksheet: Reflect on the Process and the Results to Learn

1. **Clarity and Responsibility** *What was the decision and who is accountable for it?*

2. **Ethical Reasoning** *Which values guided the decision? Why did the decision maker(s) believe it was the right thing to do?*

3. **Benefits** *What were the positive outcomes?*

4. **Costs** *What were the negative costs/consequences?*

5. **R.O.D. (Return on Decision)** *Did the benefits outweigh the costs? By how much? Rank the decision on a 5 to 0 scale (5 is a complete success and 0 is a complete failure)*

6. **Respect for Stakeholder** *How well were stakeholders concerns considered and addressed during the decision-making process? Was the decision honestly communicated to them so they could understand?*

7. **Lessons Learned** *What can we learn from the way we made this decision and the outcomes that resulted? How can we turn our mistakes into lessons (a valuable asset) that we can implement to make stronger decisions in the future? What changes will we make to improve our critical decision-making process?*

8. Health Assessment #1 Creative Collaboration – Leadership Team

Definition: CREATIVE COLLABORATION is work together that accomplishes more than is possible separately. This capacity within a leadership team is an excellent diagnostic indicator of overall organization health because the role models of leaders who work well together are essential to build a collaborative organization. When an organization collaborates well as a whole, and within its divisions and teams, the organization can adapt to challenges or setbacks and successfully implement plans that fulfill its mission. These behaviors require leadership by example. This assessment provides useful feedback to deepen your conversations about three characteristics of the culture of a healthy, collaborative organization and the use of four cornerstone practices. **For each statement, indicate your opinion of the leader or leadership team's current capacity. Some questions focus on the conditions in the organization that may reflect on the capacity of the leadership team. If you do not know or can not agree or disagree because the action within the organization is inconsistent, mark the undecided circle. Additional discussion may be needed to clarify the organization's capacity.**

Organization Culture Characteristic #1: INTEGRITY Internal (employees, staff, volunteers) and external (customers, investors/funders, community partners, and suppliers) stakeholders have a high level of trust in the organization and its leaders. They are confident that everyone will act ethically at all times.

1. The organization has well-defined core values (e.g. Integrity) with accompanying principles that set clear standards and guide the way we do our work and the way we treat others.

o	o	o	o	o
5. Strongly Agree	4. Agree	3. Undecided	2. Disagree	1. Strongly Disagree

2. Everyone on the leadership team understands how the values and principles apply to their work responsibilities.

o	o	o	o	o
5. Strongly Agree	4. Agree	3. Undecided	2. Disagree	1. Strongly Disagree

3. Members of the leadership team consistently treat each other according to our values and principles.

o	o	o	o	o
5. Strongly Agree	4. Agree	3. Undecided	2. Disagree	1. Strongly Disagree

4. The leadership team, as a group and as individuals, understand what is important to the people we serve (clients, customers, colleagues) and respect them.

o	o	o	o	o
5. Strongly Agree	4. Agree	3. Undecided	2. Disagree	1. Strongly Disagree

5. Leaders provide a clear, consistent, and ethical example at all times.

o	o	o	o	o
5. Strongly Agree	4. Agree	3. Undecided	2. Disagree	1. Strongly Disagree

6. Managers provide a clear, consistent, and ethical example at all times.

o	O	o	o	o
5. Strongly Agree	4. Agree	3. Undecided	2. Disagree	1. Strongly Disagree

7. Leaders actively encourage everyone to raise any ethical concerns and, when they do, leaders follow through to determine whether action is necessary.

o	o	o	o	o
5. Strongly Agree	4. Agree	3. Undecided	2. Disagree	1. Strongly Disagree

8. Managers actively encourage everyone to raise ethical concerns and, when they do, managers follow through to determine whether action is necessary.

o	o	o	o	o
5. Strongly Agree	4. Agree	3. Undecided	2. Disagree	1. Strongly Disagree

Organization Culture Characteristic #2: PSYCHOLOGICAL SAFETY
Leaders practice consistent behaviors that build and sustain a work environment where people speak up because everyone's contribution matters and no one's dignity is at risk.

9. In this organization, people are held accountable but mistakes are not held against people.

o	o	o	o	o
5. Strongly Agree	4. Agree	3. Undecided	2. Disagree	1. Strongly Disagree

10. As a leadership team member, I can bring up problems and tough issues.

o	o	o	o	o
5. Strongly Agree	4. Agree	3. Undecided	2. Disagree	1. Strongly Disagree

11. People in the organization are never rejected or excluded for being different.

o	o	o	o	o
5. Strongly Agree	4. Agree	3. Undecided	2. Disagree	1. Strongly Disagree

12. As a member of the leadership team and as a leader within the organization, it is safe for me to take a risk.

o	o	o	o	o
5. Strongly Agree	4. Agree	3. Undecided	2. Disagree	1. Strongly Disagree

13. It is easy to ask other leadership team members for help.

o	o	o	o	o
5. Strongly Agree	4. Agree	3. Undecided	2. Disagree	1. Strongly Disagree

14. I am confident that no one on the leadership team would deliberately act in a way that undermines my efforts.

o	o	o	o	o
5. Strongly Agree	4. Agree	3. Undecided	2. Disagree	1. Strongly Disagree

15. In my work with other leadership team members, my unique skills and talents are valued and utilized.

o	o	o	o	o
5. Strongly Agree	4. Agree	3. Undecided	2. Disagree	1. Strongly Disagree

16. The Leader engages all members of the leadership team with consistent, positive communication.

o	o	o	o	o
5. Strongly Agree	4. Agree	3. Undecided	2. Disagree	1. Strongly Disagree

Organization Culture Characteristic #3 GROWTH MINDSET Leaders practice consistent behaviors to reinforce a shared belief that everyone can continually improve the capacity to work together by learning from all mistakes and challenges.

17. Throughout the organization from the top down, when mistakes happen, people admit them, discuss them, and learn from them.

o	o	o	o	o
5. Strongly Agree	4. Agree	3. Undecided	2. Disagree	1. Strongly Disagree

18. Leadership promotes open channels of growth-promoting positive feedback and constructive criticism that flow in all directions (up, down, across departments/divisions).

o	o	o	o	o
5. Strongly Agree	4. Agree	3. Undecided	2. Disagree	1. Strongly Disagree

19. Leaders and managers focus on the well-being of employees and treat them as collaborators, as a team.

o	o	o	o	o
5. Strongly Agree	4. Agree	3. Undecided	2. Disagree	1. Strongly Disagree

20. There is a high level of employee commitment to the organization because employees believe leaders "have their backs."

o	o	o	o	o
5. Strongly Agree	4. Agree	3. Undecided	2. Disagree	1. Strongly Disagree

21. Leadership supports risk-taking and fosters innovation (putting new ideas into practice).

o	o	o	o	o
5. Strongly Agree	4. Agree	3. Undecided	2. Disagree	1. Strongly Disagree

22. In hiring, leaders emphasize potential capacity and passion for learning more than credentials and past accomplishments.

o	o	o	o	o
5. Strongly Agree	4. Agree	3. Undecided	2. Disagree	1. Strongly Disagree

23. There is an active program to engage employees (including leaders and managers) and help them develop on the job (coaching, workshops, apprenticeships). The organization regards capacity as something that will be gained through effort.

o	o	o	o	o
5. Strongly Agree	4. Agree	3. Undecided	2. Disagree	1. Strongly Disagree

24. The organization uses open forums with participation by employees to review major projects and initiatives, assess successes and mistakes, and develop lessons learned.

o	o	o	o	o
5. Strongly Agree	4. Agree	3. Undecided	2. Disagree	1. Strongly Disagree

Core Practice #1: DIALOGUE Leaders establish an environment filled with learning conversations that engage everyone's knowledge, skills, and creativity.

25. Leadership team meetings are safe forums where each member is willing to contribute their ideas and be listened to with respect.

o	O	o	o	o
5. Strongly Agree	4. Agree	3. Undecided	2. Disagree	1. Strongly Disagree

26. Leaders actively seek input from other members of the team on a range of important issues.

o	o	o	o	o
5. Strongly Agree	4. Agree	3. Undecided	2. Disagree	1. Strongly Disagree

27. Leaders seek input from employees and stakeholders and follow up with communication about how the input was used or considered.

o	o	o	o	o
5. Strongly Agree	4. Agree	3. Undecided	2. Disagree	1. Strongly Disagree

28. As a leadership team and one-to-one, we have meaningful opportunities to talk together, share ideas, and learn from each other.

o	o	o	o	o
5. Strongly Agree	4. Agree	3. Undecided	2. Disagree	1. Strongly Disagree

29. Leadership team members support the use of cross-functional teams to address challenging organization-wide issues by engaging people with different expertise and perspectives.

o	o	o	o	o
5. Strongly Agree	4. Agree	3. Undecided	2. Disagree	1. Strongly Disagree

30. Leadership team members always listen respectfully to others within and outside the team.

o	o	o	o	o
5. Strongly Agree	4. Agree	3. Undecided	2. Disagree	1. Strongly Disagree

31. The Leader (CEO/ED/President/Director) engages all members of the leadership team in two way communication to make sure they know their responsibilities and what is expected of them.

o	o	o	o	o
5. Strongly Agree	4. Agree	3. Undecided	2. Disagree	1. Strongly Disagree

32. The Leader structures and coordinates the roles and responsibilities of every member of the leadership team so that we work together effectively.

o	o	o	o	o
5. Strongly Agree	4. Agree	3. Undecided	2. Disagree	1. Strongly Disagree

Core Practice #2: PRINCIPLED NEGOTIATION Leaders respectfully and skillfully deal with conflict, disagreement and differences to make agreements that maintain organizational peace.

33. Leadership team members confidently and creatively address strong differences and disagreements when they arise with other leaders and with those they lead.

o	o	o	o	o
5. Strongly Agree	4. Agree	3. Undecided	2. Disagree	1. Strongly Disagree

34. The Leader (CEO/President/ED) confidently and creatively addresses strong differences and disagreements within the leadership team.

o	o	o	o	o
5. Strongly Agree	4. Agree	3. Undecided	2. Disagree	1. Strongly Disagree

35. If I have a conflict with someone else on the leadership team, I have the skills to work it out respectfully and directly with the other person.

o	o	o	o	o
5. Strongly Agree	4. Agree	3. Undecided	2. Disagree	1. Strongly Disagree

36. When a conflict situation is too difficult for me to resolve on my own, I can get help from someone in the organization.

o	o	o	o	o
5. Strongly Agree	4. Agree	3. Undecided	2. Disagree	1. Strongly Disagree

37. If I have a serious difference of opinion or disagreement with the Leader, I can talk with him or her directly about the issue and I know that I will be treated fairly and respectfully.

o	o	o	o	o
5. Strongly Agree	4. Agree	3. Undecided	2. Disagree	1. Strongly Disagree

38. There is little or no gossip by leadership team members. ("gossip" means spreading rumors, speculation that increases anxiety, and sharing negative information with others).

o	o	o	o	o
5. Strongly Agree	4. Agree	3. Undecided	2. Disagree	1. Strongly Disagree

39. There is little or no backbiting by leadership team members. ("backbiting" means complaining, criticizing, or speaking negatively about others when they are not present)

o	o	o	o	o
5. Strongly Agree	4. Agree	3. Undecided	2. Disagree	1. Strongly Disagree

40. Leadership team members guide and orient their respective departments, divisions, and work teams to work together cooperatively and avoid office politics, power plays, and ongoing feuds.

o	O	o	o	o
5. Strongly Agree	4. Agree	3. Undecided	2. Disagree	1. Strongly Disagree

Core Practice #3: VALUES BASED DECISION MAKING Leaders demonstrate integrity by using core values and guiding principles to make key decisions and then credibly communicate them to internal and external stakeholders.

41. Leaders use a clear process to learn from people with diverse perspectives before making a key decision.

o	o	o	o	o
5. Strongly Agree	4. Agree	3. Undecided	2. Disagree	1. Strongly Disagree

42. Leaders sincerely consider the needs of stakeholders who will be impacted by their key decisions before committing to a final decision.

o	o	o	o	o
5. Strongly Agree	4. Agree	3. Undecided	2. Disagree	1. Strongly Disagree

43. When the leadership team (or an individual leader) makes a key decision, it is clear to others who participated directly, who provided input, and who is accountable for the decision.

o	o	o	o	o
5. Strongly Agree	4. Agree	3. Undecided	2. Disagree	1. Strongly Disagree

44. When making a key decision, the members of the leadership team understand and respect the values of the stakeholders affected by our work.

o	o	o	o	o
5. Strongly Agree	4. Agree	3. Undecided	2. Disagree	1. Strongly Disagree

45. All key decisions by the Leader, the leadership team, and individual leaders are well aligned with the organization's core values and principles.

o	o	o	o	o
5. Strongly Agree	4. Agree	3. Undecided	2. Disagree	1. Strongly Disagree

46. All key decisions by managers are well aligned with the organization's core values and principles.

o	o	o	o	o
5. Strongly Agree	4. Agree	3. Undecided	2. Disagree	1. Strongly Disagree

47. Each leadership team member clearly communicates key decisions to internal and external stakeholders so they are able to understand the values and principles that guided the decision.

o	o	o	o	o
5. Strongly Agree	4. Agree	3. Undecided	2. Disagree	1. Strongly Disagree

48. When members of the leadership team communicate key decisions to internal and external stakeholders, they honestly acknowledge the downside (challenges, negative consequences, risks).

o	o	o	o	o
5. Strongly Agree	4. Agree	3. Undecided	2. Disagree	1. Strongly Disagree

Core Practice #4: WISE PLANNING Leaders commit to a dynamic, flexible plan that aligns mission, core values, and guiding principles with actionable goals that move the organization toward a shared vision of success.

49. The organization has a clear, meaningful mission statement that confirms its purpose.

o	o	o	o	o
5. Strongly Agree	4. Agree	3. Undecided	2. Disagree	1. Strongly Disagree

50. The organization has a clear, compelling vision of success that inspires sustained, shared effort.

o	o	o	o	o
5. Strongly Agree	4. Agree	3. Undecided	2. Disagree	1. Strongly Disagree

51. Every leadership team member clearly communicates to employees how the work of each part of the organization contributes to the overall vision of success.

o	o	o	o	o
5. Strongly Agree	4. Agree	3. Undecided	2. Disagree	1. Strongly Disagree

52. The organization has a clear set of major goals that organize the shared effort necessary to achieve the vision of success.

o	o	o	o	o
5. Strongly Agree	4. Agree	3. Undecided	2. Disagree	1. Strongly Disagree

53. Each major goal has one or more clear performance measures used to assess our progress.

o	o	o	o	o
5. Strongly Agree	4. Agree	3. Undecided	2. Disagree	1. Strongly Disagree

54. Every member of the leadership team understands his/her responsibility to coordinate or oversee particular goals, objectives, or actions in the plan

o	o	o	o	o
5. Strongly Agree	4. Agree	3. Undecided	2. Disagree	1. Strongly Disagree

55. Members of the leadership team regularly (at least 2 times per year) review the overall plan, assess progress on the major goals, and provide a summary update to employees.

o	o	o	o	o
5. Strongly Agree	4. Agree	3. Undecided	2. Disagree	1. Strongly Disagree

56. If there are any changes in the vision and the major goals, members of the leadership team clearly and promptly communicate the change to the employees they lead.

o	o	o	o	o
5. Strongly Agree	4. Agree	3. Undecided	2. Disagree	1. Strongly Disagree

9. Leadership Assessment Worksheet

Practices that Build Organization Health and Collaboration

DIALOGUE establish an environment of learning conversations to engage everyone's knowledge, skills, & creativity	PRINCIPLED NEGOTIATION respectfully & skillfully deal with conflict, disagreement, & differences to build unity
Strengths **Gaps/Needs Improvement**	**Strengths** **Gaps/Needs Improvement**
Possible Action Steps	**Possible Action Steps**
VALUES BASED DECISION MAKING demonstrate integrity by using core values & guiding principles to make key decisions and recommendations that are credibly communicated to stakeholders	**WISE PLANNING** commit to a plan that aligns mission, core values, & guiding principles with actionable goals to move the organization toward a shared vision of success
Strengths **Gaps/Needs Improvement**	**Strengths** **Gaps/Needs Improvement**
Possible Action Steps	**Possible Action Steps**

Integrity, Psychological Safety, and a Growth Mindset personal characteristics, attitudes, and additional dimensions of your leadership approach that strengthen the organization's culture to sustain collaboration

Strengths Gaps/Needs Improvement

Possible Action Steps

10. Health Assessment #2 Creative Collaboration – Work Team

Definition: CREATIVE COLLABORATION is work together that accomplishes more than is possible separately. When an organization collaborates well as a whole, and within its divisions and teams, the organization becomes more able to adapt, face challenges or setbacks, and continue to fulfill its mission. This assessment helps clarify the three characteristics of the culture of healthy, collaborative teams and organizations and their use of four cornerstone practices. These behaviors require leadership by example at all levels of the organization. **For each statement, indicate your opinion of the team's current capacity. Some questions focus on overall conditions and leadership behavior in the organization that may directly or indirectly affect the capacity of your team. If you are unsure, mark the "undecided" circle. Responses of 4 and 5 indicate strengths to build upon. Responses of 1 and 2 indicate weaknesses to improve. A response of 3 may be a weakness or it may only need additional discussion to clarify the reason for a non-definitive response.**

Organization Culture Characteristic #1: INTEGRITY Internal (employees, staff, volunteers) and external (customers, investors/ funders, community partners, and suppliers) have a high level of trust in the organization and its leaders. They are confident that everyone will act ethically at all times.

1. The organization has well-defined core values and guiding principles that set standards and guide the way we do our work and the way we treat others.

o	o	o	o	o
5. Strongly Agree	4. Agree	3. Undecided	2. Disagree	1. Strongly Disagree

2. Everyone on the team understands how the values and principles apply to their work responsibilities.

o	o	o	o	o
5. Strongly Agree	4. Agree	3. Undecided	2. Disagree	1. Strongly Disagree

3. Members of the team consistently treat each other according to our values and principles.

o	o	o	o	o
5. Strongly Agree	4. Agree	3. Undecided	2. Disagree	1. Strongly Disagree

4. The team, as a group and as individuals, understand what is important to the people we serve (clients, customers, patients) and respect them.

o	o	o	o	o
5. Strongly Agree	4. Agree	3. Undecided	2. Disagree	1. Strongly Disagree

5. Organization leaders provide a clear, consistent, and ethical example at all times.

o	o	o	o	o
5. Strongly Agree	4. Agree	3. Undecided	2. Disagree	1. Strongly Disagree

6. Managers provide a clear, consistent, and ethical example at all times.

o	o	o	o	o
5. Strongly Agree	4. Agree	3. Undecided	2. Disagree	1. Strongly Disagree

7. Organization leaders actively encourage everyone to raise any ethical concerns and, when they do, leaders follow through to determine whether action is necessary.

o	o	o	o	o
5. Strongly Agree	4. Agree	3. Undecided	2. Disagree	1. Strongly Disagree

8. Managers actively encourage everyone to raise ethical concerns and, when they do, managers follow through to determine whether action is necessary.

o	o	o	o	o
5. Strongly Agree	4. Agree	3. Undecided	2. Disagree	1. Strongly Disagree

Organization Culture Characteristic #2: PSYCHOLOGICAL SAFETY Practice consistent behaviors that build and sustain a work environment in which everyone's voice is heard, and no one's dignity is at risk.

9. In this organization, people are held accountable but mistakes are not held against people.

o	o	o	o	o
5. Strongly Agree	4. Agree	3. Undecided	2. Disagree	1. Strongly Disagree

10. As a team member, I can voice my questions, concerns, problems, and ideas.

o	o	o	o	o
5. Strongly Agree	4. Agree	3. Undecided	2. Disagree	1. Strongly Disagree

11. People in the organization are never rejected or excluded for being different.

o	o	o	o	o
5. Strongly Agree	4. Agree	3. Undecided	2. Disagree	1. Strongly Disagree

12. As a member of the team, it is safe for me to take a risk.

o	o	o	o	o
5. Strongly Agree	4. Agree	3. Undecided	2. Disagree	1. Strongly Disagree

13. It is easy to ask other team members for help.

o	o	o	o	o
5. Strongly Agree	4. Agree	3. Undecided	2. Disagree	1. Strongly Disagree

14. I am confident that no one on the team would deliberately act to undermine my efforts.

o	o	o	o	o
5. Strongly Agree	4. Agree	3. Undecided	2. Disagree	1. Strongly Disagree

15. In my work with other team members, my unique skills and talents are valued and utilized.

o	o	o	o	o
5. Strongly Agree	4. Agree	3. Undecided	2. Disagree	1. Strongly Disagree

16. The team leader engages all members of the team with consistent, positive communication.

o	o	o	o	o
5. Strongly Agree	4. Agree	3. Undecided	2. Disagree	1. Strongly Disagree

Organization Culture Characteristic #3 GROWTH MINDSET Practice consistent behaviors that reinforce a shared belief that we can all grow our capacity to develop by working and learning together from all mistakes and challenges.

17. Throughout the organization from the top down, people openly admit mistakes, discuss them, and learned from them.

o	o	o	o	o
5. Strongly Agree	4. Agree	3. Undecided	2. Disagree	1. Strongly Disagree

18. Organization leaders promote open channels of growth-promoting positive feedback and constructive criticism that flow in all directions (up, down, across departments/divisions).

o	o	o	o	o
5. Strongly Agree	4. Agree	3. Undecided	2. Disagree	1. Strongly Disagree

19. Organization leaders and managers focus on the well-being of employees and treat them as teammates and collaborators.

o	o	o	o	o
5. Strongly Agree	4. Agree	3. Undecided	2. Disagree	1. Strongly Disagree

20. There is a high level of employee commitment to the organization because employees believe the organization's leaders "have their backs."

o	o	o	o	o
5. Strongly Agree	4. Agree	3. Undecided	2. Disagree	1. Strongly Disagree

21. Organization leaders support risk-taking and encourage innovation (putting new ideas into practice).

o	o	o	o	o
5. Strongly Agree	4. Agree	3. Undecided	2. Disagree	1. Strongly Disagree

22. In hiring, organization leaders emphasize potential capacity and passion for learning more than credentials and past accomplishments.

o	o	o	o	o
5. Strongly Agree	4. Agree	3. Undecided	2. Disagree	1. Strongly Disagree

23. There is an active program to engage employees (including leaders and managers) and help them develop on the job (coaching, workshops, apprenticeships).

o	o	o	o	o
5. Strongly Agree	4. Agree	3. Undecided	2. Disagree	1. Strongly Disagree

24. There are open forums with participation by employees to review major projects and initiatives, assess successes and mistakes, and develop lessons learned.

o	o	o	o	o
5. Strongly Agree	4. Agree	3. Undecided	2. Disagree	1. Strongly Disagree

Core Practice #1: DIALOGUE Establish an environment of learning conversations that engage everyone's knowledge, skills, and creativity.

25. Our team meetings are open forums where each member has the opportunity to contribute and be listened to with respect.

o	o	o	o	o
5. Strongly Agree	4. Agree	3. Undecided	2. Disagree	1. Strongly Disagree

26. The team leader actively seeks input from members of the team on a range of important issues.

o	o	o	o	o
5. Strongly Agree	4. Agree	3. Undecided	2. Disagree	1. Strongly Disagree

27. Organization leaders seek input from employees and follow up with communication about how the input was used or considered.

o	o	o	o	o
5. Strongly Agree	4. Agree	3. Undecided	2. Disagree	1. Strongly Disagree

28. As a team and one-to-one, we have meaningful opportunities to talk together, share ideas, and learn from each other.

o	o	o	o	o
5. Strongly Agree	4. Agree	3. Undecided	2. Disagree	1. Strongly Disagree

29. Our organization actively uses cross-functional teams (a team of representatives from different teams across the organization) to address challenging organization-wide issues by engaging people with different expertise and perspectives in learning conversations.

o	o	o	o	o
5. Strongly Agree	4. Agree	3. Undecided	2. Disagree	1. Strongly Disagree

30. Team members consistently listen respectfully to others, within and outside the team.

o	o	o	o	o
5. Strongly Agree	4. Agree	3. Undecided	2. Disagree	1. Strongly Disagree

31. The team leader engages members of the team in two-way conversation to make sure everyone understands their responsibilities and what is expected of them.

o	o	o	o	o
5. Strongly Agree	4. Agree	3. Undecided	2. Disagree	1. Strongly Disagree

32. The team leader structures and coordinates the roles and responsibilities of every member of the leadership team so everyone can work together effectively.

o	o	o	o	o
5. Strongly Agree	4. Agree	3. Undecided	2. Disagree	1. Strongly Disagree

Core Practice #2: PRINCIPLED NEGOTIATION Respectfully and skillfully deal with conflict, disagreement and differences to maintain organizational peace.

33. Team members confidently and creatively address strong differences and disagreements when they arise with each other and with other coworkers.

o	o	o	o	o
5. Strongly Agree	4. Agree	3. Undecided	2. Disagree	1. Strongly Disagree

34. The team leader confidently and creatively addresses strong differences and disagreements within the team.

o	o	o	o	o
5. Strongly Agree	4. Agree	3. Undecided	2. Disagree	1. Strongly Disagree

35. If I have a disagreement or conflict with someone else on the team, I have the skills to work it out respectfully and directly with the other person.

o	o	o	o	o
5. Strongly Agree	4. Agree	3. Undecided	2. Disagree	1. Strongly Disagree

36. When a conflict situation is too difficult for me to resolve on my own, I can get help from my team leader or someone else in the organization.

o	o	o	o	o
5. Strongly Agree	4. Agree	3. Undecided	2. Disagree	1. Strongly Disagree

37. If I have a serious difference of opinion or disagreement with the team leader, I can talk with him or her directly about the issue and I know that I will be treated fairly and respectfully.

o	o	o	o	o
5. Strongly Agree	4. Agree	3. Undecided	2. Disagree	1. Strongly Disagree

38. There is little or no *gossip* by team members. (*gossip* means spreading rumors, speculation that increases anxiety, and sharing negative information with others).

o	o	o	o	o
5. Strongly Agree	4. Agree	3. Undecided	2. Disagree	1. Strongly Disagree

39. There is little or no *backbiting* by team members. (*backbiting* means complaining, criticizing, or speaking negatively about others when they are not present)

o	o	o	o	o
5. Strongly Agree	4. Agree	3. Undecided	2. Disagree	1. Strongly Disagree

40. Our organization's departments, divisions, and teams work together cooperatively and avoid office politics, turf conflicts, power plays, and ongoing feuds.

o	o	o	o	o
5. Strongly Agree	4. Agree	3. Undecided	2. Disagree	1. Strongly Disagree

Core Practice #3: VALUES BASED DECISION MAKING Leaders demonstrate integrity by using core values and guiding principles to make key decisions and then credibly communicate them to internal and external stakeholders.

41. Organization leaders use a clear process to learn from people with diverse perspectives before making a key decision.

o	o	o	o	o
5. Strongly Agree	4. Agree	3. Undecided	2. Disagree	1. Strongly Disagree

42. Organization leaders sincerely consider the needs of stakeholders who will be impacted by their key decisions.

o	o	o	o	o
5. Strongly Agree	4. Agree	3. Undecided	2. Disagree	1. Strongly Disagree

43. When organization leaders make key decisions, they are transparent about who participated directly, who was consulted, and who is accountable for the decision.

o	o	o	o	o
5. Strongly Agree	4. Agree	3. Undecided	2. Disagree	1. Strongly Disagree

44. When our team leader makes key decisions, he or she is transparent about who participated directly, who was consulted, and who is accountable for the decision.

o	o	o	o	o
5. Strongly Agree	4. Agree	3. Undecided	2. Disagree	1. Strongly Disagree

45. All key decisions by the organization's leaders are well-aligned with the organization's core values and principles.

o	o	o	o	o
5. Strongly Agree	4. Agree	3. Undecided	2. Disagree	1. Strongly Disagree

46. All key decisions by our team leader are well-aligned with the organization's core values and principles.

o	o	o	o	o
5. Strongly Agree	4. Agree	3. Undecided	2. Disagree	1. Strongly Disagree

47. Organization leaders clearly communicate key decisions to internal and external stakeholders so they are able to understand the values and principles that guided the decision.

o	o	o	o	o
5. Strongly Agree	4. Agree	3. Undecided	2. Disagree	1. Strongly Disagree

48. When organization leaders communicate key decisions to employees, they honestly acknowledge challenges, negative consequences, and downside risks.

o	o	o	o	o
5. Strongly Agree	4. Agree	3. Undecided	2. Disagree	1. Strongly Disagree

Core Practice #4: WISE PLANNING A dynamic, flexible plan aligns mission, core values, and guiding principles with actionable goals, uniting the organization to move toward a shared vision of success.

49. The organization has a clear, meaningful mission statement that confirms its purpose.

o	o	o	o	o
5. Strongly Agree	4. Agree	3. Undecided	2. Disagree	1. Strongly Disagree

50. The organization has a clear, compelling vision of success that inspires sustained, shared effort.

o	o	o	o	o
5. Strongly Agree	4. Agree	3. Undecided	2. Disagree	1. Strongly Disagree

51. Every organization leader and manager clearly communicates to employees how the work of each part of the organization contributes to the overall vision of success.

o	o	o	o	o
5. Strongly Agree	4. Agree	3. Undecided	2. Disagree	1. Strongly Disagree

52. The organization has a clear set of major goals that organize the shared effort necessary to achieve the vision of success.

o	o	o	o	o
5. Strongly Agree	4. Agree	3. Undecided	2. Disagree	1. Strongly Disagree

53. Each major goal has one or more clear performance indicators used to assess progress.

o	o	o	o	o
5. Strongly Agree	4. Agree	3. Undecided	2. Disagree	1. Strongly Disagree

54. Each member of our team understands how his or her responsibility relates to particular goals, objectives, or actions in the plan.

o	o	o	o	o
5. Strongly Agree	4. Agree	3. Undecided	2. Disagree	1. Strongly Disagree

55. Our team leader meets with key members of the team regularly (at least 2 times per year) to review our team's part of the overall wise plan, assess progress on our team goals, and provide a summary update to employees.

o	o	o	o	o
5. Strongly Agree	4. Agree	3. Undecided	2. Disagree	1. Strongly Disagree

56. If there are any changes in the vision and the major goals, organization leaders clearly communicate to everyone to maintain shared understanding and alignment.

o	o	o	o	o
5. Strongly Agree	4. Agree	3. Undecided	2. Disagree	1. Strongly Disagree

11. Leading Virtual Collaboration – a Checklist

Context Leaders need a strategy for the new reality of virtual operations. Management, communication, and meetings must all be intentionally coordinated and integrated.

Frame the Work and Connect the Dots

- Amidst change and uncertainty, it is more important than ever that everyone understand the organization's mission, vision, and major goals.

- The organization's core values, guiding principles, and key behaviors that implement them must be demonstrated and communicated well by leaders. They form the ethical center that holds the organization together.

- Each team must know its mission within the larger organization, have a firm grasp on its goals, and recognize how its contribution matters.

- There must be effective processes for making decisions and recommendations, sharing information, clearing up miscommunication, and turning conflicts into peace.

Integrate Technology

- Intentional use of available technologies requires selection of the most appropriate tools. Then, leaders must assure sufficient support to fix inevitable glitches, resolve connectivity challenges, and provide training. All team members must have shared expectations and sufficient capacity to effectively use the technology.

- Emphasize frequent, real-time videoconferencing to give participants the best possible opportunity to interpret non-verbal communication including gestures, posture, and facial expressions. Along with voice tone, these visual cues supply critical information to understand what spoken words mean.

- Virtual training must rise in importance. Many organizations ignore virtual training and many of those that offer training fail to make it a priority. Throwing technology at untrained people produces limited results.

Clarify Roles, Workloads, and Expectations

- Unshared and misunderstood expectations sow seeds of low morale, resentment, and conflict. Begin each project with clear explanations of each team member's role, responsibilities, and contribution.

- To avoid burnout, assess the capacity of team members to get their work done in normal hours.

- Set guidelines for scheduling that minimize early morning or late night meetings. When team members are spread across time zones, this issue becomes more challenging and more important.

- Provide organizational support for health maintenance practices. When team members have the ability to handle stress, uncertainty, and challenges, the team is better able to adapt to change and the organization becomes more adaptive as a whole.

- When conditions permit travel and in-person meetings, remember that geographically dispersed teams are challenged to sustain high levels of commitment. Regular opportunities to meet face-to-face help develop rapport and build trust.

- Right-size teams. Start with a guideline of 5-9 members.

- Be careful about assigning anyone to multiple teams. You can spread people too thin and reduce their effectiveness. This can be easy to do with your most capable, high performing members.

Design Meetings to Succeed

- Agendas rule! A well prepared agenda should be sent out ahead of time. This sets expectations for a necessary, productive meeting and prepares everyone to participate.

- Connect everyone. Make introductions if necessary. Use people's names when interacting.

- Be task oriented and generate opportunities for everyone to participate.

- Evaluate each meeting. Invite ideas or concerns to improve the process and outcomes.

- Send out meeting notes and action items that summarize the meeting outcomes and direct follow through.

Acknowledgements and Gratitude

There is a saying, "It takes a village to raise a child." A village of collaboration graced every step in the process of creating this book. I am grateful to all of you who step up to be my community of generous support.

- The seeds for this book were planted long ago. Lyman and Dorothy Bennett showed me that a library card is a passport to the world. They raised me to "always have a book under your arm."

- Celina Cavalcanti-Bennett, my life partner, was the first to set her insightful eyes on every word in this book, offering structural feedback and encouragement.

- Friends and colleagues read advanced drafts to help me step back, take the reader's perspective, and strengthen every part of this book. Tsiporah Nephesh, Aba Ankrah-Ntambwe, Laura Bassein, Deborah Dungan, Dottie Indyke, and Liz McGrath.

- My long-time professional partner, Joan McIver Gibson, collaborated with me for over a decade to grow our decision making work in Lesson Seven from a blank sheet of paper.

- My colleagues in the National Trusted Advisor network provided opportunities for me to present parts of this material.

- Erika Yocom and her team gracefully moved my work from text to press.

- My stalwart brothers of the *Year to Live* fellowship help me experience the power of uniting in an enduring community of mutual support. In this community, I continue to receive encouragement to step forward and live this wild, precious life with an open heart. For Jeff, Tony, Bill, David, Michael, Bob, Peter, Billy, Glenn, Jason, and those who moved on but are not forgotten, Burke and David

- Bob Schrei for countless depth conversations that encourage my capacity to embrace the mystery, be patient, and listen to the muse.

- Doreen Canfield for the illustrations in Lesson One.

- My children Andrew Bennett, Christopher Bennett, Isis Bennett, and my grandson, James Bennett who inspire me to contribute to a more peaceful world where people know how to work well together.

- For the leaders and staff of the organizations whose stories are in this book.

- Merle Lefkoff generously introduced me to group and organizations work.

- Judy Haas and Hector del Valle provided graphic design assistance.

- Tania Jackson at RedIdea designed the logo on the cover https://redidea.co.uk/

About the Author

Mark D. Bennett is the founder of Uniting by Design LLC, a consulting firm with a mission to help leaders unite organizations that deliver superior results, earn ethical reputations, and adapt to change.

He graduated from the University of Texas School of Law and spent the first part of his career in the organizational *emergency room*. As a trial attorney representing aggrieved employees, he began the practical study of organizational mistakes and dysfunctions.

He left the practice of law for graduate study in counseling psychology and family therapy. Then, he returned to work with organizational disputes as a mediator. For over 15 years, he handled a wide range of conflicts including individual and group cases with staff, leaders, and boards of businesses, nonprofits, government agencies, and international organizations.

Twenty-five years ago, he shifted his focus from cleaning up organizational problems to *promoting organizational health*. He serves as a workshop presenter on leadership, teaming, conflict resolution, values-based decision making, and creative collaboration. He facilitates collaboration, wise planning, and critical decision making. He offers his support as a leadership coach to many of the organizations he assists.

His publications include:

- *Uniting by Design: the Architecture of Creative Collaboration (Spring, 2021)* - a practical guide to building collaboration in organizations, leadership teams, work teams, alliances, and partnerships.

- *A Field Guide to Good Decisions: Values in Action (2006)* – the practical steps of ethical decision making to make difficult decisions with integrity, accountability, and credibility.

- *The Art of Mediation, 2d edition (2005)* – the skills of conflict resolution and principled negotiation to help people bridge differences, make agreements, and make peace.

- *Negotiation in the Practice of Law (1996)* – a training manual to improve lawyers' skills in settlement.